Healthy BREAKS

The complete guide
to health farms, hotels, spas
and centres in Britain and Ireland

Catherine Beattie

GW00597294

DISCOVERY BOOKS

English
Tourist Board

STB
SCOTTISH
TOURIST
BOARD

BWRDD CROESO CYMRU
WALES TOURIST BOARD

Northern Ireland
Tourist Board

© Catherine Beattie 1994

Discovery Books
29 Hacketts Lane, Pyrford, Woking, Surrey GU22 8PP

Production by David Simpson

Printed by
Mandarin Offset

British Library Cataloguing in Publication Data
A catalogue record for this book is available from the British Library.

ISBN 0 9518511 1 X

CONTENTS

ACKNOWLEDGEMENTS

My warmest thanks to David Simpson for his constructive ideas and production skills; to Richard Thomas for editing the photographs; to Joy Hodge for her help and encouragement; to Michael Dewing and Jane Collinson at the English Tourist Board for their continued interest and advice. I should also like to express my appreciation for the hospitality and assistance given by health farms, holiday villages and hotels.

Once again, special thanks to my husband Alec, without whose practical help and support this book would never have been written, and to my children, Julie, Clare, Kevin, Sarah, Alison, Jonathan, Thomas and Stephen, who have encouraged and inspired me throughout.

This book is dedicated with love to my mother,
who has never taken a healthy break but deserves one.

FOREWORD

Are life's stresses and strains are getting you down? Then taking a 'healthy break' might be just what you need to restore that feeling of well-being and vitality. Pampering treatments, healthy meals and enjoyable exercise routines will not only make you feel and look better, but may prompt you into a new and more active lifestyle.

As the most taxing part of any healthy break is often deciding where to go, I have written this book to make choosing the right place *for you* as easy and pleasurable as possible.

Healthy Breaks includes a wide choice of destinations throughout Britain and Ireland with ideas for everyone - individuals, couples and family groups. All entries offer accommodation combined with optional body, beauty or health treatments. Establishments range from the most homely and unusual to the ultimate in luxurious pampering, and include health farms, spa hotels, residential centres and holiday villages.

Full details and prices of all dedicated health farms in Britain and Ireland are included, ranging from the exclusive *Champneys* to the simple *Lios Dana*. Other entries have been selected on merit because they offer an alternative choice of 'healthy break,' and unlike health farms, usually have no age or dietary restrictions.

Healthy Breaks includes many hotels and self-catering holiday villages with good rates for family visits. Friendlier attitudes to children and a marked improvement in the provision of free or low cost accommodation, meals and child facilities, means a 'healthy' family break is now an affordable treat at any time of the year.

All particulars were checked for accuracy before going to press, but it is impossible to guarantee prices will not have increased by the time you use this book. *Always check current prices and facilities before making a firm booking*. It also wise to reserve optional health and beauty treatments in advance, as this keeps track of what you are likely to spend and avoids finding popular treatments booked up when you arrive.

Please mention *Healthy Breaks* when using the guide to contact any of the establishments featured.

If you would like further impartial advice on any entry in this book, please telephone either of our special numbers (details at the end of the book). If you wish, we can even take care of your booking.

I hope *Healthy Breaks* will inspire you to plan some relaxing and revitalising days away. Please write to me with your comments on any of the establishments featured, and with any suggestions for a third edition. Address your correspondence to:

Catherine Beattie
Discovery Books
29 Hacketts Lane
Pyrford
Woking
Surrey
GU22 8PP

INTRODUCTION

It is hardly surprising that healthy breaks have become so popular in recent years. Everyone needs an occasional break from the stresses of everyday life, and a relaxing few days away is a pleasant way to unwind.

Once you have felt the benefits of a healthy break, you are likely to want to repeat the experience, and may even become one of the many health farm visitors who return regularly each year to 'top up' their improved lifestyle routines.

Affordable health and fitness packages are now offered by hotels and holiday villages, where families are welcomed and menus less restrictive than at health resorts. Differences between hotels and health resorts have become less distinct in recent years, as hotels have become more health orientated and health farms less strict. A new type of 'spa' has emerged, with the accent on relaxation, health and fitness rather than strict diets and physical jerks.

Today, even the word 'spa' has become an ambiguous term used by hotels and health farms for facilities like saunas and steam rooms, and unrelated to genuine spas with therapeutic mineral springs.

With increasing competition between establishments to reduce our stress levels and body flab (not to mention our bank balances), the healthy break has become one of the fastest growing sectors of the domestic travel market. Its popularity looks like continuing for a long time to come.

Health farm, spa hotel or holiday village, what do they offer in the way of amenities and value for money?

DEDICATED HEALTH FARMS

Also known as *health resorts, centres, retreats, clinics* and *hydros,* these highly individual establishments have their own approach and philosophy.

Usually situated in historic manor houses amid acres of beautiful grounds, health farms are not as glamorous as their media image suggests. The ambience is relaxed and comfortable, rather than ritzy. Most establishments bear no resemblence to the clinically austere 'fat farms' of earlier years, offering cheerful informality and homely comforts in a nurtured and friendly environment.

After enjoying an unassailable position for many years, pandering to the whims of rich guests on reduction diets, health farms are finding attitudes to health and fitness and even their clientele, changing radically. Competition from hotels and overseas spas has caused progressive health resorts to rethink their approach and provide overall lifestyle improvement rather than just dedicated weight loss and pampering.

Today's visitor - who must be over 16 years of age - comes from a variety of backgrounds and is looking for a break from an overstressed life, unhealthy eating habits, family or other problems. Forward-looking health resorts encourage active participation in fitness programmes and offer new natural treatments and holistic therapies. More traditional establishments still favour low calorie menus combined with passive beauty and slimming treatment. Serious exercise sessions are given a low priority.

The attraction of a staying at a health farm is that it offers a chance to make a fresh start - to learn better eating habits and a healthier more relaxed and active lifestyle. Unlike hotels and holiday villages, health farms are unique because all visitors share the same goal - self-improvement.

Food & Drink

Despite the carrot juice and lettuce leaf myth, health farm food is actually plentiful, nourishing and usually well presented. All establishments serve 'healthy' dishes, some more imaginatively than others. Meals consist of a light breakfast, an adequate soup and buffet lunch and a more substantial three or four course dinner. Dishes are calorie counted and vegetarian options are always provided, as are basic foods like bread rolls and jacket potatoes. Chips, cream, chocolate biscuits and fattening snacks are notable by their absence, but tiny sandwiches and even low calorie cake are a welcome addition to afternoon tea in a number of health farms. Wine is now available with meals in some establishments (see entry page numbers for individual health farm policy).

Fresh fruit, salads and low calorie dishes are the mainstay of health farm cuisine, but only strict dieters are likely to feel the odd hunger pang. Light diet areas are set aside for slimmers, who graduate to the main dining room's more substantial menus when the desired weight loss has been achieved. Given prior notice, most health farm kitchens can cater for guests with special needs and requiring diabetic, gluten-free or other diets However, few establishments accept guests on total fasts - with the exception of *Malvern Nature Cure Centre, Shrubland Hall* and *Tyringham* who provide specialist support.

Visitors are encouraged to help

themselves to free refreshments (tea, coffee, soft drinks, mineral water) throughout the day, to replace body fluids lost during heat treatments and exercise. A few alternative establishments serve only herbal teas and mineral water. Regular tea and coffee, even decaffeinated varieties, are not available.

Accommodation

Surprisingly, en suite facilities are still lacking in some leading health farms, although bedrooms are well decorated with comfortable beds and television. However, standards of comfort vary, even within the same establishment, with luxury accommodation at one end of the price scale and basic, lower priced rooms at the other. Many 'budget' rooms are small, without a good view, and have shared bathroom facilities.

Copious supplies of bath towels are supplied, but few establishments provide towelling bathrobes, which all visitors need (lightweight and flimsy negligees are definitely not suitable). Practically everyone wears bathrobes and tracksuits throughout the day and changes into ordinary clothes for dinner. The only other essentials needed are two items of swimwear, flip-flops, trainers and exercise clothing.

All health farms have a strictly enforced no-smoking policy which extends to bedrooms too. Visitors unable to give up smoking entirely during their stay can make use of the smokers' lounge.

The routine

On arrival, visitors are checked in just like at any hotel. They are then shown around the facilities and may be asked to complete a medical questionnaire. A personal consultation with a senior therapist, nursing sister or doctor follows, and a timetable of treatments and activities arranged. A consultation might involve taking a full medical history and nutritional advice, or may be just a brief check of weight and blood pressure.

The daily routine is geared to an 'early to bed, early to rise' pattern, as the first optional activities of the day start around 7.00am with a brisk walk, early morning swim or a circuit of the jogging track. Less hardy types awaken to breakfast in bed, the morning newspaper and the day's timetable of treatments and activities.

Treatments

All health farms include some treatments in the daily tariff - the actual number often depending on the length of stay. The tariff covers accommodation, all meals and non-alcoholic refreshments, exercise classes, evening social programmes and use of leisure amenties.

Regrettably, many establishments have substantially *increased* their rates recently while *decreasing* the number of inclusive treatments provided. A daily massage and heat treatment (steam, sauna or spa bath) are often the only inclusive treatments offered. Some of the many optional treatments are very expensive, and delightful as they are, add considerably to the cost of a stay.

Health farms still offering a good allocation of inclusive treatments include *Stobo Castle*, *Inglewood*, *The Lorrens*, *Thorneyholme Hall*, *Tyringham* and *Roundelwood*. Visitors on fixed or limited budgets should try to keep to inclusive treatments and make the most of the many 'free' sports and exercise opportunities.

Weekend visitors may be unaware that not all health farms offer Sunday treatments, so these must be fitted in on Fridays and Saturdays. Most recreational facilities are available seven days a week.

Some treatment precautions

The best part of any heat treatment is the relaxation afterwards, so always rest for at least 20 minutes after a sauna or steam cabinet (*Champneys* offers the most perfect relaxation with comfortable recliners, cosy covers and a dark, quiet room).

Extremes of temperatures can cause changes in blood pressure, so heat treatments are not recommended for pregnant women nor those with high blood pressure. Other treatments cannot be combined safely, for example a sunbed after a deep facial like Cathiodermie might cause skin irritation. Visitors with low blood pressure should remember that immersing in very hot or cold water can cause dizziness, and taking a steam bath too soon after a soporific treatment like aromatherapy may result in fainting. Staff are always on hand to advise on treatment suitability.

A few health farms allow free access to saunas and steam rooms, appreciating that visitors enjoy using these facilities when taking an early morning swim or late evening dip. However, in some establishments use is restricted to one daily 'heat' treatment. Visitors requiring unlimited access should ask about this when booking.

Leisure facilities

Health farm sports and leisure amenities are generally excellent. Organised walks, cycling and jogging are popular outdoor pursuits, and most health farms have an indoor swimming pool with aquarobic sessions, supervised gym or fitness room and daily exercise classes for all ages and abilities. On-site golf, tennis and outdoor swimming are also available at some establishments.

HOTELS WITH LEISURE & TREATMENT FACILITIES

A huge improvement in standards of accommodation, food and amenities has transformed many hotels in Britain and Ireland over the last decade. Bargain weekend rates and the provision of leisure facilities have tempted many visitors to try a short break for the first time.

Greater health awareness and increased consumer demand has sparked off an unprecedented growth in the number of hotels offering leisure facilities. Although some hotel 'spas' consist of little more than a swimming pool and sauna, others offer treatments and amenities that compare favourably with the best health farms. Many of these excellent new facilities operate as private leisure clubs with membership extended to hotel residents during their stay. Amenities are usually free, although golf, squash and solaria may have nominal charges. Body and beauty treatments are paid for as taken, except when part of special health and fitness packages.

Hotel leisure clubs open early and close late. Most allow unrestricted access to pools, saunas and steam rooms - a more generous use of facilities than offered by many health farms, where extra heat treatments incur additional charges.

Hotels do not offer discussion groups, demonstrations or make-up classes in the evenings of course; these are the prerogative of the health farm. However, exercise and aerobic classes are often of a higher standard, due to the fitness of the club members who regularly attend them.

Similar treatments and standards apply everywhere, as beauticians and therapists have the same qualifications and training wherever they work. Product manufacturers also provide additional specialist training. Treatment quality is influenced by less tangible factors such as the warmth and comfort of the treatment room and the therapist's skill and personality.

Hotels are more formal than health farms and certainly livelier! Health farms are essentially quiet, restful places and their casual informality is one of the most striking differences between hotels and health farms. No hotel guest would wear a towelling bathrobe to lunch or dinner, but in health farm dining rooms this is perfectly acceptable and practical.

Hotels featured in this guide offer a good or excellent standard of accommodation which invariably includes an en suite bathroom. With very few exceptions, children are made welcome and accommodated free or at low rates when sharing with parents. Children's menus, baby-sitting and creche facilities are frequently provided in hotels.

One of the highlights of staying in an hotel is the opportunity to try out new dishes and sample delicious food - cooked English breakfasts, appetising lunches, traditional afternoon teas and memorable dinners. Slimmers, able to resist such temptations, can choose low calorie menus, vegetarian dishes, fresh fruit, vegetables and salads.

Many spa and seaside towns have palatial hotels built in Victorian or Edwardian times, now fully refurbished and renovated to a high standard. The excellent facilities on offer make these quality hotels a great choice for a healthy family break at any time, especially in low season when bargain rates apply.

SELF-CONTAINED HOLIDAY VILLAGES

All-season family resorts, or 'holiday villages' as they are sometimes called, provide an opportunity for the whole family to enjoy a healthy break together, even in inclement weather.

Villages are usually self-contained with shops, restaurants, cafes, bars and entertainments provided on site.

Sports and leisure facilities indoors and out, are excellent and varied with equipment and bicycles available for hire. Some resorts have super indoor pools with exciting features like wave machines, rivers, slides and waterfalls - fun for all ages. The pool complex may be purpose-built, as at *Center Parcs* villages, or located within the leisure area within an hotel, as at the *Lakeland Village.*

Entrance to the pool complex is included in the cost of the villa rental, but other sports and health facilities must be paid for as taken, which can prove expensive.

A multitude of child-orientated activities keeps all ages happy and safely occupied, leaving parents free to relax or use the many facilities themselves. Spa areas in the *Center Parc* villages adjoin the pool and are open to over 14s only. However, family sessions are arranged several times a week so younger children and their parents can enjoy using the saunas and steam rooms together.

Some villages offer a wide range of body and beauty treatments as well as hairdressing services, seven days a week, while in others the choice is more restricted. Advance booking is always advisable. At *Center Parcs*, treatments are carried out in the purpose built *Aqua Sana* - a pleasantly private and restful area, situated away

from the spa and pool complex.

Accommodation in holiday villages is in self-catering modern villas, lodges or apartments fully equipped down to the last teaspoon. Some lodges in timeshare resorts are especially well-equipped with luxuries like private saunas, dishwashers and microwave ovens.

Some resorts have a good selection of shops on site, at others visitors use local shops in the surrounding area. *Center Parc* villages are completely self-contained with a supermarket, newsagent and other attractive shops. These open early and close late, making shopping for food and other supplies easy and convenient.

Although holiday villages are situated in beautiful rural areas with local attractions, many visitors remain on site during their entire stay, preferring to explore the resort's own acres of landscaped grounds, nature trails and paths - on foot, horseback or bicycle.

Staying at a holiday village is a great way for parents to combine a wide range of activities and treatments with a family holiday.

PRICE CATEGORIES

The letter in the price category refers to the lowest price charged per person for accommodation on a nightly basis. In nearly all establishments this applies when sharing a twin or double room. Single room prices and supplements will be found under each establishment's tariff heading.

With some exceptions, hotel rates are lowest on weekends or when a stay includes two or more consecutive nights and often include room, breakfast and either lunch or dinner.

* Indicates that the tariff is full board and one or more treatments are included in the price. All dedicated health farms have this type of category.

Self-catering rates are not categorised - rental details are given under the tariff headings.

At-a-glance price categories are used in *Healthy Breaks* to make it easy to compare different establishments and rates. Prices were correct when this book went to press, but are subject to change at any time.

All details relating to treatments, facilities, services and prices should be checked for validity and availability before booking. It is probable some incremental price changes will occur during the life of this book.

Unless otherwise stated, prices include VAT and service charge.

£ A	£100+
£ B	£75 - £100
£ C	£50 - £75
£ D	£35 - £50
£ E	£35 or less

Entries are grouped in geographical sections and each section is preceded with a listing and area map. For easy identification, health farms are listed in **bold** type, self-catering holiday villages in *italics* and hotels and residential centres in standard type.

AMENITIES

32	Number of bedrooms *(number shown in box)*
☆	Price includes at least one daily treatment
2	Aromatherapy / massage
3	Heat treatments
4	Beauty treatments
5	Hairdressing
6	Slimming treatments
7	Alternative health treatments
8	Medical screening facilities
9	No alcohol
10	No smoking in public rooms
11	Stress management
12	Nutritional counselling
13	À la carte menus
14	Swimming pool
15	Open fires in winter
16	Outdoor sports facilities
17	Gymnasium
18	Golf available on site
C	Credit cards accepted

CENTRAL LONDON

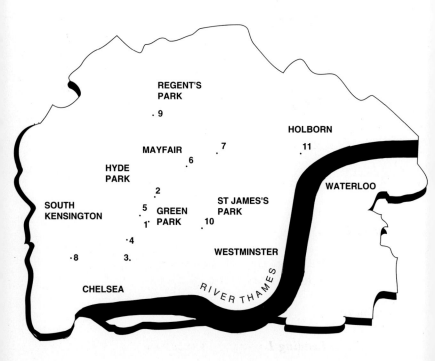

REGENT'S
PARK

. 9

HOLBORN

MAYFAIR
. 7

. 11

HYDE
PARK

. 6

WATERLOO

. 2

SOUTH
KENSINGTON

. 5
GREEN
PARK

ST JAMES'S
PARK

. 1
. 10

. 4

WESTMINSTER

. 8
3.

CHELSEA

RIVER THAMES

HEALTH, BEAUTY AND FITNESS
IN CENTRAL LONDON

The Berkeley
Wilton Place Knightsbridge London SW1X 7RL
Tel 071-235 6000   Fax 071-235 4330

| 160 | 2 3 4 5 13 14 17 C | £ A |

Exclusive and luxurious, the Berkeley is situated in fashionable Knightsbridge overlooking Hyde Park, with easy access to some of London's most prestigious shops and the West End. The Berkeley was relocated to its current site in 1972, and retains much of the charm, atmosphere and artefacts of the old hotel.

Bedrooms and bathrooms offer every luxury and comfort - many have adjoining terraces or conservatories with extensive views of London. Diners have a choice of European menus: fine French cuisine in the oak-panelled Berkeley's Restaurant or the Perroquet's exciting contemporary Italian food. Cocktails and traditional English afternoon tea are served in the foyer lounge.

Leisure amenities at the Berkeley include a private luxury cinema and a health club situated on the top floor, with a roof-top pool and gym equipped with the latest power sports equipment. The lovely pool is designed in the style of an ancient Roman bath, and its roof can be retracted on summer days to let in natural sunlight and allow open air swimming. The surrounding patio is ideal for sunbathing and on colder days is underfloor heated. Next to the pool are refreshment and relaxation areas and the gym. Individual changing rooms, two saunas and treatments rooms are one floor down on the 7th level. Fitness assessments can be arranged and hotel residents are welcome to join in the twice weekly aquarobics classes. Hairdressing, body and beauty treatments are supervised by Robert Wright, after whom the Berkeley's luxury hairdressing salon is named.

Treatments

The health club's facilities and treatments are available seven days a week. Robert's Salon is open for hairdressing, manicures and pedicures weekdays only.

Treatments include reflexology £25; facials from £25; Swedish massage £35 per hour; aroma-massage (Swedish massage with essential oils) £34; aromatherapy £21; waxing from £10; sunbed £18.50; manicure £15.50; pedicure £24.50; eyebrow/eyelash tinting £11; shampoo & blow dry £20.50; perm from £16.40.

Tariff

The special weekend rate of £150 single or £190 per couple per night applies to stays on a Friday or Saturday night and includes accommodation in deluxe room, flowers, English breakfast, use of health club facilities and a complimentary round of golf at the Wentworth Club.

Regular weekday tariff is £160 single or £220 double room and is exclusive of breakfast and VAT.

The Dorchester
Park Lane London W1A 2HJ
Tel 071-629 8888   Fax 071-409 0114

| 252 | 2 3 4 5 6 13 17 C | £ A |

Located on Park Lane in the heart of Mayfair, the Dorchester overlooks Hyde Park and is within easy walking distance of shops, theatres and other central London attractions. This great hotel re-opened in 1990 following an extensive refurbishment and renovation. Guests now enjoy the highest level of personalised service plus the most advanced modern facilities in the ambience and luxury of a bygone age.

All the Dorchester's gracious bedrooms and suites have been refurbished in luxurious and comfortable Georgian country-house style, with lavish fabrics and furnishings, triple-glazed windows, air-conditioning, Italian marble bathrooms and walk-in showers. Luxury suites, non-smoking rooms and rooms with whirlpool baths are available. All rooms have 24-hour room service and views over Hyde Park or the Dorchester's own landscaped gardens.

Three main restaurants offer a choice of Cantonese, English or French cuisine. Cocktails, light lunches and dinners are available in The Bar, and traditional afternoon tea is served each day in the Promenade lounge.

The Dorchester Spa opened in 1991 and is located beneath the hotel. The luxurious art deco design incorporates gym and workout studios, spa baths, saunas, steam rooms, hairdressing services and treatment rooms but no swimming pool. Spa members, hotels guests and day visitors enjoy the latest body and beauty treatments in the most opulent surroundings.

Treatments

This is the only salon in Europe using Elizabeth Arden's luxury cosmetics. Arden facials cost from £45; Thalgo facials from £45; body wraps £42 each; jet shower body treatment £42; body massage £42; aromatherapy massage £45; reflexology £30; anti-cellulite slimming treatments £42; eyelash tint £9; manicure from £17; pedicure from £21; waxing from £7; shampoo/blow dry £25; highlights £78; perms from £45; fitness assessment £25.

Tariff

Two- night *Romantic Weekends* (arrival on a Friday or Saturday night) cost £500 per couple. This includes two nights' accommodation for two persons in deluxe room with complimentary champagne on a dinner/bed and breakfast basis and use of the Spa. If dinner is not taken the rate is £360 per couple.

Regular nightly tariff (room only) from £180 - £215 single occupancy, £215 - £240 double, suites from £330 per night.

Eleven Cadogan Gardens
Sloane Square   London   SW3 2RF
Tel   071-730 3426   Fax   071-730 5217

| 60 | ☆ 2 3 4 6 7 8 11 13 14 17 C | £ B |

This elegant town house hotel is situated the heart of Chelsea in a quiet tree-lined square a short distance from Harrods and the King's Road.

The hotel is exquisitely decorated and furnished and retains a unique Victorian ambience. Bedrooms and suites are oak panelled and have Italian marble bathrooms, antiques and oil paintings. A butler greets guests on arrival and a chauffeur driven limousine service is available for sightseeing or shopping trips. The hotel does not have a restaurant, but 24-hour room service provides light meals and refreshments served either in your room or in the conservatory adjoining the lounge.

Just a few doors along from the hotel is one of London's most exclusive health clubs, No 1 Synergy. This luxurious club is under the same ownership as the hotel and guests are invited to make use of its many health and beauty facilities during their stay. Amenities include a fully equipped gym, exercise studio, aqua aerobic pool with swim jet, steam room, sauna, solarium and beauty clinic. The club offers fitness assessments, a wide range of complementary therapies, exercise classes and hydrotherapy.

Treatments

Treatments available at Synergy include aromatherapy £30; homeopathy £35; shiatsu £30; reflexology £30; acupuncture £35; cosmetic lasertherapy £30; paraffin body envelopment £33; body massage £31; G5 massage £15; Slendertone £14; Frigi-Thalgo £33; seaweed wrap £33; Thalgo facials from £28; waxing from £6.50; eyelash tinting £12; manicure £14; pedicure £18.

Fitness assessments with Bodystat (Body Composition Analysis, cholesterol testing and Exercise Tolerance Test with ECG can be arranged.

A non-residential beauty day costs £65 and includes 30 minute massage, facial, manicure, pedicure and use of Club facilities.

Tariff

Single rooms from £89 to £119 per night, double/twin rooms from £132 to £172 per night (two persons). Suite from £200 per night, Garden Suite with own private entrance, two double bedrooms and large drawing room overlooking the gardens £350 per night.

Continental breakfast £8, English breakfast £10.

A *Synergy Stay* incorporating three days of health, beauty and fitness costs from £400 per person.

Hyatt Carlton Tower
2 Cadogan Place Knightsbridge London SW1X 9PY
Tel 071-235 5411   Fax 071- 245 6570

| 224 | 2 3 4 5 13 17 C | £ A |

One of London's most exclusive modern hotels, the Carlton Tower is situated in the midst of fashionable Knightsbridge, with far-reaching views of London from its upper floors.

Bedrooms and suites are sumptuously appointed with luxury bathrooms and every modern amenity. Lounges and public areas have a restful ambience with green foliage plants and subdued lighting. An excellent range of menus is offered in the hotel's main restaurants - the elegant Chelsea Room serves fine French cuisine and The Rib Room is renowned for its superb beef dishes.
The Peak Health Club is situated on the ninth floor and is open to all hotel residents. Amenities include a magnificent gym equipped with a plethora of sophisticated exercise machines, saunas with television, steam room, exercise room with regular classes, refreshment lounge and bar and hair and beauty salon. All exercise areas are light and airy and have wonderful views of the city.

Treatments

Massage therapy £45 per hour; private training £30 per hour; sunbed £8; osteopathy consultation £50, treatment £38; Clarins body treatments from £30; Clarins facials from £24; manicure £15; pedicure £19; waxing from £9; eyelash tinting £10; Clarins treatment packages from £55 to £145.

Tariff

Reduced weekend rates from £150 per room per night apply to stays on Friday, Saturday and Sunday nights. Mid-week tariff from £240 per room per night. The above rates are for single or double occupancy and do not include VAT which is added to accounts at the current rate.

The Intercontinental Hotel
1 Hamilton Place London W1V OQY
Tel 071-409 3131   Fax 071-409 7461

469 2 3 4 5 13 17 C   **£ B**

Situated at Hyde Park Corner close to many of London's major attractions, this deluxe hotel is popular with business visitors and overseas tourists alike.

Rooms have every amenity and are sumptuously furnished and decorated. Diners can choose from the extensive menus of the Souffle Restuarant, or eat informally in the Coffee House. Nightly dancing is held until the early hours in Hamiltons, the Intercontinental's own nightclub.

Hotel residents enjoy free use of the health and leisure facilities in the Apsley Health Club on the first floor. Facilities include a fully equipped high-tech gym, sunbed, separate saunas, steam room, plunge pool with wave machine, large jacuzzi and treatment rooms.

Treatments

The Apsley Health Club offers a wide range of Clarins body and beauty treatments - the choice includes facials from £20; body massage £30 per hour; aromatherapy £39 for 11/2 hours; G5 massage £22 per session; manicure £11.50; pedicure £13.50; make-up £16; eyelash tint £6.50 (50% discount when combined with a facial); sunbed £10.

Various day packages using the facilities of the health club are available to hotel residents, club members and members' guests.

Top to Toe Day £75 includes a morning in the gym for a personal fitness assessment and recommended exercise programme, 30 minute massage, manicure, pedicure, relaxing facial and light make-up. The package includes use of the pool, steam room, sauna and jacuzzi.

Relax and Rejuvenate £62 includes one sunbed session, one hour massage and relaxing facial;

Beauty Bonus £36 includes a basic manicure, reviving facial and make-up.

Tariff

Heart of the City Weekends from £145 per night per double room on a Friday, Saturday or Sunday night. This includes breakfast and use of the health club for two persons.

Regular mid-week tariff is £195 for room only and unlike the weekend rate does not include VAT.

All rooms at the Intercontinental are double or twin-bedded and the above rates apply to single or double occupancy.

Depending on availability, reduced rates are sometimes offered mid-week, so ask about these when making initial enquiry.

The Mayfair Hotel
Strattan Street   London   SW5   OTH
Tel   071-629 7777   Fax   071-629 1459

| 294 | 2 3 4 5 13 14 17 C | £ B |

A sister hotel to the Intercontinental at Hyde Park Corner, the Mayfair Intercontinental is another of London's elite hotels and enjoys a prestigious location close to Green Park.

All the Mayfair's luxurious rooms have private bathroom, bathrobes, satellite television, minibar, hairdrier and other facilities. Residents can relax in the comfortable lounges and bars before dining at Le Chateau restaurant, with its extensive array of distinguished menus. Light meals and refreshments are available all day in the Coffee Shop.

Health and fitness amenities at the Mayfair are centred on the Spa Club, situated on the lower ground floor. This warm oasis offers hotel residents and club members relaxation or invigorating exercise with a lovely indoor pool with powerful aquajet, separate saunas, sunbed and a small but well equipped gym. Fitness assessments and personlised training regimes available by arrangement. The Spa Club is open from early morning until late in the evening seven days a week. Freshly prepared 'healthy' dishes and refreshments are available and served alongside the pool.

Aromatherapy, beauty treatments and hairdressing for men and women are carried out in the Panache Hair and Beauty Salon also on the lower ground floor. The salon is open seven days a week, and massage and facials can be arranged up to 11.00pm by appointment.

Treatments
Treatments in the Panache Hair and Beauty Salon include aromatherapy body massage £45; aromatherapy back massage £30; aromatherapy facials from £45; Royal Harmony slimming programme from £50 per treatment; waxing from £8; eyebrow or eyelash tinting from £6; manicure and pedicure from £20; shampoo and blow dry £12.50; cutting from £25; perms from £45; silver foil highlights from £65.

Tariff
Weekend rate £155 per room for two persons, or £140 single includes VAT and English breakfast.

Regular nightly rate (room only) £185 plus VAT or deluxe room £230 plus VAT.

The Meridien Hotel
Piccadilly London W1V OBH
Tel 071-734 8000 071-437 8114 *(Champneys Club)* **Fax 071-437 3574**

| 290 | 2 3 4 5 6 13 14 17 C | £ A |

The Meridien is situated in the heart of the West End, close to theatres, nightlife and elegant shopping thoroughfares. Edwardian splendour fused with a sprinkling of French glamour and style give this luxury hotel an unmistakable character and charm.

Bedrooms and suites are furnished with every possible comfort. Elegant lounges invite unwinding and relaxation, while the selection of bars and restaurants cater for the most discerning palate.

The Meridien is the site of one of London's most exclusive health clubs, the Champneys Club, situated on the lower ground floor. The extensive facilities include swimming pool and whirlpool spa, fully equipped gym, dance studio, cardiovascular room, squash courts, sauna and Turkish Bath, snooker tables, library and five beauty therapy rooms. The Club has a drawing room, library and its own refreshment bar.

Hotel residents are welcome to use the Club and its faciities during their stay, treatments are charged for as taken.

Treatments

The range of body and beauty treatments for men and women is extensive and includes body massage from £22; face, scalp and body aromatherapy massage £47; G5 massage £19; Slendertone £20; Aromazone £20; Clarins relaxing body treatment £45; Dead Sea Mud inch loss £50; Clarins and Rene Guinot facials from £22; manicure £20; pedicure £25; thermology/thread vein treatments prices on application; sunbed £19; waxing from £8; electrolysis from £10.

Hotel residents can take advantage of the various day treatment packages available at the club.

A *Top To Toe Day* incorporating six treatments, lunch and afternoon tea costs £175 per person.

A *Health and Fitness Day* with supervised workout, coffee, lunch and choice of beauty treatment £95 per person.

Tariff

Weekend tariff including breakfast and VAT is £160 per night single, £172 per night double or twin room.

Regular tariff is for room only and is exclusive of VAT from £190 single, £210 double.

The Regency Hotel
100 Queens Gate London SW7 5AG
Tel 071-370 4585   Fax 071-370 5555

| 210 | 2 3 4 13 17 C | £ B |

A busy hotel situated in the heart of South Kensington, with good facilities for business visitors or those enjoying a break in the capital.

En suite rooms have television, trouser press, hair drier and 24-hour room service. Light meals, coffee and afternoon tea can be taken on the terrace; the Pavilion Restaurant serves a variety of dishes with good vegetarian choices.

Residents have use of the hotel's Elysium Club with its large whirlpool bath, sauna and steam rooms, solarium, floatarium, exercise machines and vibrosauna.

Treatments
A range of beauty treatments are offered in addition to massage £15 for 30 minutes or £25 per hour; floatarium £20 per hour; sunbed £5 for 30 minutes; vibrosauna £15 for 20 minutes.

Tariff
Monday to Thursday nightly rate £95 single, £115 double room.

Weekend rate (Friday to Sunday) £80 per room per night, single or double occupancy. Rates do not include VAT which is added to accounts at current rate.

The Regent, London
222 Marylebone Road London NW1 6JQ
Tel   071-631 8000   Fax 071-631 8080

| 309 | 2 3 5 13 14 17 C | £ A |

The Regent, London opened in February 1993 and is the capital's newest world-class hotel combining the grandeur of the Victorian era with the ultimate in luxury and modern day amenities. Located opposite Marylebone Station near Regent's Park, many of London's tourist attractions, shops and theatres are within easy reach. The Regent occupies the site of the Great Central Hotel, the last of the great railway hotels, and former headquarters of British Rail from 1949 to 1986.

The £75 million transformation includes a soaring eight-storey glass-roofed atrium housing a superb Winter Garden - the only one of its kind in London.

Bedrooms and suites are situated on six floors with either outside views or

overlooking the Winter Garden. All are exceedingly spacious and luxurious, equipped with enormous beds, large marble bathrooms, full-length bathrobes, slippers, radio, satellite television, private bar and individually controlled air-conditioning. Two floors of the hotel are non-smoking.

The Regent offers a choice of restaurants, The Dining Room, serving breakfast, lunch and dinner with English and Italian menus, The Cellars Bar and Restaurant providing informal meals, hot snacks and drinks, and the Winter Garden serving lunches, full afternoon tea and cocktails. An extensive 24-hour room service accommodates the needs of guests changing time zones in their travels and requiring full meals at odd times.

During their stay, guests enjoy complimentary membership of the Regent Health Club, with its fine 15 metre heated indoor swimming pool, adjoining whirlpool, sauna, steam room, fully equipped and supervised gym and treatment rooms.

Treatments

The Regent Health Club offers a full range of massage therapies seven days a week. These include therapeutic general massage, craniosacral therapy, shiatsu, aromatherapy and reflexology. Massages cost £40 per hour or £25 per half hour.

Tariff

Special two-night breaks (dates on application) cost from £160 per room (two persons) and are inclusive of full breakfast, champagne on arrival and use of the Regent Health Club.

Regular nightly tariff from £160 single, £180 double or twin room. These rates includes service but not breakfast or VAT.

St James Court Hotel
Buckingham Gate London SW1E 6AF
Tel 071-834 6655   Fax 071-630 7587

| 400 | 2 3 4 5 6 13 14 17 C | £ C |

54 self-contained apartments

One of London's most palatial hotels, St James Court Hotel is situated in peaceful Buckingham Gate in the heart of Westminster, close to Buckingham Palace.

The hotel offers visitors three different types of accommodation all with 24 hour room service: Luxurious en suite bedrooms and suites with satellite television, mini-bar and direct dial phone; one and two bedroom suites in the high security all suite block overlooking the courtyard; self-contained serviced apartments with fully equipped kitchen, dining room, lounge, study area and up to three bedrooms.

St James Court is renowned for its fine food and has two haute-cuisine restaurants, the Auberge de Provence, winner of the coveted Michelin 3-star rating for 30 years and the Inn of Happpiness serving authentic Szechuan, Cantonese and Pekinese dishes. An informal range of international light meals and refreshments are available in the Cafe Mediterranee.

The hotel has its own modern self-contained business centre 'Chambers' offering individual office suites, reception lounges, committee and boardrooms and multi-lingual staff. Banqueting salons accommodating up to 250 people are also available.

Residents have use of the hotel's Olympian Health Club which boasts two gyms, one equipped with cardio-vascular equipment, the other with variable resistance weight machines, separate saunas and steam rooms, impulse showers, two whirlpool spas, dance studio, sunbeds, relaxation area and health food bar.

Treatments

Swedish body massage £30 per hour; aromatherapy from £20; reflexology £25; facials £20; eyelash tint £10; manicure £15; pedicure £20; sunbed £10; slimming treatment prices on request.

Tariff

Weekend nightly rate from £82.50 plus VAT per room (accommodating one or two persons).

Regular weekday tariff from £130 plus VAT per room .

Apartment studio from £175 plus VAT per night .

Other accommodation rates on application.

The Savoy Hotel
The Strand   London   WC2R OEU
Tel   071- 836 4343   Fax   071-240 6040

| 202 | ☆ 2 3 4 5 7 13 14 17 C | £ A |

Situated on the Strand in the heart of London's theatreland, the Savoy was created over a century ago by impresario Richard D'Oyly Carte following the success of the Gilbert and Sullivan operas. Its unique ambience and all-round excellence thoroughly justify its reputation as one of London's most prestigious world class hotels. Royalty, celebrities and international travellers count regularly among its clientele and every year it hosts some of the capital's most glittering social gatherings and media events.

The Savoy's luxurious bedrooms and bathrooms are decorated in a variety of styles - traditional, art deco or contemporary, and offer every convenience and comfort including 24-hour room service, fresh flowers, bathrobes and satellite television.

The Savoy has three main dining rooms: The elegant Riverside Restaurant with nightly dancing and choice of classic English or French cuisine; the Savoy Grill serving traditional British fare, and the Savoy Upstairs, a popular seafood and champagne restaurant. The Savoy's American Bar is renowned for its cocktails, while a full English afternoon tea is a daily treat in the Thames Foyer.

The Fitness Gallery is the Savoy's new health club and opened in 1993. It is built on top of the newly restored Savoy Theatre (fire destroyed the original theatre in 1990). A stunning rooftop pool is housed under a central atrium, creating a light and airy environment. A relaxation area surrounds the pool furnished with comfortable loungers and green plants. The Fitness Gallery's

other amenities include an exercise area with aerobic floor, exercise equipment and video screen, gym equipped with Keiser exercise units, separate men's and women's lounges with luxurious changing areas and lockers, showers, saunas and steam rooms.

Trained staff are on hand to advise on equipment use or to assist with personal fitness programmes. Therapeutic massage is carried out in a beautifully restful therapy room created in pale wood with pale green walls and subdued lighting.

Treatments

Various type of massage are offered in the The Fitness Gallery - Swedish body massage £40 per hour, or £22 per 1/2 hour; aromatherapy £47; reflexology £40; shiatsu £50; individual sports massage - prices on application.

An extensive range of hairdressing and beauty treatments are also available from Michael at the Savoy, the hairdressing and beauty salon. The choice includes facials from £30; body massage from £40; manicure from £16; pedicure £17.50; waxing from £7; eyelash tinting £12; shampoo/set or blow dry from £22; highlights from £45; perms from £37.

Tariff

Various short break packages are offered throughout the year from £220 per night for two persons. Breaks include accommodation in luxurious double or twin-bedded room with bathroom, English breakfast, fruit, flowers and hand-made chocolates on arrival and complimentary use of The Fitness Gallery.

The Pampered to Perfection Break, details as for short break package, plus aromatherapy or massage and two monogrammed Savoy bathrobes. The break costs £370 for two persons on the first night and £220 for each additional night.

LONDON SPAS

The Dorchester Spa
Park Lane   W1A 2HJ   Tel 071-495 7335

Luxurious spa located underneath this world famous hotel welcomes day visitors with spa baths, saunas, steam rooms, gym, workout studios, hairdressing salon and a superb range of sophisticated treatments for men and women (see *Dorchester Hotel* entry in London section).

The London Esthetique
41 Queen's Gate Terrace London SW7 5PN   Tel 071-581 3019

London's first **residential** ladies only, non-membership health spa opened in March 1994 and incorporates Turkish baths, saunas, gym and exercise studios, water therapies, innovative private treatments and personal training in hair, make-up and styling. Entrance fee £10.

The Esthetique's new in-house restaurant *Baltis* serves freshly prepared authentic Indian cuisine for lunch and dinner at reasonable prices. Breakfast and refreshments are also available in the cafe bar.

Overnight accommodation at reasonable London rates is provided in single, twin and triple bedrooms, mostly with shared facilities from £35 single, £28 per person sharing accommodation.

The Sanctuary
12 Floral Street   WC2E 9DH   Tel 071-240 9635

Tropical surroundings with lush foliage and running water create a peaceful environment in this women only health and beauty spa. Facilities include a beautifully warm therapy pool, exercise pool, relaxation areas, whirlpool, sauna and steam rooms. Food and drinks available in the restaurant areas. Wide range of exclusive body and beauty treatments and prescribed packages available to suit individual need. Open seven days a week, daily membership £37.50 (£25 after 5.00pm Wednesday - Friday) includes use of facilities and sunbed.

The Spa at Selfridges
400 Oxford Street W1A 1AB Tel 071-409 2712

Newly opened spa within the store with five treatment rooms, floatarium, hydrotherapy bath, sauna and steam room. Lifestyle planning and holistic therapies offered, as well as a super range of spa treatments priced from £15. *Health and Relaxation Days* from £51.50.

The Spa is situated opposite the hairdressing and beauty salon on the fifth floor.

LONDON HEALTH CLUBS OPEN TO NON-MEMBERS

Aquilla Health & Fitness Centre
11 Thurloe Place Knightsbridge SW7 2RS Tel 071-225 0225

Club adjoins Rembrandt Hotel with swimming pool, sauna, jacuzzi, gym and exercise studio. One treatment room offering massage and range of Elemis body and beauty treatments. £10 daily admission gives access to all facilities - treatments bookable in advance.

Livingwell Premier Health Club
4 Millbank Westminster SW1P 3JA Tel 071-233 3579

Small health club with hairdressing and Thalgo beauty salon open to non-members. Two treatment rooms. Beauty and fitness days incorporating treatments and use of club facilities arranged on request.

Mecklenburgh Health Club
Mecklenburgh Place Bloomsbury WC1 2AY Tel 071-813 0555

Well-equipped health club with swimming pool, gym, squash courts, aerobics studios, steam room, sauna and jacuzzi. Hairdressing and Elemis beauty treatments available to non-members. Day membership £20.

The Peak Health Club
Hyatt Carlton Cadogan Place London SW1X 9PY
Tel 071-235 1234

On the 9th floor of Hyatt Carlton Tower Hotel, the Peak offers state-of-the-art gym, extensive range of classes, steam and sauna rooms, solarium and club room serving healthy snacks and refreshments. Fitness assessments, massage, osteopathy and holistic treatments available, as well as full range of Clarins body and beauty treatments. Day membership £20.

The Porchester Centre
Porchester Road Queensway W2 5HS Tel 071-792 1372

Unique fitness club with Victorian spa offering separate days for men and women, couples on Sundays. Steam rooms, dry Turkish hot rooms, log sauna, plunge pool, jacuzzi, swimming pools and relaxation areas. Four therapy rooms offering great range of treatments. Also squash courts, sunbeds, large well equipped gym and exercise classes for all levels of ability. Spa Entrance £15.40, £20 couple.

Synergy Centre
1 Cadogan Gardens SW3 2RJ   Tel 071-730-0720

Luxury club with therapy pool, sauna, steam room and gym. Two therapy rooms offer thalassotherapy treatments. Yoga, Chinese herbs, acupuncture, nutritional advice, osteopathy and personal fitness trainers. Admission £20.

LEADING LONDON
HEALTH & BEAUTY SALONS

L'Avenue Decleor
17 Lowndes Street Knightsbridge SW1X 9EY Tel 071-235 3354
Busy salon offering Decleor treatments and products. Three treatment rooms.

Beverley's Beauty Room
16 Balderton Street W1Y 1TF Tel 071-355 4036
Situated off Oxford Street opposite Selfridges. Decleor body and beauty treatments offered exclusively - one treatment room.

Bharti Vyas Beauty Centre
24 Chiltern Street W1 Tel 071-486 7910
Regular beauty treatments plus a wide range of therapies requiring a holistic approach are available at this innovatative salon. Stress problems, dietary advice and other problems helped. Centre specialises in Dead Sea mud and mineral treatments. Six treatment rooms.

Clarins Studios
At Neville Daniel - 25a Basil Street
Knightsbridge SW3 1BB Tel 071-245 6151
Busy and friendly salon with four large treatment rooms situated opposite Harrods' rear entrance. Full range of Clarins body and beauty treatments for men and women, as well as complete hairdressing service from Neville Daniel. Full and half day treatment packages and refreshments available on request.

19 Long Acre Covent Garden
(Below The Garden Pharmacy) WC2E 9PA
Tel 071-379 1225
Clarins' first London Studio has four treatment rooms and a full range of body and beauty treatments for men and women.

Clarins At Selfridges - 400 Oxford Street W1A 1AB
Tel 071-629 1234
Three treatment rooms situated within the store offering complete privacy and a full range of Clarins body and beauty treatments for men and women.

Green Room Natural Health & Beauty Rooms

Green Rooms are a chain of natural treatment rooms owned by a franchisee operating seven London branches of *The Body Shop.* Seven are based within *Body Shops* and two branches are based in Kensington High Street.

Green Rooms approach to health and beauty avoids the stereotyped beauty salon image and specialises in natural face and body treatments, including massage and complementary therapies such as aromatherapy, reflexology, homœopathy and acupuncture.

Green Rooms have a fresh, attractive appearance and a friendly relaxed atmosphere. All products used are cruelty-free.

Branches of the Green Room are open six days a week with late nights on Thursdays. The Covent Garden and Kensington High Street branches also open on Sundays.

London branches of Green Rooms within *The Body Shop*:

Covent Garden - 23 Long Acre WC2
Tel   071-379 9600

Hammersmith - 8 Kings Mall   King Street   W6
Tel   081-748 7675

Portobello - 194 Portobello Road W11
Tel   071-243 8211

Putney - 3 Token Yard   77 Putney High Street   SW15
Tel   081-780 0644

Victoria - 113 Victoria Street   SW1
Tel   071-931 0575

Other London branches at:

165 Kensington High Street   W8
(Entrance in Adam & Eve Mews)
Tel   071-937 6595

The Kensington Close Hotel Health & Fitness Club,
Wrights Lane   London W8.
Tel   071-937 8170 ext. 4721

Harrods Hair & Beauty Salon
Brompton Road Knightsbridge SW1X 7XL
Tel 071-581 2021

Europe's largest beauty salon is situated on the fifth floor and was luxuriously refurbished in 1993. 32 treatment rooms, private suites and an extensive hairdressing salon offer an unrivalled choice of treatments from leading cosmetic and skin-care manufacturers. Many unusual or specialist beauty services are available including semi-permanent make-up application.

Harvey Nichols Hair & Beauty Salon
Brompton Road Knightsbridge SW1X 7RJ Tel 071-235 7207

Well established hair and beauty salon with ten beauty therapy rooms and an extensive list of body and beauty treatments using mainly Guinot products. Specialist services include thread vein removal and various nail techniques. *Top to Toe* whole day package costs £113.50 and includes body massage,facial, manicure, pedicure, shampoo and blow dry, restaurant lunch and refreshments.

Number Five Beauty Salons

5/6 Clarendon Terrace W9 1BZ
Tel 071-266 2127

Popular salon offering wide range of body and beauty treatments by Thalgo, Clarins and La Prairie. Five treatment rooms.

1101 Finchley Road NW11 1QB
Tel 081-455 1948

Extensive range of Thalgo and Clarins body and beauty treatments available. Four treatment rooms plus manicure/pedicure room.

The Ragdale Clinic and Michaeljohn Hairdressing
25 Abermarle Street W1X 3FA
Tel 071-409 2956

Large beauty salon with 14 treatment rooms and separate men's area upstairs offering huge range of beauty, body and slimming treatments by many different cosmetic houses including Sisley, Guinot, Ionithermie, Clarins, Decleor, Phytomer, Eve Taylor and Jessica Nails. This is the only salon in London offering a Phytomer facial. In addition to the many beauty treatments on offer, sunbeds, chiropody, aromatherapy and reflexology are also available.

Leading hairdresser Michaeljohn shares the premises and offers a complete range of hairdressing services by some of London's top hair stylists.

Steiner Salons

193 Wardour Street W1U 3FA
Tel 071-636 2805

Busy salon with four treatment rooms offering Elemis, Guinot, Phytomer, Ionithermie and Cathiodermie treatments. Hairdressing salon.

66 Grosvenor Street Mayfair W1X OAX
Tel 071-225 0225

Purpose built salon offering Elemis, Guinot and various specialised body and beauty treatments and hairdressing.

25a Lowndes Street Belgravia SW1
Tel 071-235 3154

Good range of treatments using Elemis, Phytomer and Mary Cohr products. Five treatment rooms, no hairdressing.

Village Affair
95 High Street Wimbledon SW19 5EG
Tel 081-946 6222

Popular salon in Wimbledon Village offering complete range of Thalgo, Guinot, Decleor and other treatments. Five treatment rooms, steam room, two sunbeds, studio area for exercising, personal training or shiatsu massage.

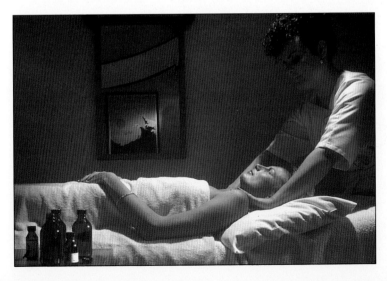

SOUTHERN
ENGLAND

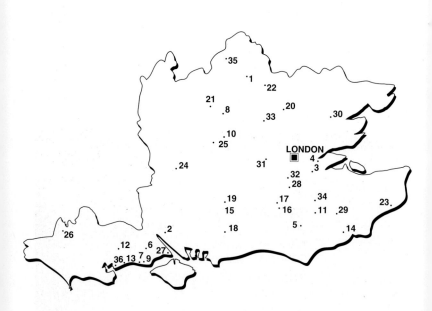

SOUTHERN ENGLAND

Beadlow Manor
Beadlow   Nr Shefford   Bedfordshire   SG17 5PH
Tel 0525 860800   Fax 0525 861345

30   ☆   **2 3 4 5 6 12 13 15 16 17 18 C**   **£ B***

Beadlow Manor is situated in rural Bedfordshire overlooking meadows and woodlands and adjoining 300 acres of championship golf courses. Guest facilities are incorporated in three main buildings on the site - the comfortable residential hotel, the country club and health farm, and the distinctive Tapestry restaurant and lounge.

Comfortable bedrooms have en suite bathroom and shower, television, radio, telephone, trouser press and tea/coffee making facilities. Visitors take breakfast and light meals in the Manor and are served dinner in the Tapestry Restaurant from à la carte and table d'hôte menus.

The Fitz Health and Beauty Club is housed in a purpose-designed building, and has a magnificent Polaris gym with an extensive array of sophisticated apparatus. No swimming pool, but steam and spa baths, separate saunas, dance studio, solaria, hairdressing salon, beauty and treatment rooms.

Beadlow Manor is essentially a golfing oasis, and has a 25 station driving range and two championship 18-hole golf courses.

Treatments

The Fitz Health and Beauty Club offers an extensive range of the latest body and beauty treatments and hairdressing, plus nutritional counselling.

G5 massage £9 per session, 3 for £23.50 or 6 for £45; Swedish body massage £11, with infra red £13.50; aromatherapy and reflexology £28; aromatherapy massage £24; Ionithermie £35 or 5 treatments for £140; body exfoliation £11; Cathiodermie bust treatment £24.50; waxing from £3.95.

A full range of René Guinot treatments are available, facials from £11, eye and neck Cathiodermie £22 each or £35 combined; make-up lesson £15; eyebrow and eyelash tint £8; electrolysis from £6; manicure £11; pedicure £14.00.

Tariff

Fitz Health Weekend breaks from £150 per person sharing a twin or double room, include a generous number of treatments with further optional ones available. *Golf Weekends* from £150.

The inclusive weekend tariff (subject to seasonal variation) includes accommodation and dinner on Friday and Saturday evenings, two full English breakfasts, snack lunch on Saturday and traditional Sunday lunch prior to departure. Facilities and treatments include sauna, steam and spa bath, use of gym, facial, G5 massage, manicure, Swedish body massage and sunbed.

Non-residential days include a *Day of Beauty* from £38.50 and a *Health and Leisure Day* from £75

Travel Directions

Take M1 motorway and exit at junction 12 or 13 and follow directions to A507 towards Shefford.

Nearest railway station Flitwick approximately 3 miles.

Botley Park Hotel and Country Club
Winchester Road Botley Hampshire S03 2UA
Tel 0489 780888   Fax 0489 789242

100	2 3 4 5 13 14 15 16 17 18 C	£ C

This attractive development in rolling Hampshire countryside lies a few miles to the east of Southampton. The hotel boasts an impressive Country Club with a beautiful swimming pool, sauna, steam room, spa bath, solaria and gym. Sports facilities are equally impressive with a challenging 18-hole golf course, two squash and three tennis courts, execise/aerobics suite, snooker, croquet and a putting green.

Bedrooms are contemporary in style with en suite bathroom, satellite television, telephone, trouser press, hair drier and tea/coffee making facilities.

Light meals and refreshments are served in the Plus Fours Leisure Lounge or in the more formal Winchester Restaurant, where dinner-dances are a popular feature on Saturday evenings.

Treatments

Treatments in the Country Club include aromatherapy body massage £25; facial, neck and shoulder massage £16; back, neck and shoulder massage £16;

regular massage £18; waxing from £4; electrolysis from £5.50, facials from £11; eyelash tint £6; cleanse and make-up £10; manicure £8; pedicure £12.50; Cathiodermie facial £22; Bio-Peel £18. A *Day of Beauty* incorporating four hours of individually chosen treatments costs £72.

Hairdressing is available in the Cutting Garden salon from £7.25 for shampoo/set or shampoo/blow dry.

Tariff

Two-night weekend breaks £58 nightly per person and include room, full English breakfast, table d'hote dinner and use of the Country Club amenities. Weekend package with golf £67.50 per person nightly.

Regular tariff from £79.50 single, £94.50 double.

Travel Directions

From M27 exit at junction 7 and follow signs to Botley for 2 miles, taking B3354 (signposted Fair Oak from centre of Botley) for 2 miles.

Nearest railway station Southampton approximately 5 miles.

Brandshatch Place
Fawkham Kent DA3 8NQ
Tel 0474 872239   Fax 0474 879652

| 29 | ☆ 2 3 4 5 6 13 14 15 16 17 C | £ C |

A mellow Georgian building, Brandshatch Place is situated at the end of a long tree-lined avenue amid twelve acres of gardens and woodlands. Such a peaceful setting in the heart of rural Kent makes it ideal for a short relaxing break. The hotel offers elegant surroundings, comfortable en suite bedrooms and friendly service with excellent food and wine.

Hotel residents have use of Fredericks, the modern leisure club in the grounds adjacent to the hotel. Facilities include three squash courts, badminton court, 17 station gym, snooker tables, table tennis and all weather tennis court. Poolside amenities include heated swimming pool, children's play pool, steam room, sauna, spa bath and two solaria with en suite showers. Fitness assesssments and and aerobic classes are available.

Treatments

Frederick's beauty salon offers aromatherapy massage £20; regular massage £18 (courses of treatment available from £45); leg and hip treatment £9, facials from £10; Decleor facials from £16 or programme of five treatments £80; make-up lesson £15; eyelash tinting £6; manicure £6; pedicure £7; waxing from £4.

Tariff

Fitness for Fun breaks for a minimum of two nights cost £54.50 per person per night and include bed/breakfast and dinner each night with unlimited use of the leisure centre and a complimentary beauty treatment. *Golfing* and *Romantic Breaks* are also available from £39.50 per person per night.

Travel directions

From M25 exit at junction 3 (junction 1 of M20), then A20 south to West Kingsdown and Fawkham Green. Hotel is 1/2 mile from village of Fawkham. *Nearest railway station Longfield 2 miles*

Bridgewood Manor
Maidstone Road Rochester Kent ME5 9AX
Tel 0634 201333   Fax 0634 201330

| 100 | 2 3 4 5 13 14 15 16 17 C | £ D |

Bridgewood Manor is a friendly modern hotel situated three miles from the historic cathedral city of Rochester, and close to the ancient Pilgrims Way - the route taken by Chaucer's pilgrims to Canterbury.

Rooms are well decorated with co-ordinated furnishings and have en suite bathroom, satellite television, hairdrier, trouser press, radio and tea/coffee making facilities. There is a choice of single, double, twin, family rooms, four suites and two rooms specially suitable for the less able.

The dining room serves fine food and wine and offers à la carte menus with daily selections of 'healthy' and vegetarian dishes. Special diets can be catered for if advance notice is given.

A splendid selection of leisure facilities is available to hotel residents: Indooors, a heated pool and spa bath, well equipped gym, snooker table, sauna, steam room, massage room, beauty treatment room, hairdressing and health assessment room; outdoors, all-weather tennis court, putting green, children's climbing frame and jogging trail.

Body and beauty treatments and hairdressing are available in the beauty salon at reasonable prices. Appointments are not always necessary.

Treatments

Swedish and holistic massage from £7.50 to £20; reflexology £10; basic facial £5.50; French facial with neck and shoulder massage and eyebrow shaping £12.50; £15; aromatherapy facial £20; Cathiodermie £20; eyelash tinting £3; waxing from £3.50; electrolysis from £3.50; manicure £5; pedicure £6; faradic toning £4; make-up £7; shampoo/set £4; perm from £16; highlights £15. *Top to Toe* package £30 includes manicure, pedicure, facial, back massage, eyebrow tidy and a wash and blow dry.

Tariff

Two night weekend break (dinner/bed/breakfast) £90 per person sharing double/twin room, £60 for child 16 or under in own room, £40 for child 12-16 sharing parents' room. Under 12s pay £15 bed and breakfast with meals charged as taken.

Bed and breakfast £30 per night, £20 per night for child 16 or under in own room, £10 for child 12-16 sharing parents' room, £7.50 for child under 12 sharing parents' room. Longer stays on half board basis from £245 per person for five days, £320 per person for seven days.

Travel Directions

From M2 exit at junction 3, from M20 exit at junction 6, (both signed Chatham) and take A229 to Rochester. At Bridgewood Roundabout take 3rd exit signed Waldersade and Lords Wood. Hotel is 50 yards on left on Waldersade Road. Nearest railway stations Rochester 3 miles, Chatham 5 miles.

Buxted Park
Buxted Uckfield East Sussex TN22 4AY
Tel 0825 732711 Fax 0825 732770

| 43 | 2 3 4 6 13 14 16 17 C | £ C |

Buxted Park is set amid 320 acres of parklands with acres of lakes stocked with rare species of ducks, swans and geese. The house and estate have a long and interesting history dating back to 1199, and the fireplaces and crystal chandeliers collected by one owner are still retained. The interior decoration of this fine house was designed by *Savoy* and *Claridges''* designer, Basil Ionides.

The elegant bedrooms are spacious and luxuriously furnished with private bathroom, satellite television, direct dial telephone and tea/coffee making facilities. Many room have direct access to the gardens and others have balconies. As well as comfortable lounges for relaxation, Buxted Park also has a private 54 seater cinema.

Diners in the elegant Renaissance Restaurant are served traditional English menus skilfully created from fresh local produce.

The facilities of Springs Health Club are complimentary to residential guests and include a lovely outdoor heated swimming pool (open summer only), well equipped gym, sauna and steam rooms, jacuzzi, sunbeds, snooker room. The grounds also have a putting green, croquet lawn and boules pitch.

Treatments
Treatments offered in the Springs Health club include facials from £13.60; eye treatment £13.65; cleanse and make-up £18; waxing from £4.75; electrolysis from £5.25; eyelash tint £6.85; manicure from £8.50; pedicure from £11.60; G5 massage £9.80; faradic toning £9.80; full body massage £20; back massage £12. A *Top to Toe* treatment costs £48 and includes full body massage, manicure, pedicure and basic facial.

Tariff
Two nights' dinner bed and breakfast from £98 per person double or single occupancy.

Regular bed and breakfast tariff from £55 single room, £78 double or twin room for two persons.

Travel Directions
From M25 exit at junction 6 and follow A22 south, signed to East Grinstead and Eastbourne. After the village of Five Ash Down take A272 to Buxted.
Nearest railway station Buxted approximately 1 mile.

Careys Manor Hotel
Brockenhurst Hampshire SO42 7RH
Tel 0590 23551   Fax 0590 22799

| 80 | ☆ 2 3 4 5 6 12 13 14 15 16 17 C | £ C |

This ivy-clad manor is situated in the New Forest, amid five acres of sweeping lawns and attractive, mature trees.

Delicious food, comfortable en suite accommodation and excellent leisure facilities guarantee an enjoyable leisure break at any time of the year. Most bedrooms are in the Garden Wing and have either a terrace or balcony. Four poster rooms and a suite are available in the Manor.

The hotel's well equipped leisure facility, the Carat Club, has a heated ozone swimming pool with jetstream, jacuzzi, sauna, steam room, impulse shower, solarium, supervised gym and rest area. Beauty treatments are available and aquarobic and exercise classes held on a regular basis.

Treatments

Thalgo body wrap £25; Frigo-Thalgo £25; aromatherapy body massage £25; reflex diagnosis £15; G5 £10; Swedish body massage £20; waxing from £3; electrolysis from £6.50; Trimtone £15; body exfoliation £15, luxury hand and nail treatment £20; manicure with massage £12; luxury foot treatment £20; pedicure with leg massage £12; Cathiodermie facials from £22; Geloid facial £20; eyelash tint £6; make-up lesson £20.

Tariff

Three night *Health* and *Beauty* breaks are held from Sunday afternoon until Wednesday morning and include accommodation, breakfast and dinner each day, use of all Health Club facilities, fitness assessment and daily exercise classes.

The Health Break costs £69 nightly per person (£53 sharing) includes daily individually supervised exercise class, cholesterol testing, nutritional consultation and daily use of mountain bike.

The Beauty Break costs £77 nightly per person (£59 sharing) includes aromatherapy treatment, exfoliant body treatment, Geloid facial and daily sunbed.

Regular bed/breakfast tariff from £59 single £99 double.

Travel Directions

Take M3 and follow signs to Bournemouth, joining M27 westbound and exiting at junction 1 (New Forest). Follow A337 to Brockenhurst (signed Lyndhurst and Lymington).

Nearest railway station Brockenhurst less than 1/2 mile.

Carlton Hotel

East Overcliff   Bournemouth   Dorset   BH1 3DN

Tel   0202 552011   Fax   0202 299573

| 65 | ☆ 2 3 4 5 6 13 14 17 C | £ B |

Located in a prime position on Bournemouth's East Cliff, this independent and luxurious hotel offers many enjoyable short breaks which include use of the facilities of the Health Spa.

Friendly service, an elegant dining room serving a variety of interesting menus, and spacious en suite bedrooms with spectacular sea views are notable attractions of this luxurious Edwardian hotel.

The Health Spa's facilities include steam cabinets, sauna, whirlpool spa, solaria and a new gym equipped with the latest electronic apparatus. Yoga classes are also arranged. The Health Spa does not have an indoor pool, but the outdoor heated pool is open April to October and has a sunbathing area with loungers, conveniently accessible from the Health Spa. Fitness clothing and beauty products are available from the Spa's well-stocked boutique. Healthy refreshments are obtainable throughout the day.

Treatments

The Health Spa offers an excellent selection of treatments and hairdressing including body massage from £12 to £20; aromatherapy from £14 to £22; G5 massage £13; Slendertone £10 per session, £80 for 10; Decleor facials from £21.50; Hollywood facial £38.50; Cathiodermie £19; Super Cathiodermie (2 hours) £43; manicure £7.50; pedicure £10.50; eyelash tinting £7.50; waxing from £4.50.

Tariff

Special rates for stays of two nights or more from £79 per person per night include luxury room, early-morning tea and newspaper, full English breakfast, four course table d'hote dinner and free use of the Health Spa.

Travel Directions

From central Bournemouth follow signs to East Cliff. East Overcliff Drive is on the sea front. east of the pier.

Nearest railway station Bournemouth Central less than a mile.

Champneys Health Resort
Wiggington Tring Hertfordshire HP23 6HY
Tel 0442 863351 & 873153 *(reservations)* **Fax 0442 872342**

82 ☆ 2 3 4 5 6 7 8 10 11 12 13 14 15 16 17 C   £ A

Champneys - Britain's most famous health resort - is situated in the Chiltern
Hills amid 170 acres of attractive parkland, close to the village of Tring in
Hertfordshire. It attracts wealthy visitors from all over the world who come to
enjoy its unique ambience and outstanding range of treatments and amenities.
These include heated indoor swimming pool, whirlpool bath, steam cabinets,
sauna and outdoor jacuzzi, dance studio, squash courts and fully equipped
gym. Leisure activities include tennis, badminton, croquet, putting, giant
chess, golf driving range, bicycling, nature walks and jogging trails.

On arrival everyone has a consultation with a medical adviser and individual
programmes and diets are arranged. Special programmes help with particular
medical problems such as back pain or cardiovascular disorders, with qualified
physiotherapists, dieticians and lifestyle consultants on hand to give advice
and treatments.

Medical screening, stop-smoking programmes, back-care courses, stress
management and alternative health therapies such as acupuncture and
osteopathy can all be arranged. Treatments are carried out in the Japanese
aromatherapy suite.

The dance studio has classes suitable for all levels of fitness, and the
beautiful indoor pool provides further opportunities for exercise with
swimming lessons and aquarobics classes.

A full activity programme runs from 8.00am to 10.00pm each day, and offers
cookery classes, beauty demonstrations, painting, talks on varied topics, back-

care classes, organised walks and cycle rides. However, guests can relax and do nothing at all, if that is their preference.

Eating - even dieting, is one of the pleasures of a stay at Champneys with a choice of two dining rooms - the Sundial for dieters, and the adjoining Trellis Room, serving larger portions of exquisitely prepared food and wine with dinner.

Accommodation is on a par with the best offered in deluxe hotels, although some single rooms still lack en suite facilities. Rooms and suites are individually designed with co-ordinating furniture, prints and furnishings. Bathrooms are luxurious, some have individual jacuzzis.

Treatments

A vast range of optional treatments, hairdressing and alternative therapies is available daily including aromatherapy £39; Cathiodermie facial £35; Aromazone leg therapy £24; Slendertone £13; Thai massage £45; reflexology £25; underwater massage £21; G5 massage £21; waxing from £6; manicure £15; pedicure £16; eyebrow and eyelash tint £16; low intensity sunbed £9; high intensity sunbed £20.

Non-residential day programmes include *Health and Fitness Day* £75; *Aroma-Day* £80 and *Health and Beauty Day* £115.

Tariff

Rates start at £150 per night for small single room with shared facilities or from £220 single occupancy in en suite room. Sharing en suite double room from £165 per person per night. Suites from £450 to £650 per night single occupancy, £275 to £380 per person per night sharing.

The minimum length of stay is two nights. Daily tariff includes accommodation and full board, daily heat treatment and body massage (except on arrival day and Sunday), initial consultations, exercise and relaxation classes, lectures and social activities, use of the leisure craft centre, sports and recreational facilities.

Health for Life membership is now available - full details on application. Members enjoy special lower tariffs and other privileges.

Travel Directions

Leave M1 at junction 8 and take A41 signposted Hemel Hempstead and Tring for approx 12 miles. At Tring look out for sign to Wiggington and Champneys, approximately 4 miles.

Nearest railways stations Tring 4 miles, Berkhamsted 12 miles.

Chewton Glen
New Milton Hampshire BH25 6QS
Tel 0425 275341 *(hotel)* **0425 277674** *(health club)* **Fax 0425 272310**

| 62 | 2 3 4 5 7 8 12 13 14 15 16 17 18 C | £ A |

This delightful establishment is undoubtedly one of England's leading country house hotels and has received many accolades over the years. It stands in 70 acres of gardens, parklands and woodlands, a ten minute walk from the sea. The atmosphere of a large private house pervades the tastefully decorated rooms, furnished with antiques and fresh flowers. Bedrooms and bathrooms are individually designed and furnished with many thoughtful extras.

The Marryat Restaurant's food and wine are legendary. Imaginative classical cuisine is combined with a choice of lighter dishes for guests on a diet, or availing themselves of the health and fitness amenities of the superb Health Club. The outstanding facilities include an ozone-treated swimming pool, steam room, separate saunas, spa pool, sunbed, treatment rooms and a fully computerised gym. Additional sporting facilities include a billiard room, 9-hole golf course, outdoor jogging track, outdoor pool and tennis court. Two indoor courts with a continental Marka grain surface are housed in a separate complex.

Treatments
A wide range of health and beauty treatments are available and carried out in specially appointed rooms. These include full body massage £32; G5 £20; French hydrotherapy massage £32; aromatherapy £42 initially with

consultation, £32 subsequently; Frigi-Thalgo £32; Clarins Paris massage for body and bust £40; sunbed treatments from £10; full fitness assessment £20; facials for men and women from £32; manicure £17; pedicure £20; Clarins make-up £20; eyelash tint £8; waxing from £6.

A full range of hairdressing services for men and women is available at various prices from £10.75 for a shampoo/set or wash/blow dry.

Alternative health treatments are available by special appointment and include chiropody, osteopathy, homœopathy, stress management, psychotherapy, naturopathy, shiatsu, nutrition, acupuncture, physiotherapy and Alexander Technique.

Non-residential *Pamper Days* from £79.

Tariff

Healthy Packages cost from £165 per person per night sharing a room for three nights. Rate includes breakfast, dinner, use of amenties and a generous number of body and beauty treatments.

Regular room only tariff from £178 per room (two persons)

Travel Directions

Take M3 and A33, turning before Southampton onto M27 signposted to Bournemouth. Take A337 to Lyndhurst and follow one-way system onto A35 for Bournemouth. Drive for 10 miles ignoring signs to New Milton, turning left for Walkford and Highcliffe (opposite Cat & Fiddler pub). Continue through Walkford and up Chewton Farm Road.

Nearest railway station New Milton 5 miles.

Cliveden

Taplow Buckinghamshire SL6 OJF

Tel 0628 668561   Fax 0628 661837

| 31 | 2 3 4 5 6 7 13 14 15 16 17 C | £ A |

Stately Cliveden, former home of royalty and the Astor family stands on the banks of the Thames in 376 acres of National Trust private gardens and parkland. It has been skilfully transformed into a sumptuous hotel offering a wide range of health, leisure and sporting activities. These include a health spa, indoor and outdoor heated swimming pools, squash court, one indoor and two all-weather tennis courts, croquet, boating, horse riding and golf practice holes.

Cliveden's public rooms are breathtaking in their size and grandeur, as are the palatial bedrooms and suites with their luxury furnishings and precious antiques. Two dining rooms cater for all tastes with imaginative contemporary cooking. Light lunches and salads are also served in the Pavilion, a luxurious spa situated within a walled garden adjacent to the main house. Facilities include an indoor pool, large steam room, separate saunas, plunge pool, Canadian hot tub, spa bath with underwater massage, swim jet trainer, solarium, air conditioned gym and four treatment rooms for health, body and beauty treatments. A specially designed room has been created for full body treatments.

Treatments

Aromatherapy massage, seaweed body wrap, body exfoliation, G5, Swedish massage, Slendertone, reflexology, manicure, pedicure, waxing, facials, cleanse and make-up, Cathiodermie and many more.

Prices are based on the length of treatment - £26 for 30 minutes, £36 for 60 minutes and £46 for 90 minutes. Treatments lasting less than 30 minutes cost from about £10.

Tariff

The Cliveden Weekend £550 per couple includes accommodation for two nights with continental breakfast, dinner for two on both evenings and use of all sport and leisure facilities.

Relaxation, Fitness and Fun Break £215 per guest, includes bed and continental breakfast for two nights, lunch in the Pavilion, three massages or beauty treatments per guest and use of all amenities.

Regular nightly tariff per room for two persons from £208.

Travel Directions

Only 25 miles from London via M4. Exit at junction 7, or the M40 junction 2. Cliveden is on the B476, 2 miles north of Taplow.

Nearest railway stations Taplow 2 miles, Maidenhead 4 miles.

Dale Hill Hotel
Ticehurst Wadhurst East Sussex TN5 7DQ
Tel 0580 200112   Fax 0580 201249

| 25 | 2 3 4 13 14 16 17 18 C | £ D |

This luxurious new hotel is situated in 300 acres of beautiful gardens with its own established golf course, high on the Weald on the East Sussex/Kent borders. It is an ideal quiet spot for a pampered short stay, and golfers will particularly appreciate the challenge of the attractive 6,000 yard course.

Bedrooms are spacious with quality co-ordinated furnishings and en suite bathrooms with generous toiletries and unlimited supplies of towels. Most rooms have balconies overlooking the golf course and countryside, all have satellite television, trouser press, hairdrier, direct dial telephones and 24 room service.

The elevated restaurant has panoramic views and a relaxed atmosphere and serves à la carte and table d'hôte menus using fresh quality produce. Calorie counted dishes are available for slimmers.

All visitors to Dale Hill should find time to relax in the hotel's well equipped Health Club with its small but delightful pool, sauna, solarium and state of the art fitness room. The Beauty clinic offers body and beauty treatments six days a week. There is also a snooker table.

Dale Hill's 6,000 yard golf course is for players of all abilities, and has been upgraded over the last few years with excellent practice facilities, golf school and a comfortable clubhouse, all open to hotel residents. Trout fishing and leisurely walks through the ancient bluebell woods can also be enjoyed in this lovely part of sourthern England.

Treatments
Herbal body massage £18; back and neck massage £10; exfoliating massage £21; electrolysis from £3; waxing from £3; facials from £15; cleanse and make-up £10; eyelash tint £5; manicure £7.50; pedicure £9.

A *Top to Toe* treatment costs £38 and includes a rehydrating facial, manicure, pedicure, back massage and sun-bed session.

Tariff
From £45 per person bed and breakfast, dinner £15 per head. A day's golf costs £15.

Travel Directions
From M25 exit at junction 5 and take A21 signed to Hastings. At Flimwell Crossroads turn right and drive for about two miles.
Nearest railway station Wadhurst about a mile.

The Dormy Hotel
New Road Ferndown Dorset BH22 6ES
Tel 0202 872121   Fax 0202 895388

| 130 | 2 3 4 6 13 14 15 16 17 C | £ C |

This friendly hotel stands in 12 acres of landscaped gardens on the edge of the New Forest adjoining the Ferndown Championship Golf Course.Log fires, oak panelled lounges and bars create a warm and relaxed atmosphere.

Guests have a choice of traditional style rooms and suites (four posters available) or modern style rooms, some adjoining for family use. All bedrooms have en suite bathroom, satellite television, telephone, tea/coffee making facilities, trouser press and hair drier.

Leisure facilities are excellent - large heated indoor pool, spa bath, saunas, solaria, steam room, computerised gym with instruction, dance studio, two squash courts, all weather tennis court, putting green, golf driving net and snooker - all free to hotel residents. Special arrangements can be made for hotel residents to play over the adjacent Ferndown golf course.

Treatments

Clarins body and beauty treatments include aromatherapy body massage £25; G5 massage £7; facials from £15; manicure £6.50; pedicure £9.50; waxing from £3.50.

Touch of Luxury half day £60 comprising body massage, basic facial, manicure, body scrub and oils, make-up and lunch.

Tariff

Two night or weekend breaks cost £67 per person per night and include dinner/bed/breakfast, Sunday carvery lunch and use of leisure facilities

Travel Directions

Within easy reach of M4 or M3, then take A33 to M27. Exit at junction 1 and continue down A31 to Ferndown, turning left at roundabout after Smugglers Inn.

Nearest railway station Bournemouth 6 miles.

Durley Hall Hotel
Durley Chine Road Bournemouth Dorset BH2 5JS
Tel 0202 500100   Fax 0202 500103

| 80 | ☆ 2 3 4 5 6 7 13 14 17 C | £ D |

A great range of 'healthy breaks' packages is offered at this popular West Cliff hotel, a short walk from Bournemouth town centre.

The Durley Hall offers comfortable en suite accommodation in modern

rooms with satellite television, telephone, hair drier and tea/coffee making facilities.

The Starlight Room Restaurant serves five course table d'hôte and à la carte dishes with 'Healthy Eating' and vegetarian options. Snacks and lights meals are available from Le Cafe Boulevard and Conservatory Lounge throughout the day.

Residents have use of the Below Decks leisure club's excellent facilities. These include heated swimming pool, children's splash pool and slide, jacuzzi, steam room, sauna, table tennis, Shapemaster toning table, hairdressing, solarium, three beauty treatment rooms and coffee lounge. Exercise classes are held regularly and the heated outdoor pool is open April through September.

Treatments

A complete range of treatments is included in the *Healthy Breaks* packages (see tariff). Optional extra treatments include Matis Bio-Lift facial £25; Dead Sea mineral mud treatment £15; collagen mask facial £15; collagen eye treatment £9; eyelash/brow tint and eyebrow shape £6.

Non-residential *Pamper Day* with treatment choice, lunch and use of facilities from £18.50 to £65.50.

Tariff

Healthy Breaks packages from £167 per person for two nights (three day programme), £457 for seven nights (eight day programme). All programmes include accommodation, meals and a generous number of treatments and activities.

Travel Directions

From M27 exit at junction 1 and take A31 and then A338.
  Nearest railway station Bournemouth 2 miles.

The Flackley Ash
Peasmarsh Near Rye East Sussex   TN31 6Y11
Tel 0797 230651   Fax 0797 230510

| 32 | ☆ 2 3 4 5 6 7 13 14 15 17 C | £ C |

Situated in the little village of Peasmarsh in the depths of rural Sussex, Flackley Ash welcomes visitors with comfortable accommodation and a varied range of short stay packages.These include a selection of treatments and use of the hotel's indoor leisure complex.

All bedrooms have double or twin beds, en suite bath or shower, satellite television, hairdrier, phone and tea/coffee making facilities. Three four-poster rooms and two suites are available as well as a special family room sleeping up to four people.

Visitors can sip pre-dinner drinks in the cosy bar with its cheerful log fire before dining in the non-smoking candlelit restaurant. Meals are prepared from quality fresh ingredients and seasonal vegetables, grown in the kitchen gardens. The home-made desserts are especially good!

The leisure complex boasts heated indoor swimming pool, saunas, solarium, mini-gym, saltwater floatation tank, hairdressing and two treatment rooms offering a basic range of body and beauty treatments.

Treatments

Floatation tank £20 (1 hour session); aromatherapy massage (full body) £25, back only £15; reflexology £20 initially then £17.50; remedial body massage £20, back only £12; self-tanning massage and moisturiser £15; faradic treatment £10 or £90 for course of ten; manicure £6.50; pedicure £8; eyelash tint £5.50; waxing from £2.50; facials from £17; mini-facial with make-up £10. Hairdressing prices available on application.

Tariff

Two night (three day) *Sane Man or Woman Breaks* from £149 per person weekends or £135 weekdays include shared accommodation, breakfast, dinner, use of leisure facilities, two solarium sessions, 1 hour floatation, full body massage or aromatherapy, wash/blow dry or shampoo/set.

Early arrival on Day 1 and afternoon departure on Day 3 necessary to allow time for all the treatments. Accompanying partners not wanting health break stay at regular *Getaway* rates from £57 per person per night. Special offer - shampoo/set or blow dry plus facial £22.50 if booked with accommodation.

Travel directions

From M25 exit at junction 5 south (signed for Hastings) and take A21 to Filmwell then A268 Rye road.

Nearest railway station Rye 3 miles.

Forest Mere
Liphook Hampshire GU30 7JQ
Tel 0428 722051 Fax 0428 723501

| 66 | ☆ 2 3 4 5 6 7 9 10 11 12 14 16 17 C | £ C* |

This peacefully situated health farm is located at the end of a long private drive, which winds through woodlands and around a picturesque lake.

Although the staff are friendly and helpful, the approach to health and stress management is serious. No alcohol is allowed, and guests are encouraged to avoid business and social pressures and limit their driving during their stay. Forest Mere is essentially a quiet haven for relaxing and unwinding.

The men's facilities have been improved and include a new spa area with power showers and a hydrotherapy bath. There is a small but pleasantly warm indoor pool and a beautifully sheltered outdoor pool surrounded by gardens and sunbathing terraces - ideal in the heat of the summer.

After an initial consultation to discuss medical background and lifestyle, a beneficial programme of treatments, diet and exercise is planned for each guest. The tariff includes daily sauna or steam bath with therapeutic massage and osteopathy (if required) and use of all leisure amenities and exercise classes.

Classes for most levels of fitness are held daily in the exercise studio alongside the supervised gym. Other leisure activities include tennis, badminton, boating on the lake, cycling, snooker, billiards, table tennis and a nature trail with fitness stations. For golfers, several local courses welcome Forest Mere guests.

The daily schedule of treatment times, newspapers and the day's post are served alongside breakfast in bed each morning. All other meals are served in

Forest Mere's two dining rooms which produce a delicious selection of fresh and nourishing meals. The Light Diet Room serves freshly made soups, fruit and home-made yoghurt for lunch and supper, the main Dining Room offers a buffet lunch with a choice of salads, fresh fruit and yoghurt, and more substantial meals in the evening.

No smoking is allowed in the public rooms and guests are requested not to drink alcohol during their stay. Guests contravening this rule may be asked to leave. This underlines the serious approach to correct diet and self discipline at Forest Mere, where the aim is to achieve rest, lifestyle improvement and stress control.

There are no signed celebrity pictures on display, Forest Mere is above all discreet, which is probably why it has more than its fair share of well-known visitors including royalty every year.

Treatments

Treatments for both sexes include aromatherapy £30; Cathiodermie facial £30.50; back Cathiodermie £38; Bio-Peel £20; Clarins facial £20; Paris Method facial £30; Paris Method body massage £31; seaweed body treatment for women £22; waxing from £4.50; eyelash dye £8.50; solarium £5; chiropody £12; manicure £10; pedicure £12 ; reflexology £15; hairdressing at various prices. Lifestyle improvement talks have proved popular with guests, and counselling is now offered on a one-to-one basis with colour analysis for £30; dietary therapy £20 and hypnotherapy £32.

Forest Mere has a fully equipped physiotherapy department, and can offer interferential therapy, ultrasonics, faradism, wax baths, hydrotherapy and infra red treatments. Guests wishing to take advantage of these treatments should ask their own doctor to write to the physician at Forest Mere.

Physiotherapy charges (between £16.50 and £18 per session) can be claimed back on some health insurance policies when supported by a doctor's certificate.

Tariff

The choice and price of rooms at Forest Mere is somewhat confusing, with five categories of accommodation. All rooms have wash-basin, television, telephone and electric blanket, and some rooms have wc, shower and bidet

Basic single room from £220 for three nights; £294 for four nights and £515 weekly. Sharing a basic twin bedded room costs from £216 per person for three nights, £288 per person for four nights and £505 per person weekly.

The most expensive accommodation costs £503 single occupancy, £379 per person sharing for three nights; £671 single occupancy, £505 per person sharing for four nights; £1,175 single occupancy £885 per person sharing weekly.

Arrivals and departures are on Sundays and Wednesdays only. Visitors are asked to arrive in the afternoon and leave immediately after lunch on the day of departure.

Travel Directions

Take A3 to just beyond Hindhead, then B2131 signposted Liphook/Haslemere into Liphook village. Go over both mini roundabouts and follow signs to Peterfield and Portsmouth. Forest Mere is 400 yards on the right after the railway bridge.

Nearest railway stations Liphook 2 miles and Haslemere 7 miles.

Gatwick Europa Hotel
Balcombe Road Maidenbower Nr Crawley West Sussex RH10 4ZR
Tel 0293 886666   Fax 0293 886680

211	2 3 4 5 6 13 14 17 C	£ E

This attractive modern hotel is designed in hacienda style and stands in six acres of landscaped gardens and grounds with mature trees. The whitewashed walls and terracotta roof create a Spanish flavour, echoed indoors with a wealth of exotic plants, terrazzo and marble floors and dark mahogany furniture. A high proportion of bedrooms are situated on the ground floor because of the unusual low lying design of the building.

All rooms have television, telephone, mini-fridge, tea/coffee making facilities, trouser press, hair drier and bathroom scales. Non-smoking, disabled and special ladies' rooms (offering complete security and additional amenities such as iron and ironing board) are available on request.

Hotel residents have complimentary use of Studio 4, the hotel's private health and fitness club, which incorporates a comprehensive range of the latest facilities for pleasant relaxation or vigorous exercise. Amenities include a 12 metre heated indoor pool, sauna, steam room, sunbeds, spa bath, dance studio with full range of classes to suit all levels of fitness. Studio 4 has a juice bar, sun lounge with relaxation area, conservatory lounge, gym, treatment rooms and hairdressing.

Three restaurants, including The Silk Trader, a stylish Chinese à la carte

restaurant, cater for all tastes and appetites.

Car parking is free whilst in residence, and £3 daily thereafter. A courtesy coach service runs to and from Gatwick airport six miles away.

Treatments

Ionithermie £30.00 (course of 5 treatments recommended); back, neck and shoulder massage £10.95; aromatherapy body massage £25.00; Decleor facials from £20.50; eyelash tinting £6.95; manicure from £6.95; pedicure £10.95; waxing from £3.50; electrolysis from £4.25; hairdressing from £5.75.

Tariff

Weekend nightly rate £60 per room (two persons) includes breakfast. Discounted rates throughout the year usually available on request.

Regular room only tariff from £100 per room (one or two persons). Executive rooms £120 per night - accommodate parents and up to two children.

Travel Directions

From M23 motorway exit at junction 10 and turn onto B2036 Balcombe Road. The hotel is 5 minutes from motorway exit and approximately 2 miles from centre of Crawley.

Nearest railway stations Crawley 2 miles, Three Bridges 1 mile.

Gatwick Ramada Hotel
Povey Cross Road Horley Surrey RH6 0BE
Tel 0293 820169   Fax 0293 820259

| 260 | 2 3 4 13 14 17 C | £ E |

Situated by Gatwick Airport, the Ramada Gatwick offers good value to travellers or visitors wanting to avail themselves of low rates, excellent leisure facilities and a choice of dining venues. Free transfers to and from the airport are provided.

All rooms have private bath and shower, double glazing, air conditioning, fridge, direct dial phone, hairdrier, radio, satellite television, room service and tea/coffee making facilities. Two dining rooms serve an international selection of dishes and the Brighton Belle Bar is popular for a relaxing drink.

Entry to the Ramada Gatwick's leisure centre is free to hotel residents, and offers outstanding sports and health facilities. These include heated indoor swimming pool, whirlpool spa, sauna, well equipped gym, two squash courts, exercise classes, solaria, massage and beauty therapy. Aerobic classes cost £3, Step classes £3.50, table tennis £2.50 and squash courts £3 per session.

Treatments

A wide choice of Clarins body and beauty treatments is offered including facials from £12; bronzing treatment £21; full body contour wrap £55; body massage £21; eyelash tint £7.50; manicure £9; pedicure £11; waxing from £4.50; electrolysis from £5.

A luxurious *Top to Toe Beauty Day* costs £46 and lasts three hours and includes facial and eyebrow shaping, back, neck and shoulder massage, manicure and pedicure. It can be incorporated into a full *Health Day* for a total of £59 and includes lunch, gym work out and use of swimming pool, sauna and jacuzzi

Tariff

The nightly tariff is £35 per person sharing a double room. Up to two children up to age 16 can stay free of charge in the same room.

A *Travel and Park* package of £80 per room per night is offered to travellers using Gatwick Airport. Guests staying a night in the hotel before flying off to their destinations can park free of charhe, for up to 14 days.

Travel Directions

Exit M23 at junction 9 and follow signs to Gatwick. Keep straight across the two roundabouts into the south and north terminals, and at turn left at the A23 roundabout signed to Horley and Redhill. Povey Cross Road is the first road on the left.

Nearest railway stations Gatwick and Horley, both within 2 miles.

Goodwood Park Hotel
Goodwood Chichester West Sussex PO18 OQB
Tel 0243 775537 Fax 0243 533802

| 90 | 2 3 4 5 6 13 14 16 17 18 C | £ C |

This pleasant hotel enjoys a unique setting on the 12,000 acre Goodwood Estate, close to the famous racetrack and Goodwood House, home to the Dukes of Devonshire for over 300 years.

The building has been sympathetically developed in keeping with the character of the surroundings, and many of the stylish bedrooms have been named after famous racehorses. Rooms are attractively furnished and have en suite bathroom, colour television, trouser press, hair drier and tea/coffee making facilities.

The Dukes' Restaurant serves English and international cuisine from a choice of table d'hôte and à la carte menus. Lighter meals and snacks can be taken in the Waterbeach Bar and Grill.

As with all Country Club Hotels, sporting and leisure facilities are first rate and hotel residents have complimentary membership of the Country Club (golf and treatments extra charge). Goodwood Park has a large heated indoor pool, jacuzzi, sauna, steam room, solaria, snooker room, gym and a hairdressing and beauty salon. Sports facilities include a fine 18-hole golf course, practice grounds, two squash courts, two tennis courts and table tennis.

Treatments

An excellent range of body and beauty treatments is available many using Clarins products. Facials from £14; aromatherapy first treatment with consultation £25, subsequent treatments £20; firming body treatment £17; body massage £21.50; faradic toning £10.50 per session; G5 massage £10.50; electrolysis from £5.50; waxing from £3.25; manicure £9; pedicure £10; hairdressing prices and services on application.

Tariff

Weekend Break (minimum stay two nights) from £55 per person per night sharing a double or twin-bedded room. Rate includes dinner, bed and breakfast. *Golf Break* £68, terms as above, includes one round of golf per day.

Weekend bed and breakfast rate from £45 per person sharing double room per night.

Travel Directions

From Chichester take A285 out of town for approximately 3 miles and follow signs to Goodwood Park.

Nearest railway station Chichester 3 miles.

Grayshott Hall Health Fitness Retreat
Headley Road Grayshott Nr Hindhead Surrey GU26 6JJ
Tel 0428 604331   Fax 0428 605463

75 | ☆ 2 3 4 5 6 7 8 9 10 11 12 14 15 16 17 18 C   £ A*

This established health retreat is situated in some of Surrey's most picturesque National Trust countryside. The well-preserved Victorian house, once the home of great poet Alfred Lord Tennyson, is surrounded by 47 acres of gardens with lakes and immaculately manicured lawns, an hour's drive from London.

Guests enjoy a highly personalised service and have a detailed consultation with one of the medical team on arrival, ensuring treatments are compatible with individual condition and state of health.

A wonderful choice of sporting and leisure activities is offered, including 9-hole golf course, outdoor and indoor tennis courts (two new indoor courts have recently been built), exercise studios, gym, outdoor badminton (summer only), whirlpool and indoor swimming pool.

The luxurious spa incorporates all treatment areas under a central atrium with a hydrotherapy centre, floatation room, six additional beauty rooms and a new hairdressing salon. The steam room can be enjoyed free of charge. Between or after treatments, a visit to the Relaxation Room is a must, with its total silence, subdued lighting and reclining beds. This is pampering at its best!

The daily exercise classes are held in an airy studio and include T'ai-chi, circuit training, stamina development, tummy trimmers, stretch and relax classes, rebounders and many more. Current timetables are displayed on the notice board in the treatment and reception areas and in all rooms. Evening talks, demonstrations and discussion groups are held regularly, and partners for bridge or tennis can be acquired by advertising on the notice board in the treatments reception lounge.

Grayshott is renowned for its delicious and healthy cuisine. Breakfast is served in your room or taken in the Light Diet Room, lunch is a vast buffet of various dishes and appealing salads, and dinner an appetising choice of meat, fish and vegetarian dishes. All dishes are calorie counted. A number of specific diets are served in the Light Diet Room with calorie intake totally controlled..

Day time dress is informal - tracksuits, trainers and leisure wear - most guests wear ordinary clothes at dinner.

Treatments

An extensive choice of optional body, beauty and health treatments is offered to both sexes including facials from £25; manicure £15; pedicure £20; hairdressing from £10; aromatherapy £37; reflexology £21; G5 massage £17; algae or herbal body wrap £30; lifestyle counselling £35; hypnotherapy £85; fitness assessment £19; individual exercise training £12 or 3 sessions for £32; physiotherapy £20; osteopathy £28; cholesterol screening £14; floatation room session £30; hydrotherapy bath £35.

Tariff

The daily rate includes initial consultation on day of arrival with routine medical check, nutritional consultation, all meals and refreshments, choice of heat treatment and massage (excluding day of arrival) all sports and leisure facilities.

Main wing - First floor basic single room with wash-basin and wc £150 per night, £525 four nights, £900 seven nights. Sharing basic twin/double room £116 per night, £406 four nights, £696 seven nights.

Ground floor basic single room with shower £166 per night, £581 four nights, £996 seven nights. Sharing twin/double with shower £132 per night, £462 four nights, £792 seven nights.

Century wing - Single occupancy room with shower £190 per night, £665 four nights, £1140 seven nights; or sharing £150 per person per night, £525 four nights, £900 seven nights.

Main house - from £150 - £298 single occupancy , £525 - £1043 four nights, £888 - 1788 seven nights, or sharing from £120 to £235 per person per night, £406 to £826 four nights, £696 to £1416 seven nights.

Travel Directions

Take A3 London to Portsmouth road as far as Hindhead. Drive through the village and turn right onto B3002 to village of Grayshott. Grayshott Hall is approximately to miles further on from the village on the left hand side.

Nearest railway station Haslemere 5 miles.

Hanbury Manor
Thundridge Nr Ware   Hertfordshire SG12 OSD
Tel 0920 487722   Fax 0920 487692

| 98 | ☆ 2 3 4 5 6 13 14 15 16 17 18 C | £ A |

Hanbury Manor is a magnificent baronial manor transformed into an exclusive country house hotel with superb health, leisure and beauty facilities, on a par with the best available at any health farm.

The Jacobean style manor was originally built in 1890 for the Hanbury family, and until recently was an exclusive girls' convent and boarding school. Standing in 200 acres of Hertfordshire countryside with delightful woodland and meadow walks, there are acres of spectacular gardens to explore including an exquisite walled garden and a 'secret garden'.

Everything about Hanbury Manor is outstanding - luxurious rooms with beautiful bathrooms, toiletries and bathrobes, imaginative food from a choice of three restaurants, sumptuously furnished public rooms with oak panelling and tapestries, enormous log fires, numerous plants and dried flower arrangements and exceptionally friendly staff.

All bedrooms are tastefully furnished and decorated with luxury bathroom, television, telephone, mini-bar, hair drier, bathrobes and trouser press. Some rooms have four poster beds.

Visitors can luxuriate in the state of the art Health and Fitness Club skilfully designed to complement the Jacobean style architecture. Amenities include a spectacular indoor swimming pool, squash courts, Polaris equipped gym with experienced staff on hand to help and supervise, mirrored aerobics and dance studio with fully sprung floor, sauna and steam rooms, jacuzzi, solarium and comfortable changing and locker facilities with copious supplies of towels.

Outdoor leisure amenities include three all weather tennis courts, croquet lawns, fitness jogging trail and an 18-hole championship standard golf course designed by Jack Nicklaus II.

Health and beauty treatments are taken in the relaxed surroundings of the Health Club's five treatment rooms with three aromatherapy baths, hand painted ceiling murals and mood music.

Treatments

Aroma-massage £27; reflexology with aromatherapy £50; G5 massage £16; exfoliation treatment £27; Decleor slimming programme of 5 treatments £125; sunbed £8; aroma bath £10; Decleor holistic facials from £27; Cathiodermie facial £29; waxing from £5; make-up £16; eyelash tinting £9.50; manicure from £12; pedicure from £17; electrolysis from £9.50; hairdressing from £7.

Tariff

A two night stay on the *Decleor Beauty Programme* from £160 per person per night sharing double room. This rate includes accommodation in Executive Room, full English breakfast, evening Menu du Jour in one of two restaurants, personal consultation with beautician to plan treatment programme, full use of the Health Club facilities and Aroma-massage, Decleor facial and aroma-bath.

One and two day *Golf and Beauty for Couples* breaks include the above programme for ladies, two rounds of golf, golf practice, bag/shoe clean and storage, aroma-massage, facial, manicure or massage for men - from £170 per person per night including accommodation and meals as detailed above.

Day health and beauty packages include use of the Health Club's facilities: *Top to Toe Day* (lunch included) £150; *Health & Body* £65; *Body & Face* £75; *Beauty & Relaxation* £55; *Relax & Bathe* £33; *Relax, Tan & Bathe £38.*

Travel Directions

From M25 exit at junction 25 and take A10 Cambridge road to Ware. Hanbury Manor is 4 miles north of Ware, 25 miles from London.
Nearest railway station Ware 4 miles.

Hartwell House
Oxford Road Aylesbury Buckinghamshire HP17 8NL
Tel 0296 747444 Fax 0296 747450

| 47 | 2 3 4 5 6 13 14 15 16 17 C | £ B |

Once home to the exiled King of France, Louis XVII, Hartwell House is now an exclusive country house hotel with a wealth of carefully preserved historic features. The hotel enjoys a rural situation two miles from the market town of Aylesbury amid 90 acres of landscaped parklands including a lake.

Accommodation is luxurious and well appointed with many exceptionally large rooms, 32 in the main house and 17 in Hartwell Court, the former stables

and riding school. Two dining rooms offer an impressive array of imaginative menus complemented by fine wines.

The Hartwell Spa is impressively housed in a splendid new building some 100 yards from the main house and has a large heated indoor pool, hairdressing and beauty salon, whirlpool spa bath, steam room, two saunas, solarium and a gym. Refreshments and light snacks are served in the Buttery overlooking the pool. The extensive grounds offer opportunities for interesting walks, fishing in the trout-stocked lake, croquet and tennis on two new all-weather courts.

Treatments
The hairdressing and beauty salon is open seven days a week and offers a wide choice of treatments including full body massage £22; Slendertone £12; G5 massage £12; aromatherapy £26; sunbed £6; facials from £12; eyelash tint £8; waxing from £6; electrolysis from £8; wash/blow dry £10. *Health and Beauty Day* £86, *Half Day* £30 includes treatments, lunch (full day only) and herbal tea in the Buttery.

Tariff
Winter & Spring Champagne Breaks from £92 per person per night (from £97 on Saturdays) include early morning tea, cooked breakfast, £38 allowance towards dinner and half bottle of champagne.

Regular tariff (room only) from £90 single, £135 double room. Continental breakfast £7.75, cooked breakfast £10.75.

Travel Directions
Exit M40 motorway at junction 2, taking A355 to Amersham, then A413 and A418 (signed Oxford) for two miles. Alternatively exit at junction 7 and follow A329 and A418 Thame/Aylesbury roads.

Nearest railway station Aylesbury approximately 2 miles.

Henlow Grange Health Farm
Henlow Bedfordshire SG16 6DP
Tel 0462 811111   Fax 0462 815310

| 90 | ☆ 2 3 4 5 6 78 10 14 15 16 17 C | £ C* |

Britain's largest health resort, Henlow Grange is a spacious red brick Georgian manor house set in the Bedfordshire countryside 40 miles from London. The grounds include an elegant garden with tennis courts and a winding stream complete with waterfall.

Owned and managed by the Purdew family, Henlow Grange has been established over 25 years and offers a complete fitness and exercise programme for every age, along with an extensive choice of body, slimming, hairdressing and beauty treatments. A £3 million extension and refurbishment completed in December 1993 has greatly enhanced the facilities. Improvements include a new 25 metre ozone treated indoor swimming pool and whirlpool, gym with the latest cardiovascular and weight equipment, separate saunas, steam rooms, plunge pools and changing facilities, new boutique, card room, coffee bar and dining rooms. Twenty additional treatment rooms have been built, plus a solarium centre, hydrotherapy and floatation rooms and a lecture theatre.

Sports and exercise facilities are good - exercise bikes and individual trampoline rebounders, exercise studio, tennis (floodlit court), table tennis, badminton, croquet, golf practice net and boats. The quiet villages in the area are worth exploring and mountain bikes can be hired at reception. A new countryside walk around the grounds has been designed, and trails around the local countryside for longer strolls marked out.

A new format for consultations has been devised, according to the length of visit. Guests staying four or more days have an initial meeting with a qualified nurse or senior therapist followed by an in-depth consultation on either fitness, slimming or skincare. This enables a personalised fitness programme and choice of treatments to be worked out to meet individual need. Visitors can join in as much or as little as they wish of the exercise and relaxation programmes, which include classes in jazz ballet, aerobics, men's workouts, yoga, relaxation, supervised jogs and walks, gym instruction and body alignment. Talks, demonstrations and make-up classes are held in the evenings.

Visitors have a choice of dining rooms - calorie-counters can opt for the light diet room, away from the temptations of the main dining area where more substantial meals and wine are served. Coffee and tea are available throughout the day and a new coffee bar remains open until late every evening.

The majority of bedrooms have private facilities, all have satellite television and are reasonably appointed. The recently completed extension includes 26 new en suite rooms.

Treatments

The huge range of optional body and beauty treatments uses products by Thalgo, Decleor, Clarins, Guinot, Kanebo and Henlow Grange's own in-house brand La Zouche . The choice of treatments includes aromatherapy £32.50; faradic toning £14.25; special wax bath £25; Decleor facials from £33.50; G5 massage £10; sunbed £7.50; Swedish body massage £18.50; make-up £15; manicure £14.85; pedicure £18.50; wash/blow dry from £10.75 and many more. Toning tables sessions last an hour and cost £9.75 each.

Tariff

The daily rate varies from £89.95 single or £67.95 per person sharing a twin bedded room without bathroom to £129.95 single en suite, £99.95 per person sharing twin bedded en suite premier room. The daily rate includes full body massage, facial (or neck/shoulder massage), sauna or Turkish bath as well as full use of all sporting amenities, complete exercise and relaxation programmes, evening demonstrations and lectures. All accommodation includes standard breakfast, buffet luncheon (Sunday lunch is also included) dinner and tea/coffee throughout the day. Many other breaks are offered at Henlow Grange with special deals for long weekends and weekly stays.

Day guest facilities have been improved and are available every day. A non-residential *Top to Toe Day* costs £65 and includes introductory talk with coffee, sauna and steam, Swedish body massage, facials or neck/shoulder massage, pedicure or manicure, sauna and steam bath, G5 massage, three course lunch, use of swimming pool, gym and sports facilities.

Travel Directions

Henlow Grange is approximately 40 miles from London and can be reached via M25 exit 23 and A1(M). Exit A1(M) at junction 10, then take A507 north to Henlow for 4 miles.

Nearest railway stations Hitchin 11/2 miles and Arlesley 11/2 miles.

The Hythe Imperial
Prince's Parade Hythe Kent CT21 6AE
Tel 0303 267441   Fax 0303 264610

| 100 | 2 3 4 5 13 14 16 17 18 C | £ C |

The splendid Hythe Imperial was built over a hundred years ago, and dominates the seafront of this pleasant Kent resort. Standing in its own 50 acre estate with gardens and a golf course, it combines the elegance and tradition of a past age with modern comforts and amenities.

The hotel was extensively improved in 1992 and offers great value accommodation with outstanding sporting and leisure facilities. Children are welcomed with free cots, baby listening service, junior menus, playroom and a safe outdoor playing area. Inter-connecting rooms are available for families, as well as two-bedroomed suites and rooms with bunk beds. Puzzles and quizzes are thoughtfully provided at meal times to keep children amused. On Saturdays and certain other dates, a child minder is available for up to three hours to give parents a break .

Sporting and leisure amenities can be enjoyed all year round. Even in inclement weather there is scope for exercise and fun, thanks to the excellent facilities which include a large heated indoor pool and spa pool, two mini gyms, two snooker tables, health assessment room, two squash courts and a Scalextric race track. Outdoors are four grass and two all-weather floodlit tennis courts, a 9-hole 18 tee par 68 golf course, putting, croquet, all-weather karting and a children's climbing frame.

Comfortable en suite rooms are equipped with satellite television, radio, trouser press, hair drier and tea/coffee making facilities. The dining room serves a choice of à la carte dishes, with vegetarian and 'healthy' menu choices.

Health and beauty facilities include steam room and sauna suites, sunbed, massage and two beauty treatment rooms, relaxation area and hairdressing room.

Two experienced freelance therapists provide hotel guests with a wide range of treatments and hairdressing at reasonable prices.

Treatments

Swedish and holistic massage from £7.50 to £20; reflexology £10; Cathiodermie treatments from £20; basic facial £5.50; French facial with neck and shoulder massage and eyebrow shaping £12.50; eyelash tinting £3; manicure £5; pedicure £6; waxing from £3.50; faradic treatments £4 per session; make-up £7; wash and blow dry £5.50; perm from £16; highlights £15.

Tariff

A two night weekend costs £120 per person for dinner/bed and breakfast and is based on sharing a double or twin bedoom.

Weekend dinner/bed and breakfast rate for children aged 16 or under in own room £60. Children aged 12-16 sharing parents' room pay £40 per child - under 12s sharing parents room pay reduced £15 bed and breakfast rate with other meals charged as taken. All residential stays include use of leisure facilities - hairdressing, treatments and weekend golf have additional charges. Golf is free during the week and £10 per person at weekends.

To make the most of weekend stays, a special *Sunday Plus* is recommended, enabling guests to keep their room until 5.00pm and enjoy Sunday lunch. It costs £10 per adult, and a small meal charge for children.

Travel Directions

Hythe is easily reached from M20. Exit at junction 11 and follow signs to Hythe. Nearest railway station Folkstone Central 4 miles.

Inglewood Health Hydro
Kintbury   Berkshire   RG15 OSW
Tel 0488 682022   Fax 0488 682595

| 72 | ☆ 2 3 4 5 6 7 8 10 11 12 14 15 16 17 C | £ C* |

Inglewood's history dates back to the days of the 12th century Crusades when it was one of the great houses of the Knights Templar. Today, the historic mansion set in 50 acres of Berkshire countryside, is one of Britain's leading health hydros with a wide range of health, fitness, beauty and dietary programmes to suit everyone.

The atmosphere is unhurried and informal. Everyone has a personal consultation on arrival with a health consultant who prescribes an individual programme of diet, treatments and exercise. There are programmes to help particular problems such as back pain, with qualified physiotherapists,

osteopaths and dieticians on hand to give advice and treatments.

Weight loss and diet are specialities at Inglewood. Advice from the resident dietician is free, with diets devised to suit personal needs and lifestyle. Two separate restaurants enable guests on lower calorie diets to keep away from the tempting, more generous portions in the main dining room, where a limited amount of alcohol is served in the evenings.

Sporting and leisure amenities include croquet, tennis, clock golf, cycling, whirlpool spa, indoor swimming pool, gym and aerobics studio. Newly purchased mountain bikes and supervised jogs on country trails provide good exercise opportunities in addition to the daily classes held in the exercise studio, gym and indoor pool. The day's activities carry on into the evening when a variety of talks and demonstrations take place in the lounge.

Inglewood's spacious interior is tastefully decorated reflecting the ambience of a stately home with gracious public rooms including a lounge with open fire. The gardens are a delight and well worth exploring, as is the surrounding area with its quaint little villages. The accommodation ranges from the palatial luxury of the Inglewood Suite to budget rooms. All accommodation has telephone, radio and television and most rooms have en suite bath or shower. In addition to the 72 bedrooms in the main house, there is a five bedroomed lodge in the grounds.

Treatments

All residential stays except weekend breaks include four treatments daily (two on midweek arrival and departure days) chosen from a wide range including G5, Slendertone, massage, hydrotherapy baths, sauna/steam, osteopathy and physiotherapy.

Further optional treatments can be taken - G5 massage £10; sauna or steam cabinet £7 each; peat bath or aroma oil bath £8 each; Slendertone £10; physiotherapy from £12; osteopathy £16; massage and sauna £20; solarium £5; aromatherapy £36; reflexology £20; facials from £23.50 (men's facial £21);

eyelash tinting £8.20; manicure £13.80; pedicure £16.85; waxing from £7.65; electrolysis from £8.50; hairdressing starts at £9.50.

The appointments system works well - the spa treatment rooms are adjacent to the pool and in the mornings guests relax on poolside loungers awaiting the therapists' call.

Tariff

Nightly accommodation rates start at £62 single budget room - £58 per person sharing twin budget room with no bathroom (one week bookings only).

Economy single room with shower and wc costs £305 for a three night stay (single rooms only in this category).

Standard room with shower and wc costs £325 single or £268 per person sharing a twin room for a three night stay.

The most expensive accommodation is the Inglewood Suite - this costs £190 per night for single occupancy or £160 per person sharing.

Travel Directions

Kintbury is just off the A4 Hungerford to Newbury road, not far from junction 13 of M4.

Nearest railway station Kintbury 1 mile (free collection) or Newbury 7 miles.

Kirtons Resort Hotel and Country Club
Pingewood Reading Berkshire RG3 3UN
Tel 0734 500885   Fax 0734 391996

| 81 | 2 3 4 13 14 16 17 C | £ D |

Nestling on the shores of its own private lake, Kirtons Resort Hotel is a secluded sporting hotel with a beautiful setting and great facilities for those wanting a healthy break. It is also an internationally renowned sporting venue, host to many televised waterskiing events including the European Championships.

The hotel is modern in style - all rooms have en suite bathroom, trouser press, hairdrier, satellite television, radio, baby listening device, direct dial phone and tea/coffee making facilities. A choice of table d'hôte dishes and à la carte menus are availabe in the Pavilion Restaurant (table d'hôte dinner from £17.50) with informal snacks and drinks served in the Lakeside Brasserie and Piano Bar.

Leisure facilties include five all-weather tennis courts, three squash courts, indoor swimming pool, dance studio, snooker tables, gym, solarium, steam room, sauna, jacuzzi and creche. Water skiing and jet skiing by arrangement from £8.50 per session. Helen's Health and Beauty Clinic offers a good range of treatments, and there is also a hairdressing salon.

Kirtons Resort Hotel is one of several Resort hotels offering health, leisure and treatment facilites. Further details on 0345 313213.

Treatments

Clarins facials from £14; eyelash tint £5.50; manicure £8.50; nail extensions £32 for full set or £3.50 per nail; pedicure £10; electrolysis from £4; waxing from £3.50; sunbed with shower £3.80; full body massage £20; bust treatment £15; G5 massage £9 per session.

Tariff

Bed/ breakfast Friday to Sunday from £36 per person per night. Dinner/bed/ breakfast any day from £48 per person per night.

Minimum stay at weekends is one night, midweek (Monday to Thursday) two nights. Up to two children accommodated free when sharing room with parents - meals charged for as taken.

Travel Directions

From M4 exit at junction 11 and take A33 signed to Basingstoke. At first traffic island turn right and take second road on the right. Drive for approximately two miles down this country lane to traffic lights. Hotel is just beyond the lights.

Nearest railway station Reading 6 miles.

Middle Piccadilly Natural Healing Centre
Holwell   Sherborne   Dorset   DT9 5LW
Tel 0963 23468

6   ☆   2 7 9 10 11 12 15   £ D*

Middle Piccadilly Natural Healing Centre is a 17th century thatched farmhouse set in the pretty Dorset countryside offering a uniquely restful break in lovely surroundings. There is a sauna and jacuzzi - no swimming pool or beauty treatments - just a caring atmosphere where a range of holistic therapies promote the process of self-healing.

Proprietors Jo and Gerry Harvey have successfully created a homely and peaceful oasis, away from the pressures of modern life. A stay at Middle Piccadilly helps restore body balance depleted by stress, lack of exercise, unhealthy eating habits and pollution. This philosophy is enhanced by a strict 'no smoking anywhere' policy and the absence of external influences such as newspapers, radios and television - even use of the telephone is discouraged.

Accommodation is in pleasant bedrooms, including some four poster rooms, each one decorated in a different shade and furnished with natural wood furniture and floral prints. Most of the bedrooms have wash-hand basins and shared bathroom facilities.

Delicious vegetarian wholefood cuisine is served at Middle Piccadilly -

homegrown organic produce in season is used whenever possible.

After dinner the cosy lounge with blazing open fire invites relaxation, or the picturesque surrounding countryside and Dorset coast can be explored.

Treatments

Remedial yoga, massage, aromatherapy and Neydharting Moor baths complement a wide range of alternative health treatments. These include acupressure, Bach flower remedies, counselling and regression therapy, creative visualisation, dietary therapy (with food allergy testing if necessary), reflexology, energy balancing, Metamorphic Technique and alignment therapy.

Each guest's life pattern is investigated and the most appropriate treatment planned. Sometimes a combination of therapies may be prescribed, with a series of treatments given at progressively less intervals, to help retrain the body into a healthier way of life.

Tariff

The daily rate of £46 per person includes accommodation and full board. Treatments are charged at £19 per hour.

Several holistic healing breaks are now offered incorporating various treatments with accommodation and full board. *Holistic Body Intensive* packages cost £168.50 per person for two days, £240 for three days and £310 for four days. Guests staying for the four day package have a choice of de-stress relaxation or energising-recharging programmes.

Travel Directions

Take motorway network and A30 to Sherborne, then A3030 road to Bishops Caundle and Holwell.

Nearest railway station Sherborne 4 miles.

Miracles Swim School, Health & Beauty Activity Centre
Little Church 51 Anglesey Road Alverstoke Gosport
Hampshire PO12 2DX
Tel & Fax   0705 601144

2 3 4 5 7 13 14 16 17 C   **£ B**

Miracles is a unique swimming school and activity centre situated yards from the shores of the Solent with lovely views towards the Isle of Wight.

Based in Little Church, an award winning conversion of a former private church of unusual design, Miracles boasts an enticingly warm swimming pool with swim jet, sauna, sunbed, beauty treatment room, aromatherapy/air bath and toning tables. Many of the original church features have been carefully preserved and are integrated into the conversion, including the stained glass windows and the organ, creating a unique backdrop to the swimming pool.

Miracles' wide choice of facilities have the most unusual of settings imaginable. Outstanding health, fitness and quality swimming tuition courses are organised with accommodation provided at local hotels.

Healthy Awaybreak rates include bed and breakfast at the Belle Vue Hotel, Lee-on-Solent (3 miles away); *Swim Break* rates include half board accommodation at nearby historic Anglesey Hotel which was completely refurbished in 1992.

Little Church's own beauty salon, Heavenly Bodies, offers colour analysis and image updating as well as an extensive range of beauty and slimming treatments. Sports injury massage is available by appointment.

Two splendid new ladies gyms have recently been added - the Figure Shaping Suite has the latest high-tech equipment, and Calorie Countdown Centre is equipped with Shapemaster calorie burning machines. Other amenities include a coffee and tea bar, relaxation lounge with satellite television and movies, table tennis, pool table, patio and garden with sun-loungers and croquet.

Nearby sporting facilities include a 9-hole coastal golf course and an 18-hole course at Lee-on-Sea, squash, tennis and windsurfing.

Treatments

Heavenly Bodies offers a wide range of beauty, health and slimming treatments including therapeutic massage from £12; sports massage therapy and injury clinic 1/2 hour session £15, 1 hour session £30; aromatherapy/air bath £2.50; facials from £11.25; make-up £7; eyelash tint £4.50; waxing from £3; manicure £6.50; pedicure £7.75; reflexology £14.25.

Top to Toe treatment with manicure, pedicure, facial and massage £34.

One-to-one aquarobic tuition £17.50 by appointment, aquacise/ aquarobics/ superfit sessions £3.50 per session - 6 sessions for £19.50. All pool exercise sessions include a sauna.

Tariff

Healthy Awaybreaks cost £395 per person for two and a half days (2 nights in hotel), £595 per person for five days (4 nights in hotel), and includes body

check and lifestyle appraisal, figure improvement programme, 1 hour's supervised exercise session (or extra beauty treatments), daily heat and body treatments. Bed/breakfast accommodation provided at the Belle Vue Hotel, Lee-on-Sea. All courses start at noon on the first day.

Nutritional analysis, swimming lessons, tennis and squash lessons and games are available at a supplementary charge.

Swim Breaks £245 per person for the two and a half day course (7 hours' tuition and 2 nights in Anglesey Hotel - Monday to Wednesday or Wednesday to Friday) or £395 per person for five day break (14 hours' tuition and 4 nights in hotel). Swimming courses are usually for a maximum of four pupils. One-to-one courses £395 for two and a half days, £595 for five day break. Rates are inclusive of full English breakfast and 3-course table d'hote dinner at the Anglesey Hotel, starting after the first day's swimming. Swimming courses start at noon on the first day.

All course participants have full use of the leisure facilities at Little Church, including treatments and massage at reasonable rates.

Tennis, Squash and *Windsurfing Breaks* are available throughout the year, prices on application.

Travel Directions
From M27 exit at junction 11 and follow signs to Gosport and Alverstoke village.
Nearest railway station Portsmouth approximately 9 miles.

Nutfield Priory
Nutfield Redhill Surrey RH1 4EN
Tel 0737 822066   Fax 0737 823321

| **52** | **2 3 4 6 7 13 14 15 C** | **£ C** |

Situated high on Nutfield Ridge, Nutfield Priory enjoys panoramic views over the beautiful Surrey and Sussex countryside

Once the home of a Yorkshire MP, the Priory has been carefully restored, retaining much of the original intricate stonework, wood carving and stained glass windows.

Every bedroom has been individually designed and decorated, with en suite bathroom, television, telephone, trouser press and hair drier. Fresh fruit, homemade chocolates and luxurious bathrobes are thoughtful extra treats.

Within the Priory is the Cloisters Restaurant with amazing views and imaginative award-winning cuisine. Pre-dinner drinks and coffee are served in the elegant lounges with cosy open fires on cooler evenings. Book lovers will enjoy browsing in the antique filled library.

Adjacent to Nutfield Priory is the Health and Fitness Club, an extensive sports and leisure complex with beautiful indoor pool, spa bath, steam room, sauna and two solaria with en suite showers, 17-station gym, badminton court, three squash courts and two full sized snooker tables. Aerobic and Step classes (extra charge) are held most days. The club has a comfortable lounge area with bar and restaurant and supervised creche.

Treatments

Body massage £20; back massage £11.50; G5 massage £13.50; red vein removal from £20; waxing from £5.50; eyelash tinting £8.50; Cathiodermie

£27; mini-facial £13; manicure £10; pedicure £12.50; Top to Toe Treat £45.

Tariff

Two night short breaks cost from £65 per person per day sharing a double room or £77.50 per day single. These rates include accommodation, 3-course dinner with coffee, English or continental breakfast, daily newspaper and temporary membership of the Leisure Club.

The regular tariff includes continental breakfast only (full breakfast £5.25 supplement) and costs from £90 single or £110 double room for two persons.

Travel Directions

M25 to junction 6 or M25 to junction 8. Nutfield Priory is situated between the two junctions just outside the village of Nutfield on the A25.

Nearest railway station Redhill 11/2 miles.

Old Batts Barn
High Street   Hawkhurst   Kent   TN18 4PS
Tel 0580 754121   Fax 0580 754014

| 6 | ☆ 2 3 4 7 14 15 | £ C* |

This pretty little health farm opened in 1991 (when it was known as *Sawyers*) and is set in a spacious 16th century country house, on the Kent/Sussex borders amidst vineyards and orchards.

Old Batts Barn combines homely comforts like cosy lounges with log fires and inglenook fireplaces with modern exercise and treatment facilities. Amenities include steam room, hydro spa baths, small heated outdoor pool (summer only), mini-gym, solarium and mountain bikes.

Tennis, squash, windsurfing, fishing, golf, visits to local vineyards, sightseeing and even hot-air ballooning are all available locally. Personal one-to-one fitness training can be arranged.

Bedrooms are attractively furnished with lots of chintz and exposed beams. All have private bathroom with quality toiletries and use of bathrobes.

Meals are served in the pleasant dining room with the emphasis on healthy eating with low fat menus, fresh vegetables and fruit. Guests wanting to lose weight will be encouraged to do so with low calorie menus, although strict fasting and starvation diets are not recommended.

Old Batts Barn aims to look after the individual needs of each guest, with amenities chosen via a detailed questionnaire completed prior to arrival.

Treatments

A range of body, beauty and alternative health treatments are carried out by experienced practitioners and include aromatherapy, holistic massage, facials, reflexology, osteopathy and chiropody.

Tariff

A three-night break with all meals costs from £199 per person and includes treatment consultation and two body massages.

Non-residential day programmes from £55 include consultation with nutritionist on arrival, refreshments, hydro spa bath or steam, relaxation, lunch, relaxation (or treatment if required), sunbed, afternoon tea and departure.

Travel Directions

Take M25 and exit at junction 5, taking A21 and then A268. Hawkhurst is 3 miles from junction of A21 and A268.

Nearest railway station Tunbridge Wells approximately 12 miles.

Pontlands Park
West Hanningfield Road Great Baddow
Nr Chelmsford Essex CM2 8HR
Tel 0245 476444   Fax 0245 995411

| 17 | 2 3 4 5 6 13 14 15 C   £ D |

Pontlands Park's origins date back to 16th century, and the present mansion standing in attractive gardens was built in 1879. The Bartella family converted the Victorian building into a country house hotel in 1981 adding a new wing and a health club, since when it has won various prestigious awards.

Bedrooms are named after flowers and are fully appointed with en suite bathroom, television, trouser press and hair drier. Four poster rooms are available on request. An excellent choice of menus is served in Trimmers Restaurant with informal snacks and refreshments available in the Terrace Wine Bar.

Hotel residents have use of Trimmers Health and Leisure Centre and facilities include Park Studios hairdressing and beauty salon, heated indoor and outdoor swimming pools, indoor and outdoor jacuzzis, sunbeds, sauna and Garden Coffee Shop.

Treatments

The Park Studios offer an extensive range of Decleor body and beauty treatments, as well as basic beauty services such as waxing, make-up, manicures and pedicures. Thread vein removal treatment, toning tables and a full range of hairdressing options are also available.

Tariff

Weekend breaks inclusive of breakfast and use of leisure facilities from £70 per double room per night for two persons.

Regular nightly tariff (room only) Monday to Thursday from £70 single £105 double room.

All prices quoted are inclusive of VAT but do not include 10% service charge.

Travel Directions

A12 (Chelmsford By Pass) to Great Baddow Intersection (A130). Take first left slip road off A130 and keep left for Great Baddow, taking first left into West Hanningfield Road.

Nearest railway station Chelmsford approximately 4 miles.

Runnymede Hotel and Spa
Windsor Road Egham Surrey TW20 0AG
Tel 0784 436171   Fax 0784 436340

| 172 | 2 3 4 5 6 7 11 12 13 14 16 17 C | £ D |

Standing on the banks of the River Thames, within easy reach of some of England's most historic sites and tourist attractions, the Runnymede Hotel and Spa is just minutes from Heathrow Airport and transport links into central London.

The hotel has been extensively refurbished in recent years, and all the en suite rooms are equipped with satellite television, in-house video, trouser press, hair drier, bathrobes and tea/coffee making facilities. Riverside views and rooms with jacuzzi bath are available on request.

The River Room Restaurant is the hotel's main dining room and serves excellent à la carte and table d'hôte menus, using fresh seasonal produce. Light meals and refreshments are also available in Charlie Bell's bar overlooking the river, or in the Conservatory, which serves a delicious traditional afternoon tea.

Hotel residents have use of Runnymede's outstanding £3.8 million health and fitness Spa. The many amenities include a beautiful heated indoor swimming pool with separate supervised children's pool, sauna, jacuzzi, plunge pools, marble steam room and wet and dry relaxation areas.

A full range of classes for all ages and levels of ability is held in the dance studio, and personalised fitness programmes and instruction provided in the high tech gym. The Spa also includes the Therapy Centre with six treatment rooms, a hair salon, fitness assessment room, fast tanning waterbed solarium and Garden Room serving healthy snacks and refreshments.

Outdoor facilities include putting, croquet and scenic riverside walks.

Treatments

A vast choice of Thalgo, Clarins and Rene Guinot body and beauty treatments and products are available to men and women, including body massage £27.50; instant inch loss cold wrap £27.50; G5 massage £16.50; seaweed envelopment £27.50; aromatherapy with consultation £44, follow up £33; facials from £16.50; manicure £13; pedicure £16; eyelash tint £5.50; waxing from £5.50; electrolysis from £11; hairdressing from £9.50.

Attractive day packages can be booked by non-residents and include lunch, afternoon tea, a variety of treatments and full use of the spa facilties - the *Vitality Day* costs £95, the *Indulgence Day* £95 and the *A La Carte Day* £35.

Tariff

Weekend rate (room only) £40 per person per night, or £60 per person per night dinner/bed and breakfast.

Health and Beauty Weekend Break £99 per person per night includes table d'hôte dinner, accommodation, continental breakfast and three beauty treatments.

Family Break (for every full paying adult, one child under 12 can stay free in their own room) £87 per adult includes dinner, bed and breakfast and entrance tickets to *Thorpe Park* and *Windsor Castle.*

Weekend supplement for executive room £15 per night.

Regular week day rate (room only) from £108 single standard room £130 standard double room. English breakfast £10.95, continental breakfast £8.95.

Travel Directions

From M25 exit at junction 13 and follow signs to A308 Egham and Windsor. Nearest railway station Egham 3 miles.

Selsdon Park Hotel
Sanderstead South Croydon Surrey CR2 8YA
Tel 081-657 8811   Fax 081-651 6171

| 170 | 2 3 4 6 7 13 14 15 16 17 18 C | £ C |

This deservedly popular and well-established hotel stands in 200 acres of parkland and offers visitors a multitude of facilities for a short healthy break.

The Tropical Leisure Complex boasts a heated swimming pool, sauna, steam room, jacuzzi, sunbeds, treatment rooms, gym, squash courts, billiards room with four tables and poolside bar. Selsdon Park's excellent sportiing amemities include an 18-hole championship golf course, putting green, driving range, outdoor pool, croquet lawn, boules, jogging trail and four tennis courts - two grass courts and two with floodlights.

Bedrooms are furnished to a high standard with en suite bathroom, television, hair drier, trouser press, mini bar and tea/coffee making facilities. The restaurant offers delicious à la carte and table d'hôte menus and a weekend dinner dance.

Treatments

A wide range of treatments is available in the leisure centre's beauty salon and options include one hour body massage £29; back massage £19; Decleor facials from £26; manicure from £15; pedicure from £16; eyelash tinting £9; *Top to Toe* treatment package £64.

Tariff

Two night weekend breaks from £55 per person per night are inclusive of accommodation, dinner, breakfast, Saturday evening dance and use of leisure facilities. Round of golf can be booked for £15.

Regular mid-week rates from £50 per person per night are for room only, breakfast extra.

Bargain rates and special interest packages are offered from time to time during the year. Reduced rates apply during August, details on application.

Travel Directions

From London take A23 to Purley, then A22 Eastbourne road and Downs Court Road for approximately 3 miles.

Selsdon Park can also be reached via M25. Exit at junction 6 taking A22 to Whyteleafe. Turn right onto B270 then first left onto B3269 Limpsfield Road. At roundabout take third exit onto A2022 to Selsdon.

Nearest railway station East Croydon approximately 3 miles.

Sopwell House Hotel, Country Club and Spa
Cottonmill Lane Sopwell St Albans Hertfordshire AL1 2HQ
Tel 0727 864477   Fax 0727 844741

| 90 | 2 3 4 5 6 11 12 13 14 17 C | £ C |

Former home of the Mountbatten family, Sopwell House Hotel is an elegant and peaceful country house hotel standing in 11 acres of landscaped gardens and grounds. The hotel overlooks a golf course and the pleasant Hertfordshire countryside, yet is a few minutes' drive from four major motorways and just 30 minutes by road from central London.

An extensive refurbishment has enhanced the country-style ambience, lounges have leather furniture and richly coloured drapes, bedrooms have en suite marble bathrooms and are equipped with every amenity. Imaginative cuisine is served under mature magnolia trees in the award-winning Magnolia restaurant or in Bejerano's Brasserie, where an innovative menu provides a variety of quality informal meals and refreshments from early morning to

late evening.

The superb Country Club and Spa offers hotel residents and private members facilities and services on a par with the best health resorts, and promotes an enhanced quality of life using exercise, diet and relaxation holistically. Facilities include a spectacular ozone treated pool, spa bath, sauna, steam room, relaxation area and sun terrace, solaria, supervised health and fitness suite with the latest high tech equipment and personal programmes, six treatment rooms, hairdressing, poolside cafe and snooker room. Bejerano's Brasserie, overlooking the pool and gardens serves healthy meals and snacks, and caters for dieters and vegetarians.

Treatments

Decleor, Thalgo and Clarins treatments are offered in the Country Club and Spa. The range includes Vital Harmony £25; body exfoliating treatment £17; Prescription facial £30; refining facial and back treatment £19; Paris body treatment £32; Paris facial £34; Thalgo wraps and hydrotherapy £25 cellulite treatment £25; relaxation and moisturising £25; G5 massage £14; underwater massage £14; massage bath £14; Slendertone £11.50 per session; Decleor facials from £25; make-up £12; waxing from £7; eyebrow and eyelash tint £9; ladies manicure from £7; gents manicure £7; pedicure from £9. Half day and full day *Top to Toe* programmes from £50. The club has a hairdressing salon with a full range of services.

Tariff

Two-night weekend breaks include table d'hote dinner, luxury accommodation, full English breakfast and use of country club facilities.

Getaway break from £132 per person; *The New You* (with body massage, mini-facial, sun-bed) £164 per person; *Sheer Indulgence* (with body massage, mini facial, manicure, pedicure and make-up) £195 per person; *The*

Stressbuster (with body massage, stress monitoring or lifestyle evaluation, personal fitness rountine with trainer) £188 per person.

Regular nightly tariff (room only) £94.50 week days/ £67.50 weekends single, £107.75 weekdays/£82.75 weekends double (two persons). Light breakfast £5.95, full English breakfast £7.95. All residents have use of leisure facilities during their stay.

Travel Directions

Easily accessible from M1, M10, M25 and A1(M), take A1081 or A414 Hatfield to St Albans road.

Nearest railway station St Albans approximately 2 miles.

The Spa Hotel
Mount Ephraim Tunbridge Wells Kent TN4 8XJ
Tel   0892 520331   Fax 0892 510575

75	2 3 4 5 6 7 13 14 15 16 17 C	£ C

Established over a century ago, the Spa Hotel enjoys a peaceful setting in 14 acres of parkland, landscaped gardens and lakes in the elegant spa town of Tunbridge Wells.

Accommodation is in comfortable en suite rooms and suites equipped with television, hair drier, telephone and tea/coffee making facilities.

Imaginative menus using fresh produce from Kentish farms are served in the ornate splendour of the Chandelier restaurant, and a traditional English afternoon tea is served daily in the lounge beside a cheerful open fire.

Within the hotel is the appropriately named Sparkling Health - a luxurious health club overlooking the gardens with a wide choice of health, leisure and sporting amenities. These include a heated indoor swimming pool, spa pool, saunas, sunbeds, gym with high-tech apparatus, mirrored exercise room, beauty therapy clinic, hairdressing salon, floodlit tennis court, fitness trail, children's adventure playground and a games room.

Treatments

Full body massage £25 back massage £15; aromatherapy £33; body paraffin wax £27.50; reflexology £20; G5 massage from £11.50 per session; Slendertone from £10.50 per session; waxing from £4.95; electrolysis from £6; Cathiodermie £27; facial treatment with steam £20.50; aromatherapy facial £21; cleanse and make-up £12.50; eyelash tinting £8; manicure £12; pedicure £15.50.

Various day treatment packages are offered - *Top to Toe* £70; *Health & Beauty* £70; *Pre-Holiday* £58; *Pre-Honeymoon* £35.

Tariff

Residential Beauty Weekends cost £115 per person and are inclusive of dinner and overnight stay on Friday in superior luxury room, breakfast and snack lunch on Saturday, exercise classes, use of Sparkling Health facilities, half-hour back massag and pedicure. The stay can be extended to include Saturday night (dinner/bed and breakfast) for an additional £60 per person. A back-massage and anti-stress facial are offered at combined price of £22.50 on Sundays. Other treatments and specialist dietary requirements can be arranged in advance.

Regular nightly tariff for accommodation only - from £69 single, £84 double room. Full English breakfast £8.50.

Travel Directions

Mount Ephraim is to the north of the town centre of Tunbridge Wells. Nearest railway station Tunbridge Wells Central less than a mile.

Tyringham Naturopathic Clinic
Newport Pagnell Buckinghamshire MK16 9ER
Tel 0908 610450

46	P 2 3 4 5 6 7 8 9 10 11 12 14 15 16 17	£ E*

Tyringham, the UK's largest residential naturopathic clinic, is situated in a pleasantly secluded part of rural Buckinghamshire, and offers a comprehensive range of naturopathic treatments and therapies. Standing in 30 acres of gardens, woodlands and farmlands, the Georgian mansion is easily reached from the M1 motorway, and is two miles from Newport Pagnell.

This is not a beauty-orientated health farm, although some pampering treatments are available. Tyringham is more clinical than luxurious with the emphasis firmly on the naturopathic approach to health and re-education of lifestyle habits. Guests are therefore accepted for a minimum stay of a week, with three weeks recommended for maximum benefit.

Wholesome vegetarian fare is served in a somewhat austere dining room reminiscent of a school refectory - basic cutlery, glasses and condiments on the tables, but no flowers or table cloths. Menus are compiled for variety and nutritional value with special diets prescribed when necessary. Some inflexibility has been reported in the serving of these special diets, so visitors should always insist on receiving their individual food choices.

When undertaken, therapeutic fasting is supervised with monitored low intakes of food and drink. Caffeine addicts please note - herbal teas and mineral water are the only refreshments available - regular tea and coffee are not served at Tyringham.

There are many leisure facilities available on site - swimming, badminton, tennis, croquet, putting, crazy golf, table tennis and a variety of card and board games. Tyringham boasts Europe's largest private outdoor pool which although unheated, is enjoyed by many hardy individuals in the summer months.

Treatments

Visitors suffering from a variety of complaints are accepted and treated with a broad spectrum of alternative treatments - specific therapies are selected to meet individual needs. Qualified practitioners supervise all treatments, and qualified nurses are on call at all times.

Tyringham specialises in hydrotherapy, with sitz baths, Scottish douche, salt water and mineral baths available. A heated therapeutic pool is used for exercise in conjunction with a jacuzzi and sauna.

Tariff

Tyringham is a registered non-profit making charity. Generously reduced fees for deserving cases are possible through the Needy Patient's Fund and apply to dormitory accommodation, normally costing from £230 per person per week.

Other accommodation is in single and double rooms, the majority having en suite facilities and charges range from £293 to £420 per person sharing a double room, £369 to £492 single room per week.

The weekly tariff includes consultations and treatments as prescribed - separate charges are made for X-rays, blood tests, ECGs, injections and medications.

Outpatients can enjoy a *Tyringham Day*, staying at the Swan Revived Hotel, in the charming town of Newport Pagnell. Accommodation, English breakfast, lunch at Tyringham, and a full day's health programme and dinner costs £62 per person - bookings to be made via Tyringham.

Staff at Tyringham are friendly and helpful, and the atmosphere is less formal than the brochure suggests.

Travel Directions

From M1 exit at junction 14 and take A509 to Newport Pagnell and B526 to Tyringham.

Nearest railway stations Wolverton 5 miles, Milton Keynes 8 miles.

Verde

167 Seabourne Road Southbourne Bournemouth
Dorset BH5 2HH
Tel   0202 428404

| 4 | 2 3 4 5 6 7 11 12 C | £ C* |

Verde Bodycare Holidays offer an intensive week of health, beauty and fitness treatments at the Verde Studios in Southbourne, a suburb of Bournemouth.

You can learn to keep healthy and trim with dietary counselling, aromatherapy remedial massage and fitness lessons. Visitors have an initial consultation with Verde's owner, Mrs Annabelle Lazenby, to plan a personalised schedule of treatments and counselling for the forthcoming week.

Accommodation is arranged at St Wilfred's Hotel, a short walk from the Seabourne Road salon, in twin-bedded rooms with shared bathroom facilities. All meals are carefully selected with the emphasis on health and nutrition.

Treatments

Skin care is based on French Collection's seaweed products known for their anti-ageing properties. Hairdressing and hair care treatments use natural ingredients such as juniper, burdock and sesame.

Daily fitness lessons £3.75; thalassotherapy £6.75; hydrotherapy bath £4.95; remedial massage £16.50; G5 massage with slenderising gel £9.95; waxing from £3.95; facials from £6.95; manicure £4.95; pedicure £4.95; eyebrow/eyelash tinting £4.50; ear piercing £6.75; shampoo/blow-dry from £5.50; cut from £3.95; perms from £18; tinting from £15.

Tariff

The daily tariff per person sharing a twin-bedded room from 1 May to 30 October is £70, £360 weekly. From 31 Octoer to 30 April the daily rate is £65, £345 weekly. These prices include accommodation with full board, daily treatment, instruction and seminars.

Single supplement £5 per night

Travel Directions

Verde Bodycare Holidays are situated in Bournemouth close to the beaches and within walking distance of the shopping centre.

Nearest railway station Bournemouth approximately 2 miles.

SOUTH WEST
ENGLAND

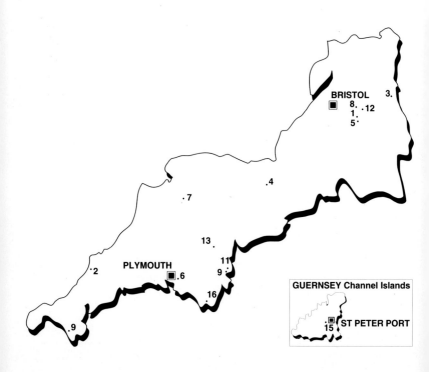

BRISTOL

3.

8. .12
1.
5.

.4

.7

13.

PLYMOUTH
.6

11
9.

.2

16.

.9

GUERNSEY Channel Islands

ST PETER PORT
15.

SOUTH-WEST ENGLAND

Bath Spa Hotel
Sydney Road   Bath   Avon   BA2 6JF
Tel   0225 444424   Fax 0225 444006

103	**2 3 4 6 11 13 14 15 16 17 C**	**£ A**

The Bath Spa Hotel is situated amidst acres of landscaped gardens overlooking the city, a ten minute walk away. The 19th century mansion re-opened after a mammoth renovation in 1990, restoring its former glory as a luxury hotel in the grandest English tradition.

Spacious bedrooms have en suite bathroom, telephone, satellite television, mini-bar and 24-hour room service. English and international cuisine is served in the gracious Vellore restaurant, designed in classic Roman style.

As befits the premier hotel in a city that was once England's leading spa, good health and leisure facilities are available in the hotel's health club, although Bath's spa water is not used for treatments or bathing. The Laurels has a large heated indoor swimming pool, jacuzzi, two saunas, fully equipped gym with instruction and personal assessment availability, outdoor tennis court and croquet lawn.

Treatments

A comprehensive range of body treatments is offered in the Beauty Salon including full body massage £25; aromatherapy £35; back, neck and shoulder massage £20; facials from £17; cleanse & make-up £15; eyelash tint £7.50; quick-slim body wrap £45; Slendertone £12; G5 massage £12; manicure £12; pedicure £15; waxing from £5; electrolysis from £8.50; red vein treatment £20.

Tariff

Leisure breaks on Friday and Saturday cost £99 per person for a minimumn stay of two nights and based on two people sharing a twin/double room.

The price for a two night break Sunday/Thursday is £89 per person per night. These rates include dinner in the Vellore Restaurant and full traditional breakfast.

The nightly room only tariff is presently £129 single room, £169 double/ twin room and £199 for a four poster room.

Travel Directions

From M4 - exit at junction 18 taking A46 to Bath approximately 8 miles, following signs for city centre.

Nearest railway station Bath approximately 1 mile.

Bedruthan Steps Hotel
Mawgan Porth   Cornwall   TR8 4BU
Tel 0637 860555 Fax 0637 860714

| 100 | 2 3 4 5 6 7 10 13 14 15 16 17 C | £ E |

This modern and friendly resort hotel is situated in five acres of grounds above a golden sandy beach on the spectacular north Cornish coast.

It would be difficult to find a more family/child orientated hotel than this, with a children's dining room, baby shop, en suite bedrooms with baby alarm, indoor and outdoor swimming pools, adventure playground, cinema, sandpits, holiday clubs and activities and baby sitting.

Extensive health and fitness amenities (nominal charges) include hydro spa, plunge pool, saunas, jacuzzi, fitness room, solaria, steam cabinets, exercise classes, hairdressing and a beauty salon. Sporting facilities are mostly free of charge - tennis, squash, racquet ball, table tennis and full sized snooker and pool tables. Sports tournaments, football, rounders and netball matches are regularly organised for all age groups.

Separate restaurant for adults (children cared for by nannies during dinner) with extensive choice of home-produced Cornish dishes including vegetarian options. Special diets catered for by prior arrangement.

Treatments

Aromatherapy massage with hot oils £25; Clarins Prescription body treatment £18; G5 massage £10; aromatherapy steam cabinet £10; reflexology £18; facials from £15; waxing from £4; eyelash tinting £6.50; manicure with polish £8.50; pedicure £7; hot paraffin wax treatment for arthritic hands £5. Complete hairdressing service available in the hair salon.

Tariff

Several types of accommodation are available with daily rate per person from £29 - £46.50 in rear view room, £32 - £48.50 hotel suite, £34 - £50.50 in villa or apartment suite. Rates include accommodation, continental breakfast and dinner. Children's terms and free child offers on application.

One week family holiday (2 adults 2 children under 8) from £525 to £693 depending on time of year and type of accommodation.

School holiday weekly rates (2 adults and 2 children under 8) in interconnecting villa back rooms from £647.50 to £805 per family.

Self catering cottages from £190 to £620 per week depending on time of year.

Travel Directions

Via motorway network signed towards North Cornwall and Newquay. Mawgan Porth is on B3276, off the main A30 Bodmin to Penzance road, a few miles north of Newquay.

Nearest railway station Newquay approximately 6 miles.

Blunsdon House Hotel
Blunsdon Swindon Wiltshire SN2 4AD
Tel 0793 721701   Fax 0793 721056

| 88 | 2 3 4 5 6 13 14 15 16 17 18 C | £ C |

Blunsdon House Hotel is situated two miles north of Swindon in spacious private grounds of 30 acres. Originally a farm guest house, Blunsdon House has grown in size and status over the years, and is now one of Wiltshire's leading country house hotels.

The Clifford family have created a fine establishment with excellent accommodation, cuisine and outstanding leisure facilities. The hotel makes an ideal choice for a relaxing short break with or without the family.

The leisure club's extensive facilities include an indoor swimming pool, spa bath, toddlers' splash pool, sauna and steam rooms, sunbeds, well-equipped gymnasium, squash courts, 9-hole par 3 golf course, snooker tables, skittles, darts, 'artificial' grass tennis court, woodland walk/jogging track and a computer games room. A supervised crèche operates at advertised times.

The comfortable bedrooms are spacious and all have en suite facilities. Children sharing parents' room stay free with meals paid for as taken. Reception can 'baby listen' during the evenings for parents in the hotel and baby-sitting can be arranged with advanced notice.

Ground floor accommodation, four poster rooms and 'Prestige' rooms with spa bath are available on request.

The hotel offers a choice of three bars and two restaurants - The Ridge Restaurant serving à la carte and table d'hôte English menus, and Carrie's Carverie offering a selection of dishes in an informal setting.

Treatments

The Reflections Beauty Salon is open seven days a week and offers a wide range of body and beauty treatments. Qualified therapists are happy to offer advice and free consultations without obligation.

Treatments include various exclusive Sothy facials from £16 to £28; eye contour treatment £10; cleanse and make-up £12; body massage from £20; back massage £12; back scrub with skin peel and mask £17.50; 20 minute Niagara treatment on vibrating therapy table to help alleviate aches and pains, tension and exhaustion £8; manicure from £9; pedicure from £11.50; eyelash tint £6; waxing and epilation £3.50 to £18. Body treatments for cellulite and slimming will be available soon.

Various day programmes are available including *The Health and Fitness Day* £38; *The Relaxation Day* £50; *The Skin Deep Day* £60 and *The Makeover Day* £60.

All programmes include lunch, use of leisure facilities and a range of pampering treatments

Tariff

Getaway Weekends from £59.50 per person per night inclusive of accommodation, breakfast, one night carverie dinner and one set price à la carte dinner. A reduced half board charge of £32.50 per person applies when Sunday is taken as a third night.

Standard accommodation charges for bed and breakfast start at £72.50 single and £92.50 for a double/twin room. The standard prices include VAT but not service charge.

Travel Directions

From M4 exit at junction 15, then take A419 dual carriageway towards Cirencester for 7 miles, turning right at sign to Broad Blunsdon.

Nearest railway station Swindon 4 miles.

We have received particularly good reports from readers staying at Blunsdon House with young families. Dining-room staff were especially singled out for their friendliness and consideration.

Cedar Falls Health Farm
Bishop Lydeard Taunton Somerset TA4 3HR
Tel 0823 433233 & 433338 *(reservations)* **Fax 0823 432777**

| 36 | ☆ 2 3 4 5 6 7 10 11 12 14 15 16 17 18 C | £ B* |

Cedar Falls is situated on the outskirts of the little village of Bishops Lydeard, close to Exmoor National Park. The red stone mansion house is set in a 44 acre estate with landscaped gardens, lakes and woods, and offers visitors extensive health, beauty and sports amenities, including golf.

The accent is very much on relaxation, and visitors are taught the specific techniques of stress management. Although there are many exercise classes and activities, visitors can be as active or as lazy as they choose.

All stays commence on arrival with a brief medical and beauty consultation when dietary and other goals are discussed. Two pleasant dining rooms cater for most types of diet, with the emphasis on raw and natural foods. Salad lunches are served buffet style, and a good choice of main courses is offered at dinner. Food is plentiful and satisfying, and complimentary beverages are available throughout the day.

Visitors have unlimited use of the many facilities including outdoor badminton, swimming pools (indoor and outdoor), whirlpool, gym, tennis, trim-track, croquet, putting, cycling, fly-fishing in the trout-stocked lake and an 18-hole par 3 golf course. Exercise classes and aquarobics are held daily and alternative health treatments - acupuncture, iridology, osteopathy, reflexology and hypnotherapy arranged on request. Evenings are taken up with interesting talks on health, lifestyle and general interest topics as well as beauty and cookery demonstrations.

The atmosphere at Cedar Falls is relaxed and informal with most guests wearing track suits or bathrobes during the day and slightly more formal wear at dinner. Casual and informal clothing and sportswear, books, toiletries and gifts can be purchased from the boutique.

Treatments

As with all health resorts, many optional body and beauty treatments are available in the beauty salon and clinic. The choice includes facials from £12.50; Cathiodermie from £34.95; Frigi Thalgo £28.95; body massage £16.50; G5 body massage £16.50; Clarins Paris Method body massage £27.25; algae body wrap £26.95; aromatherapy £36.95; Slendertone £12.25 or 5 for £49.25; solarium £3.75; sauna £7.50; steam treatment £7.50; Ionithermie £44.50; waxing from £4.95; manicure £11.75; pedicure £17.25.

Cedar Falls also has a hairdressing salon offering a complete range of hair treatments and services.

Tariff

Four categories of rooms are offered, all with en suite facilities, satellite television and telephone.

Rates start at £150 per person sharing twin room for a two night weekend, £225 for three nights, £300 for four nights, £525 for seven nights. The most expensive room, the Churchill costs £256 per person sharing for a two night weekend, £345 for three nights, £460 for four nights and £799 for seven nights. Single room supplement £10 per night.

Tariff includes accommodation, breakfast, lunch, dinner, beverages and use of facilities. The number of inclusive treatments depends on the length of stay, but all rates include exercise classes, conducted walks, relaxation sessions, brief medical and beauty consultation and daily sauna or steam bath, body or G5 massage, special peat or aromatherapy bath and a solarium.

Several non-residential day programmes are offered: *Top to Toe Day* £59 (full body massage, sauna or steam, solarium, 1/2 hour facial); *Special Beauty Day* £70 (1/2 hour facial, manicure, pedicure, make-up).

Travel Directions

Leave M5 at junction 25 and take A358 to Minehead. Ignore right-hand signs into Bishops Lydeard and continue for 1/2 mile, turning right over a small bridge. Cedar Falls drive is immediately on the left.

Nearest railway station Taunton (5 miles).

Combe Grove Manor
Brassknocker Hill   Monkton Combe   Bath   Avon   BA2 7HS
Tel 0225 834644   Fax 0225 834961

45	2 3 4 5 6 7 8 13 14 15 16 17 18 C	£ C

This gracious English manor house is situated on the hillside site of a Roman settlement, amid 82 acres of gardens and woodlands with extensive views over the Limpley Stoke valley. On a clear day the famous White Horse of Westbury is visible, 16 miles away.

The present owners purchased Combe Grove Manor in 1985 and have carefully preserved its unique 18th century elegance while renovating and transforming it into a luxurious hotel and country club with modern comforts and unrivalled sports, health and leisure facilities.

Accommodation is provided in either the Manor House itself or the charming Garden Lodge adjacent to the Country Club. Bedrooms are individually designed in delightful country house style, with luxurious bathroom, bathrobes, satellite television, telephone and tea/coffee making facilities.

Interesting and substantial table d'hôte and à la carte menus are served in the elegant Georgian restaurant which has lovely views across the wooded valley, or less formally in the Manor Vaults Bistro, which has a good choice of dishes and bar facilities.

The Country Club amenities include indoor and outdoor swimming pools, Nautilus gym with cardio-vascular equipment, aerobics studio with fully sprung wooden floor, hydro spa heated to 101°F, steam room, saunas, solarium and beauty salon. Sporting facilities are equally good - one covered and three all-weather tennis courts, 5-hole par 3 golf course, 9-hole mini putting course,

19-station two tiered driving range and a woodchip jogging trail through estate woodlands. Hotel residents have full use of all facilities, and are welcome to join in aerobic and fitness classes. Body and beauty treatments should be reserved in advance to avoid disappointment.

Treatments

Full aromatherapy and reflexology (2 hours) £39; standard body massage £21; back massage £11.50; Slendertone £11.50 per hour, 8 for £78; Clarins Prescription body treatment £25; Clarins firming bust and neck treatment £23; Clarins Prescription facial £27; Clarins relaxing facial £27; Paris Method facial £32; make-up lesson £18; eyelash tinting £6.50; manicure £12; pedicure £14; electrolysis from £7.

Tariff

Mini-breaks from £170 per room (two persons) per night (minimum two nights stay) include continental breakfast, dinner in the Georgian Restaurant and unlimited use of the sports and leisure facilities.

Clarins Top to Toe Breaks £75 supplement per person on mini break price, and including facial, body treatment, manicure and pedicure.

Health and Fitness Breaks (minimum two nights) incorporate a full programme of leisure activities and sports tuition from £230 per room (two persons) per night and include dinner and accommodation on the first evening, continental breakfast, lunch in the Manor Vaults Bistro, dinner and accommodation on day two, and a continental breakfast on the morning of departure. Specialist calorie controlled menus provided on request. A fully co-ordinated fitness programme is organised for the visit and can include tennis, squash, swimming and gym personal coaching. A body massage is also included.

Standard hotel tariff starts at £130 for a standard double/twin room in the Garden Lodge or £165 for a standard double room in the Manor House. Deluxe bedrooms, four poster rooms and suites are available at supplementary cost.

Travel Directions

Exit M4 at junction 18 and follow signs to Bath for 10 miles. Combe Grove Manor can be reached taking either the A3062 or the A36 from Bath city centre, approximately 2 miles.

Nearest railway station Bath approximately 2 miles.

Elfordleigh Hotel and Country Club
Colebrook   Plympton   Devon   PL7 5EB
Tel 0752 336428   Fax 0752 344581

| 20 | 2 3 4 6 13 14 15 16 17 18 C | £ C |

Elfordleigh Hotel and Country Club lies on the edge of Dartmoor amid 65 acres of gardens and woodlands, with extensive views over the lovely Plym Valley. The hotel has been refurbished and extended to offer the visitor comfortable accommodation and outstanding facilities.

The hotel has 20 double en suite rooms furnished in country house style, with satellite television, Teasmade and telephone. Four comfortable lounges and several bars are ideal for relaxation after energetic sporting activities or with a drink before dinner in one of the two main restaurants. Light snacks and refreshments are also served in the coffee lounge.

Elfordleigh's outstanding country club is at the disposal of all residents and boasts a Roman style indoor heated pool with pine ceiling, jacuzzi, palm trees, sauna, solarium, steam room, fitness room/gym and jogging track. Sports facilities include an outdoor heated pool with sunbathing patio, glass-backed squash court, three floodlit tennis courts and tennis pavilion, croquet lawn, full sized snooker table and games room complete with table tennis, darts and pool tables. Golfers will appreciate the 18-hole par 68 golf course with its practice area and putting green which they enjoy free of charge.

Treatments

The beauty room offers a range of body and facial treatments at competitive prices - full details on application.

Tariff

A two night weekend break costs from £99 per person sharing a twin or double room and includes accommodation, dinner, bed and breakfast and full use of health and leisure facilities including free use of the golf course (to guests showing official handicap). Extra night (half board) either side of the weekend £45.

Daily tariff for accommodation and full English breakfast £55 single, £75 twin or double and £86 family room. Children under 10 sharing parents' room have meals at 50% reduction.

Travel Directions

Take A374 Plympton road from Marsh Mills roundabout, turning left into Larkham Lane and into Crossway. At Boringdon Hill, turn left and continue for a further mile.

Nearest railway station Plymouth 7 miles.

Highbullen Hotel
Chittlehamholt Umberleigh North Devon EX37 9HD
Tel 0769 540561   Fax 0769 540492

| 35 | 2 3 4 5 13 14 15 16 18 | £ D |

Highbullen is an interesting Victorian Gothic mansion situated in wonderful seclusion amid 60 acres of parkland. The hotel stands on high ground and enjoys extensive views over the surrounding countryside.

Only 12 of the 35 bedrooms are based in the main house. Most accommodation is in adjacent outbuildings which have been discreetly converted into groups of comfortable guest rooms. All have central heating, private facilities, television and direct dial telephone.

The extensive cellar area now houses the bar (opening onto the courtyard), a small dance floor and the restaurant, which like the breakfast room is non-smoking. The intriguing main house has many quiet hideaways for a solitary read or relaxation, including a library, lounge and conservatory.

The active visitor will not be disappointed with the sports facilities: Heated indoor and outdoor pools, squash court, 9-hole par 31 golf course, indoor and outdoor tennis courts, croquet and billiards, sauna, spa bath, sunbed, steam room table tennis and indoor putting green. A comprehensive sports shop and an interesting lace and linen shop are also located on the premises.

Treatments
A limited number of body and beauty treatments and hairdressing are available including massage £9 per half hour, manicure £4.50; pedicure £7.50 and facials from £12.

Tariff
Rates are per person per night sharing a twin or double room - midweek tariff from £47.50 to £65, weekends £52.50 to £70. Rates include light breakfast and three course dinner with coffee. Small extra charge for full English breakfast.

Discounted rates are sometimes offered, such as three nights for the price of two and subsequent nights at half price. Ask about these when booking.

Nominal charges are made for the use of the sauna, sunbed, steam room, spa bath, treatments and indoor tennis - all other facilities, including golf are free to residents. The hotel is not suitable for children under the age of 8. No pets.

Travel directions
Take M5 and exit at junction 27 onto A361 to South Molton. Here take B3225 for 5.2 miles and turn right uphill to Chittlehamholt. Highbullen is half a mile after the village.

Nearest railway station King's Nympton approximately 4 miles (ask the guard to stop the train).

Hinton Grange Hotel
Nr Dryham Hinton Wiltshire SN14 8HG
Tel 0272 372916   Fax 0272 373285

| 17 | 3 4 6 13 14 15 16 17 C | £ D |

Hinton Grange is a delightful small hotel standing in six acres of grounds in the southern Cotswolds. The original building dates back to 1416 and was once a large farmhouse. It has now been lovingly converted and extended into an intriguing small hotel decorated in Victorian style and furnished with many genuine antiques. The charming grounds include ponds and a tiny island used for barbeques and picnics in the summer.

All bedrooms at Hinton Grange have a unique feature guaranteed to make any stay special - they all have individual open fires that can be lit prior to arrival to give a warm and memorable welcome. Rooms have dining areas and some have private patios. Many have antique four poster beds and Victorian bathing alcoves in view of the open fire - deluxe rooms have an additional en suite shower. All rooms have television, hair drier, trouser press and mini-bar.

In the Old Inglenook Restaurant, romantic candle-lit dinners are served beside a blazing log fire. Only the highest quality ingredients are used in the outstanding international and vegetarian à la carte menus and table d'hôte menus. All dishes are freshly prepared and cooked to order. Pre-dinner drinks, dining and (on some nights) dancing can be enjoyed in the tropical ambience of the Palm Court conservatory with its sparkling blue pool, floating candles, tropical plants and Victorian piano.

Indoor leisure facilities include a small heated swimming pool, sauna, mini gym and solarium. Outdoor activities include fishing, croquet, lawn tennis and an unflagged 9-hole pitch and putt course.

Treatments
Ultratone cellulite treatments are given in the privacy of one's room and cost £7 per session (first session £6). A course of 10 treatments (over two days) costs £60 and gives good results. A complete day of pampering can be arranged on request with healthy/slimming menus specially devised.

Tariff
Two night leisure breaks including dinner and a delicious champagne breakfast cost from £48 to £90 per person per night sharing a double room on weekdays, £61 to £97 per person on Fridays and Saturdays.

Travel directions
Take M4 and exit at junction 18, taking A46 towards Bath After almost a mile turn right to Hinton village. Turn first right at the bottom of the hill and the lane leads to Hinton Grange.

Nearest stations Bristol Temple Meads and Bath both approximately 10 miles.

Imperial Hotel

Park Hill Road Torquay   Devon TQ1 2DQ

Tel 0803 294301   Fax 0803 298293

| 167 | ☆ 2 3 4 5 13 14 16 17 C | £ C |

Standing in five acres of beautiful gardens in a sheltered clifftop position, the Imperial Hotel enjoys unrivalled views over the Torbay coastline. As one of Torquay's most prestigious hotels, the Imperial boasts luxurious en suite accommodation (most rooms have a balcony overlooking the sea), relaxing lounges and bars, a nightclub and the renowned Regatta Restaurant.

Leisure facilities are first rate and the Imperial's Health & Fitness Club is open to residents seven days a week. Amenities include indoor and outdoor heated swimming pools, fully equipped gym, separate saunas, solarium, spa pool, tennis and squash courts.

Hairdressing and body and beauty treatments are available at competitive prices in the Health Club.

Treatments

Aromatherapy massage £25; body massage £18; G5 massage £10 (with contour oil £12); Slendertone £10 per session; Cathiodermie facial £22; Geloid Prescription facial £20; GM Collins facials from £10; epilation from £5; waxing from £3.50; manicure £8.50; pedicure £9.50; eyelash tint £4.50; reflexology £20.

Tariff

Health & Fitness Breaks from £120 per person per night based on sharing a double or twin room for a minimum of two consequetive nights. Tariff includes dinner, bed and breakfast, fitness evaluation, two body massages, two sunbeds, facial and use of all health club facilities.

Regular room only tariff from £78 single, £98 double room.

Discounted rates are occasionally offered during the year, so ask about these when making enquiries.

Travel directions

Travel by M5 (and M4 from London) towards Bristol, taking A380 to Torquay. Nearest railway station Torquay approximtely 2 miles.

Center Parcs Longleat Forest Holiday Village
Near Warminster Wiltshire BA12 7JN
Tel 0272 244 744 *(brochure)* 0623 411 411 *(reservations)*

| 600 | self-catering villas 2 3 4 5 6 7 13 14 15 16 17 C

Longleat Forest is the third Center Parcs village to be built in England and opens in the summer of 1994. Situated in rural Wiltshire, the new village extends over 400 acres of rolling woodlands on the magnificent 10,000 acre Longleat estate, a short distance from the elegant town of Bath.

Many of the popular and successful features of *Sherwood Forest* and *Elveden Forest* have been incorporated in the new village, including safe car-free roads. Central focus is the Subtropical Swimming Paradise - open until 10pm and a balmy haven of relaxation and exhilaration with breathtaking water slides, flumes, rivers and quiet pools set amid palm tress and tropical plants. There is even a sandy beach area in the children's pool with poolside loungers alongside for parents' relaxation.

The Parc Plaza's is the village's main shopping area, with shops restaurants and cafes designed in Mediterranean style with whitewashed walls, terracotta pots and brightly coloured flowers. The Village Square continues the continental theme, and is the site of Longleat's gourmet restaurant Le Caprice.

A pleasant walk or cycle ride through the beautiful Longleat forest brings the visitor to the Jardin des Sports, where indoor and outdoor activities combine to create a Country Club for all the family. The Jardin des Sports is situated in a lovely valley at the head of the sports lake where canoes and pedalos can be hired. Indoor and outdoor tennis, badminton, snooker and table tennis are available here, as well as classes and tuition in the airy aerobics and fitness studios. Drinks and meals are served in the Sports Bar and Country Club restaurant, which has play areas for children.

All Center Parc villages offer an amazing choice of sporting activities. In addition to the sports already mentioned, visitors can try ten-pin bowling, cycling, racket ball, rollerskating, short tennis, squash, soccer coaching, five-a-side football, mini-golf, petanque and target archery. Bowls, croquet and volleyball are available in season. Off-site activities such as pony trekking, clay pigeon shooting, field archery and horse-riding can be arranged locally.

Close by the Country Club and Jardin des Sports is Aqua Sana, Center Parcs' own spa and health farm, designed in Roman style with saunas, Turkish baths, and warm whirlpools to complement the relaxing array of health and beauty treatments on offer.

Longleat's range of self-catering villas suits all needs - from honeymoon villas with four poster bed, jacuzzi and luxury dining area to spacious four bedroom/ two bathroom villas accommodating up to eight people, complete with a kitchen equipped with two refrigerators. Villas are centrally heated, well equipped and furnished. Gas, electricity, bedlinen, radio, television and video films included in the rental. All villas have a private patio with patio furniture as well as a high chair, combination cot and playpen suitable for babies up to two years. Towel hire and a daily maid service (included in executive villa rental) are available for an additional charge. For the less able visitor, some three-bedroomed villas are adapted with wider doors and a special modified shower room.

Treatments

A full range of treatments and hairdressing is available in the Aqua Sana including aromatherapy massage, facials, reflexology and high speed sunbeds. (Full treatment details and prices not available when we went to press, but will be similar to those at *Elveden Forest* and *Sherwood Forest* - see Central England section of *Healthy Breaks*.)

The Spa's facilities include saunas, Turkish baths, plunge pools, warm whirlpools and quiet relaxation areas.

Tariff

Villas can be booked for whole weeks (start and finish on Fridays), mid-week breaks (start on Monday finish on Friday), or weekends (start on Friday finish on Monday) and rental costs vary with the size and facilities of the villa and time of year. A weekend break for four persons in a two-bedroom villa in early December costs £188, rising to £292 in July and £391 over the August bank holiday weekend. The villa's weekly rental is £691 during late July and August when all rentals are on a weekly basis only.

Travel Directions

From M4 exit at junction 17 taking A350 to Warminster and A362 signed to Longleat, or exit at junction 18 taking A46 to Bath then A36 and A362.
From M5 exit at junction 25 and take A361 towards Frome then A362.
Nearest railway station Bath approximtely 12 miles.

Lorrens Health Hydro
Cary Park Babbacome Torquay Devon TQ1 3NN
Tel 0803 323740

| 10 | ☆ 2 3 4 6 7 9 10 12 17 | £ C* |

Pleasantly situated some 500 yards from Babbacombe Downs in lovely Devon, The Lorrens Health Hydro is England's only coastal health farm and one with a difference - it caters exclusively for women with the emphasis on total relaxation, pampering and slimming in a stress-free environment.

Owned and managed personally by Valerie, Peter and Steve Vickerstaff with the assistance of a friendly and enthusiastic staff, The Lorrens provides a personalised service accommodating a maximum of 20 guests at any one time.

The facilities include a large beauty salon complex, jacuzzi, steam room, sauna, solarium, fully equipped gym and spacious exercise studio (Step Reebok a speciality), as well as an outdoor heated swimming pool and sun terrace (summer only).

Everyone has a consultation with a qualified therapist on their first morning when personal needs, dietary requirements and aims are discussed and a suggested programme devised. A computerised fitness assessment lasting an hour is also carried out to analyse aerobic capacity,cardio-vascular fitness and ideal body-weight. This helps in devising a personalised exercise programme for the visit which can be continued at home. Several exercise classes with qualified instructors are organised each day.

With the emphasis on good health and weight loss, a well-balanced, calorie-controlled de-toxification diet is provided including fresh vegetables, fish and chicken dishes, salads and fresh fruits. Delicious vegetarian meals are served every day.

All rooms have en suite facilities and are very comfortably furnished and decorated. Matching toiletries and large bath towels are provided and all rooms have television and tea/coffee making facilities.

The Lorrens is a non-smoking establishment, smoking is not allowed anywhere in the building including the bedrooms.

Guests travelling long distances can extend their stay by arriving the evening before their first day of treatments. Rooms cost an additional £25 per person and are available from 4pm onwards.

Treatments

The tariff includes the following daily treatments and activities:

Supervised gym workout; sauna; faradic treatment; G5/vacuum suction; jacuzzi; steam treatment and body massage, plus Sixtus Pedicure on one day and anti-stress massage on first day of treatments.

Optional treatments include Rene Guinot facials from £22, Tip-Top treatment £40; Bio-Peel £22; Cathiodermie £25; aromatherapy facial £20; make-up lesson £18; contour wrap £55; G5, faradic toning, vacuum suction or galvanic treatment £15 or £120 for 8 sessions; aromatherapy massage and reflexology £28; anti-stress massage £17; aerobic/step class £3.50 or £12.50 for 5; manicure £10.50; Sixtus pedicure £11.50; electrolysis from £6.50; waxing from £5.

Good value non-residential days include *Pamper Day* £70 and *Fitness Day* £60 - both days include lunch and a variety of treatments and activities.

Tariff

Weekend Pamper Break £195 single, £175 sharing twin room;

   3 Day Slimaway £240 single, £216 sharing;

   5 Day Slimaway £375 single, £337.50 sharing;

   7 Day Slimaway £510 single, £459 sharing.

Rates are per person and include accommodation, all meals, treatments and activities prescribed (at least 6 each day with the exception of the last day). Extra days (room, meals and treatments) £70 per person.

Travel Directions

From central Torquay follow signs to Babbacombe. Carey Park can be accessed off Reddenhill Road or Manor Road.

   Nearest railway station Torquay 3 miles.

Lucknam Park
Colerne Wiltshire SN14 8AZ
Tel 0225 742777   Fax 0225 743536

| 39 | 2 3 4 5 6 13 14 15 16 17 C | £ B |

Built in 1720 in countryside on the southern edge of the Cotswolds, Lucknam Park has been converted into a luxurious and elegant country house hotel with first class health and leisure facilities.

An impressive mile-long avenue lined with beech trees leads up to the Georgian mansion, decorated and furnished in period style with an abundance of fresh flower arrangements. Housed within the walls of the old garden is the Leisure Spa with heated indoor swimming pool, whirlpool spa, steam room, sauna, gymnasium, solarium, beauty salon, hairdresser and snooker room.

Outdoor sports facilities include floodlit tennis courts, croquet lawn and many pleasant walks in the grounds. Golf, fishing, boating, horse riding and even hot air ballooning can be arranged in the locality.

The spacious bedrooms are individually designed with splendid views and beautiful furnishings, all have en suite bathroom, television and telephone. Four poster rooms and a number of suites are available.

The restaurant has been awarded a Michelin star for a second year and serves a frequently changing menu of modern English cuisine, complemented by an impressive wine list. The dining room is non-smoking.

Treatments

Body and beauty treatments are available in the Beauty Salon seven days a week. Hairdressing can be arranged Tuesday to Saturday. The choice of treatments includes full body massage £27; aromatherapy £32; back and neck massage £15; solarium £5 per 1/2 hour; facials from £24; manicure and pedicure £14 each; waxing from £4.50; cut/blow dry £17.

Tariff
Two night breaks from £195 per person sharing a twin/double room on half board basis - includes full use of the leisure facilities.

Travel Directions
From M4 exit at junction 17 or 18 and follow signs to A420. Continue for 4 miles and at Ford turn onto Colerne road. Lucknam Park is 1/4 mile on the right.
Nearest railway station Bath 6 miles.

Passage House Hotel
Kingsteignton   Newton Abbot Devon YQ12 3QH
Tel 0626 55515   Fax 0626 63336

| 40 | 2 3 4 13 14 17 C | £ D |

This attractive new hotel has been specially designed to take advantage of the superb river views and the countryside. Even the interior colour schemes were chosen to reflect the calmness of the river and give a feeling of space and light.

All rooms have lovely views and are well equipped with modern comforts. The Penthouse rooms are especially luxurious and have a private terrace.

The best of fresh Devon produce is used for the preparation of local recipes, all beautifully presented and served with an excellent wine list.

Hotel residents have use of the modern Leisure Club and facilities include a clover-leaf shaped heated indoor pool with hydro-massage spa and jet-stream, sauna, steam room, gym and beauty salon.

Treatments
The Beauty Salon opens every day and treatments include aromatherapy £20; facials from £12; eyelash tint £4; manicure£5; pedicure £6; full body massage £15; back and shoulder massage £10; solarium £4; waxing from £3.50; electrolysis from £4. *Top to Toe* with aromatherapy, Geloide Prescription facial, manicure, pedicure and lunch £55.

Tariff
Special offer two night stay from £47 per person per night, includes dinner, accommodation and breakfast and use of the Leisure Club.

Travel Directions
The hotel is next to Newton Abbot racecourse. From A380 take A381 and follow sign to the racecourse and turn left at the mini-roundabout.
Nearest railway station Newton Abbot approximately 2 miles.

Polurrian Hotel
Mullion Lizard Peninsula Cornwall TR12 7EN
Tel 0326 240421   Fax 0326 240083

| **40** | 2 3 4 5 10 13 14 16 17 C | **£ D** |

Dramatically situated 300 feet above a secluded sandy cove in 12 acres of gardens and grounds, this friendly hotel offers great seaside holidays with lots of activities and facilities for all the family.

En suite bedrooms are well appointed, some with stunning sea views. Flowers and a glass of sherry on arrival are extra welcoming touches. Self-catering apartments and bungalows are equipped down to the last teaspoon.

A varied choice of menus using fresh local produce is served in the restaurant. Cream teas on the lawn are a popular feature on summer afternoons.

All guests have use of the Leisure Club's many facilities with younger visitors' needs particularly well catered for. Amenities include indoor pool, spa bath, sauna, solarium, refreshment bar and gym. Heated outdoor pool, tennis, badminton, croquet and mini-golf are available on site and the 18-hole golf course at Mullion is just two miles away. Safe sea-bathing can be enjoyed from the hotel's own sandy cove and many other beaches in the area.

Treatments
Hairdressing and beauty treatments available on request. Body massage with essential oils £12.50 per 1/2 hour, £20 per hour, or £25 per 11/2 hours. Reflexology is also available.

Tariff
Daily half board rate from £42 - £76 per person per night sharing double room

(non-sea view), from £52 to £86 per person sharing sea view room. Children up to 5 years of age stay free when sharing parents' room with breakfast and high tea provided when parents are on half board basis. Details on application.

Weekly tariff for self-catering apartments and bungalows based on four people sharing, from £150 in low season and from £450 in high summer.

Special rates offered at certain times of the year- apply for dates and details.

Travel Directions

From Helston follow A3083 signed to The Lizard for 6 miles, turn right onto B3296 to Mullion. Drive through village 1/2 mile to Mullion Cove.

Nearest station Redruth approximately 25 miles (ccmplimentary chauffeur-driven car service to and from Polurrian for guests staying 7 nights or more).

St Pierre Park Hotel
Rohais St Peter Port Guernsey Channel Isles
Tel 0481 728282   Freephone 0800 373 321 Fax 0481 4191662

| 134 | 1 2 3 4 5 6 13 14 16 17 18 19 | £ C |

Guernsey's leading hotel is set in 45 acres of attractive parkland a few minutes' drive from the Island's charming capital St Pierre Port. The hotel's superb health club Le Mirage, is the most luxurious and well equipped on the island, with a large heated indoor pool, high-tech gym, snooker room, saunas, solarium, jacuzzi, steam rooms, hairdressing salon and treatment rooms.

The en suite bedrooms are luxuriously furnished and have either a terrace or balcony overlooking the grounds. All rooms have satellite television, radio, telephone, baby listening service, trouser press, hair drier, 24-hour room service and tea/coffee making facilities.

The hotel has six bars and three delightful restaurants - La Fontaine serving a splendid daily breakfast buffet, the Cafe Renoir for informal dining and children's meals, and the elegant Victor Hugo French Restaurant for special occasions.

Excellent sporting and leisure facilities include a nine-hole par three golf course, putting green, driving range and pro-shop, three all-weather tennis courts, archery, croquet, boules and a trim trail with exercise stations, winding round the acres of parkland. There is also a super children's playground.

Treatments

Le Mirage has treatment rooms and a hairdressing salon. Treatments include Clarins and Guinot facials from £11.50; Cathiodermie from £11.50 to £24; body massage with essential oils £24; G5 massage £9; toning table session £6; waxing from £3.50; electrolysis from £3; manicure £8.50; pedicure £11; high-speed sunbed £4; eyelash tint £6.50; trim/blow dry £15.50; perms from £25.50; men's hairdressing from £6.50. *Health and Beauty Day* with lunch included £60.

Tariff

Three night *Health and Fitness Breaks* £183.50 per person sharing luxury double or twin-bedded room, £258.50 single occupancy.
Price includes full buffet breakfast, use of leisure facilities, sunbed, golf or tennis, 30 minute massage, beauty treatment of choice, early morning tea and orange juice. The break is not available during July and August.
   Regular bed/breakfast tariff from £95 single, £135 double room.

Travel Directions

Guernsey is served by daily flights from over 20 UK airports and 11 European destinations. Frequent car ferries operate from Poole in Dorset.

The Tides Reach
South Sands Salcombe Devon TQ8 8LJ
Tel 0548 843466   Fax 0548 843954

| 38 | 2 3 4 5 6 13 14 16 17 | £ D |

The Tides Reach stands on a sandy cove in glorious south Devon and combines comfort and friendly service with an excellent array of leisure facilities.
   Attractive en suite bedrooms are well equipped and most overlook the Salcome Estuary.
   Menus are prepared from fresh local produce and served in the Garden Room Restaurant, complemented by a reasonably priced wine list.
   Leisure facilities include indoor swimming pool, spa bath, sunbed, sauna,

multi-gym, squash court, dinghy sailing, windsurfing, full size snooker table, games room, beauty treatments and hairdressing. Golf, riding, water-skiing and tennis are available locally.

Treatments

The Beauty Salon's range of treatments includes body massage £22; eyelash tinting £6.50; cleansing facial with brow shape £16.25; make-up £9.50; manicure £7.50; pedicure £8.50; cut/ blow dry £13.25; *Top to Toe* package £30.

Tariff

From £48/£70 (low season) to £57 /£96 (high season) per person per night sharing a double room on half board terms with use of leisure facilities. Special children's tariff, but no babies or children under 8 years of age.

Travel Directions

Take M5 to its southern limit then A38 to Ashburton and Buckfastleigh. Take A384 and A385 road signed towards Totnes, then A381 to Kingsbridge, Salcombe and South Sands.

Nearest railway station Plymouth 26 miles.

CENTRAL ENGLAND

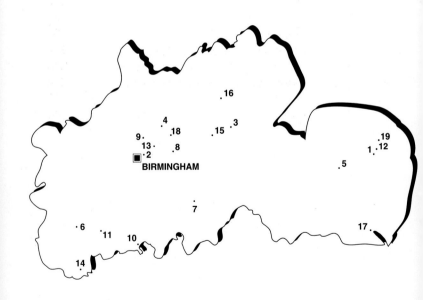

CENTRAL ENGLAND

Barnham Broom Hotel
Barnham Broom Norwich NR9 4DD
Tel 0603 759393   Fax 0603 758224

| 52 | 2 3 4 5 13 14 16 17 18 C | £ C |

Barnham Broom is a comfortable modern hotel situated in 250 acres of Norfolk countryside. It boasts excellent health, leisure and sporting facilities including two 18-hole par 72 golf courses.

Bedrooms are well appointed with en suite bathroom or shower, television, radio, telephone, trouser press, hair drier and tea/coffee making facilities.

The Flints Restaurant offers a varied selection of hot and cold breakfast dishes, a lunchtime carvery and a choice of table d'hote and a la carte dinner menus. Snacks and refreshments are available all day in the Sports Bar Buttery.

Leisure facilities available to hotel guests include the heated indoor swimming pool, sauna, steam room, solarium, fully equipped gym, tennis and squash courts and full size snooker table. Green fees are charged £17.50 per round.

Hairdressing is available on site and the health and beauty salon offers a range of reasonably priced pampering treatments.

Treatments
Body and beauty treatment choice includes two hour aromatherapy session with consultation £25, one hour session £20; mini-facial including massage £14; other facials from £16.50; full body massage £18.50; facial and back massage £15; back massage £10; G5 massage £8; Dermoessence anti-stress back treatment £17; manicure £8; pedicure £9; waxing from £4.50; electrolysis from £5.50; full body peel £11.50. Hairdressing prices on application.

Tariff
Getaway Leisure Break from £109 per person sharing accommodation, inclusive of dinner/bed and breakfast for any two consecutive nights. *Getaway Golf Break*, details as *Getaway Break* but including up to four rounds of golf over the courses with pre-booked tee times - from £159 per person sharing accommodation. A 10% discount is given on Sunday to Thursday bookings.

Regular nightly bed/breakfast tariff from £59.50 single, £82 double room.

Reduced seasonal rates are offered in July and August and from 1 November 1994 to 13 March 1995 (excluding Christmas and New Year), details on application.

Travel Directions
The hotel is situated 10 miles south/west of Norwich between the A47 and A11 main roads.

Nearest railway station Norwich approximately 10 miles.

The Belfry
Lichfield Road Wishaw Warwickshire B76 9PR
Tel 0675 470301   Fax 0675 470178

| 219 | 2 3 4 6 13 14 16 17 18 C | £ C |

The Belfry is set in 300 acres of grounds overlooking its own lake, and is renowned as the venue for golf's Ryder Cup. It is also a complete sports and leisure complex and makes an ideal choice for a family leisure break.

All bedrooms have the latest comforts and services, including en suite bathroom, radio, television, telephone and tea/coffee making facilities.

A French Restaurant and Carvery are just two of The Belfry's four main restaurants. The hotel also has three bars in addition to those in the Bel Air nightclub.

At weekends, games and activities are organised by The Belfry Children's Club and all 6-14 year old visitors invited to join in the fun.

All hotel residents have use of the Leisure Club's facilities during their stay. These include an indoor swimming pool, spa bath, sauna, gym, aerobic sessions, squash and an all weather tennis court. Some facilities have nominal charges. Squash, tennis and swimming lessons are available, as well as golf tuition and a driving range. Clarins body and beauty treatments are available in the beauty salon.

Treatments
Body massage £20; aromatherapy face and body massage £29.50; Prescription body treatment £20; Prescription facial £20; cleanse and make-up £10; make-up lesson £14.25; eyelash tint £6.75; waxing from £4.25; electrolysis from £5.25; G5 massage from £8.50; manicure £8; pedicure £10.

Tariff
Two nights' dinner/bed and breakfast in shared twin/double room from £75 per person per night. Children sharing with parents stay free, with meals charged as taken.

Generous discounts are offered during school holidays, details on application.

Golfing breaks from £210 per person sharing half board accommodation for two nights - includes two rounds of golf.

Travel Directions
Follow motorway network to M42 and exit at junction 9 (signed Belfry Golf Centre). Follow A446 signed to Lichfield, for a mile.

Nearest railway station Birmingham International approximatley 5 miles.

Belton Woods

Belton Nr Grantham Lincolnshire NG32 2LN

Tel 0476 593200 Fax 0476 74547

96	2 3 4 5 6 13 14 16 17 18 C	£ C

Belton Woods is an exciting golf and leisure resort situated in over 400 acres of parkland and lakes. It offers luxurious accommodation with outstanding facilities for health, leisure and sport, including a superb pool complex with waterfalls and a children's pool.

All bedrooms in this modern hotel are furnished and equipped to a high standard, with private bathroom, satellite television, telephone, hair drier, trouser press and tea/coffee making facilities.

Belton Woods offers a choice of two dining rooms - the elegant Manor Restaurant overlooking the golf courses and serving specially created à la carte and table d'hôte menus, or the popular Plus Fours Restaurant for traditional dishes and refreshments.

The many exercise and sporting opportunities include aerobics, aquarobics, supervised gym with fitness assessments and circuit training, two squash courts, snooker, floodlit tennis courts and driving range, three golf courses (two 18-hole, one 9-hole), putting green and a nature trail (nominal charges made for some facilities). Guests can relax in the pool, spa bath, steam rooms and saunas before being thoroughly pampered in the hairdressing and beauty salon.

Treatments

An extensive selection of Clarins treatments includes full body massage £18; shoulder and back massage £10; G5 massage £7; faradic muscle toning £10; facials from £11 - £21; cleanse and make-up £10; make-up lesson £15; sunbed from £3; eyelash tinting £6; manicure with polish £7; pedicure £12; electrolysis from £8; thread vein removal 10; skin tag removal £10; waxing from £5.50; bleaching from £4. Hairdressing prices on application.

Day packages include *Belton Woods Leisure & Beauty Day* £75; *Top to Toe Day* £70; *Pre Holiday Special* £35; *Bridal Package* £40.

Tariff

Leisure Break from £70 per person per night sharing twin/double room (minimum two nights) on dinner/bed and breakfast basis.

Summer Specials (Sunday to Thursday) during August from £110 per person for two nights package, details as above.

Children up to age 14 stay free when occupying parents' room, meals charged for as taken.

Travel Directions

Take A1 to Gonerby Moor Services and Great Gonerby.Take B1174 signed to Manthorpe/Belton and turn left onto A607.

Nearest railway station Grantham approximately 3 miles.

Breadsall Priory Hotel, Golf and Country Club
Moor Road Morley Nr Derby Derbyshire DE7 6DL
Tel 0332 832235   Fax 0332 833509

92	2 3 4 5 6 13 14 15 16 17 18 C	£ C

Breadsall Priory is a 13th century mansion set in 200 acres of mature parkland and approached by a long parkland drive. Its historic past is still much in evidence with battlements, huge doorways and tall elegant windows. Inside, log fires and a minstrel gallery complement modern amenities - bars, restaurant and leisure facilities. It is now one of ten Country Club Hotels offering leisure and sporting facilities, including golf.

All bedrooms are en suite with attractive furnishings and overlook the golf course or small courtyard.

Pre-dinner drinks can be enjoyed beside a log fire in the cocktail lounge, before trying out the imaginative table d'hôte and à la carte menus served in the Elizabethan Priory Restaurant.

The Golf and Country Club offers a whole range of excellent amenities. Indoor, a swimming pool, fitness studio, steam room, sauna, solarium, spa bath, two snooker tables, two squash courts and a poolside grill. Outdoors - children's play area, trim trail, two all-weather tennis courts, five-a-side football pitch and two challenging 18-hole golf courses, the original Priory course and the new Moorland course. Sporting activities are charged at nominal rates, squash £2 - £2.60 per session, tennis £3.20 per hour (floodlit £5), snooker £3, fitness studio £2.25. Green fees £20, juniors £8.

Treatments

Clarins 1 hour body massage treatments, firming, contouring or exfoliating

£20; body massage with infra-red £15 for 30 minutes; Clarins bust treatment £16; faradic muscle toning £11 for 30 minutes or 6 for £55; G5 massage £11 for 30 minutes or 6 for £55; Paris Method facial £26, bust treatment £21, body treatment £26; make-up £10; make-up with lesson £14; eye treatments from £4.50; Clarins 1 hour facial treatments £19.50 each; reviving 30 minute facial £12; manicure £11.50; pedicure £14.50.

The Health and Beauty Clinic also offers a complete *Health Farm Day*, available Monday to Friday at an inclusive cost of £63.

Tariff

Weekend Leisure Breaks £65 per person per night sharing a twin/double room (minimum two nights) inclusive of accommodation, breakfast and dinner.

Golf Breaks (Monday to Sunday) £85 per person per night, details as above, but including one round of golf per day.

Travel Directions

3 miles north of Derby just off A38 on the edge of Breadsall village. Turn left at the off-licence and follow Moor Lane for 2 miles, Breadsall Priory is on the left.

Nearest railway station Derby approximately 3 miles.

Center Parcs Elveden Forest Holiday Village
Brandon Suffolk IP27 0YZ
Tel 0272 244744 *(brochure)*　0623 411 411 *(reservations)*

680 self-catering villas　90 apartments

2 3 4 5 6 7 13 14 15 16 17 18 C

Elveden Forest opened in 1989 and is the second Center Parcs village in the UK. The villas and facilities are set in ancient Suffolk woodlands around attractively landscaped lakes. Thousands of trees and shrubs have been planted to conserve and encourage the wildlife population.

Most indoor activities take place in the Parc Plaza, a futuristic leisure area incorporating tropical gardens with wildlife and waterfalls, the Jardin des Sports (a huge indoor sports area), supermarket, shops, restaurants, bars, Spa and the Subtropical Swimming Paradise. This popular recreational pool is open every day and attractions include wildwater rapids, slow river, flumes, slides, salt pool, and a wave pool. Small children have their own paddling pool. Whirlpools, solarium and poolside chairs are provided for relaxation. Disabled visitors have special changing cabins and easy access to the poolside.

Accommodation is in serviced apartments and modern one to four bedroomed villas, centrally heated and fully equipped. Several villas are adapted for

disabled visitors. The Sheldrake apartments have double room, private bathroom with spa bath, television, radio and telephone.

On top of the Sheldrake is Le Caprice, a revolving French restaurant with panoramic views of the village and an extensive choice of gourmet menus served by friendly staff.

After unpacking, cars must be left in designated car parking areas to ensure the safety of bike riders and pedestrians in the village. Non-bikers should reserve villas within walking distance of the village centre.

Only entry to the Subtropical Swimming Paradise is included in the villa rental, all other activities and sports are paid for as taken, with nominal charges for equipment hire. Popular sports like badminton, tennis and squash should be pre-booked a day in advance. A bicycle is essential, bring your own or hire one from the bike shop. Weekend charges £7.45 for an adult bike, £4.25 for a child's bike, and £6.90 for a large BMX.

The Spa is accessed via the pool or Jardin des Sports, and is a pleasant, restful area. It has two spacious saunas, steam room, plunge pools, drench pail, hot and cold showers, warm footbath, indoor and outdoor pools, hydro spa and rest area with log fire and refreshments. Sunbeds and massage are available in the Spa.

Swimsuits are optional for all sessions except continental ones when none are worn. Children are admitted to the Spa only during family sessions. Spa entry £6.15 per session, child £2. 15 minute Spa tours are conducted several mornings a week. Session details and tariffs available from the Pool Desk.

An exhilarating cycle ride or walk to the far side of the village leads to the Country Club, which boasts a French colonial style restaurant, snooker and tennis tables, dance studio and fitness room, children's play activity centre and the Aqua Sana - Elveden Forest's holistic health and beauty centre with adjoining hair salon.

The newly opened 9-hole, par 3 golf course is situated next to the Country Club. Green fees £5, juniors £2.50. Other outdoor activities include archery, pony trekking, clay pigeon shooting, tennis, canoeing and windsurfing - to name but a few.

Treatments

The Aqua Sana's six treatment rooms are open every day including Sunday. Treatments include seaweed body wrap £28.50; 90 minute aromatherapy £39.95; exfoliating massage £22.50; reflexology £27; Ionithermie £38; thalasso facial £13.50 for 30 minutes or £26 for 60 minutes; holistic facials £29.90 each; eyelash tint £6.50; waxing from £5.

The hair salon offers a complete hairdressing service - wet cut £7.75, with blow dry £14.50.

Tariff

Rates vary depending on time of year and villa size. A weekend stay (Friday afternoon until Monday morning) in early December in a three-bedroom villa costs £218 and rises to £378 for the August bank holiday weekend. The weekly rental for the same villa during the school summer holiday period when all villas are rented out weekly is £699.

A weekend in a Sheldrake apartment (two persons maximum) costs from £119 in early December to £222 for the August bank holiday weekend.

Fitness Motivation Weekends are held during June and September each year, and include exercise classes, Spa sessions, beauty and cookery demonstrations, fashion shows and nutritional advice. The cost for participation is just £30 per person on top of the villa rental. Full details and dates on application.

Travel Directions

Elveden Forest Holiday Village is reached via the motorway network to the A11 signposted Thetford and Norwich. Turn onto B1106 signposted Brandon and the entrance is half a mile on the left.

Nearest railway station Thetford approximately 4 miles.

Goodships Relaxation Farm and Swiming School
Avenbury Bromyard Herefordshire HR7 4EZ
Tel 0885 482735

4	2 3 6 10 14 15	£ E

Goodships Relaxation Farm is situated in 35 acres of fields and farmland in the pretty Herefordshire countryside. The farm offers relaxing short breaks and residential adult swimming courses in a delightfully rural setting - the farm has its own ducks, sheep, lambs and peacocks.

Comfortable accommodation is provided in the farmhouse in single, double and twin rooms and visitors can opt for full board or bed and breakfast terms. Meals are prepared from fresh farm produce and served in the farmhouse, which also has a cosy lounge with an open fire.

The purpose built relaxation suite can be booked for private use, and facilities include sauna, jacuzzi, sunbed and steam-tube and has access to the beautifully warm swimming pool kept at a constant temperature of 93^0 F. Hydrotherapy, aquarobic sessions and swimming tuition are available in the pool which accommodates up the 15 persons maximum.

Treatments

Aromatherapy steam-tube, sunbed, sauna and jacuzzi from £3.50 per session, or course of five sessions £15.75. Reflexology, aromatherapy and sports massage £18 per hour, £10 per half hour; faradic slimming treatments £11 per session, five for £48; ten for £90; G5 massage £8 per session, ten for £50; aquarobics £2.75; swimming lesson (shared with two others) first session £10, then £3.50 per half hour; private swimming lesson £10 per half hour.

Half-day Break includes private use of Relaxation Suite, full body massage, swim or aquarobic session and a substantial salad lunch £45 per person, £65 for two, £80 for three.

The Goodships Relaxation Suite can be hired for exclusive use for periods of one to three hours for two to ten persons, and includes free swimming. The hire charge ranges from £18 to £25 per hour depending on the party number and length of hire.

Tariff

Luxurious bed and breakfast accommodation £25 - £35 per person per night.

Relaxation Two- Day Break with all meals provided and use of facilities £185 single, £285 for two persons.

Goodships also offers residential swimming tuition courses at reasonable rates with or without full board. Prices and details on application.

Travel Directions

Exit M5 at junction 5 or 6 and take A44 Leominster road to Bromyard. Turn onto A465 for approximately 1/2 mile and turn onto B4214 signed to Ledbury. Goodships Farm is the first drive on the right..

From M50 exit at junction 2 and follow A417 towards Ledbury and B4214 for approximately 20 miles.

Nearest railway stations Hereford and Worcester both approximately 13 miles.

Hellidon Lakes Hotel & Country Club
Hellidon Nr Daventry Northamptonshire NN11 6LN
Tel 0327 62550 Fax 0327 62559

| 25 | 2 3 4 6 13 15 16 17 18 C | £ C |

Nestling in over 240 acres of rolling countryside, this comfortable modern hotel is within easy reach of the M40 and M1 motorways, and offers lake views and good leisure facilities.

Bedrooms are tastefully furnished and have en suite bathroom, satellite television, telephone, hair drier, trouser press, fridge and tea/coffee making facilities.

Hotel residents have a choice of two restaurants, the wood panelled Lakes Restaurant with open fires and excellent à la carte and table d'hôte menus, and the cosy Club Bar Restaurant providing informal tasty snacks and full bar meals.

Leisure facilities include a spectacular 18-hole golf course, covered driving range, practice areas and putting green, fully equipped gym with swim spa and jacuzzi, bio sauna and solarium, beauty treatment rooms, snooker room, nature walk, tennis, horse-riding and fly fishing.

Treatments
An extensive range of treatments is available including basic facials from £15; Decleor holistic facials from £22; Decleor body treatments from £22; full body massage £17; G5 massage from £5 for 15 minutes; faradic toning from £9.50 for 30 minutes; eyelash tint £4.75; basic facial £15; manicure £6.50; pedicure £8.50; waxing from £2.75; electrolysis from £4.50.

Tariff
Leisure Breaks from £65 per person (minimum two nights) sharing twin/double room inclusive of accommodation, dinner and full breakfast.

Golf Breaks from £75 per person per night, details as above, but with one round of golf per night's stay. Extra round of golf £10 during the week and £15 at weekends.

Regular bed/breakfast tariff from £85 single, £110 twin/double room.

Travel Directions
From M40 exit at junction 11, taking A361 towards Daventry. Turn onto Hellidon road at Charwelton. From M1 exit at junction 16 and take A45 to Daventry. Follow A361signed to Banbury, turning onto Hellidon road at Charwelton.

Nearest railway stations Rugby, Banbury and Northampton, all approximately 14 miles.

Hinckley Island Hotel

Watling Street Hinckley Leicestershire LE10 3JA

Tel 0455 631122   Fax 0455 634536

| 302 | 2 3 4 5 6 13 14 15 17 C |

£ D

This large modern hotel stands in 13 acres of tranquil parkland and landscaped gardens with a lake, yet is only yards from the M69 motorway. Catering mainly for the business and conference market during the week, it offers good value weekend breaks making use of the recently refurbished leisure facilities.

Hinckley Island's leisure complex is designed in Carribean style, with indoor kidney-shaped swimming pool, spa pool, steam room, sauna, solarium and pool-side bar. Other features include exercise and dance classes, snooker, hairdressing and a beauty salon.

Bedrooms are well furnished with en suite bathroom, satellite television, trouser press, hair drier, telephone, radio and tea/coffee making facilities. Rooms equipped for the disabled visitor, deluxe rooms and suites arc also available. Child minding can be arranged.

The Lakeside Restaurant and Iron Brasserie cater to all tastes and appetites, and there is also 24 hour room service.

Treatments

Studio Five is Hinckley Island's independently run health and beauty salon. Various treatments offered include full body massage £18; neck and shoulder massage £8; eyelash tint £4.50; eyebrow shape £4.50; manicure £6.50; pedicure £8.50.

The unisex hairdressing salon offers a complete hair service including ladies' cut and blow dry £9.50; men's cut and blow dry £7.50.

Tariff

Two night weekend rates (must include a Saturday night) from £41.50 per person per night sharing a twin/double room, and inclusive of dinner (in Iron Brasserie) bed and breakfast.

Regular bed/breakfast tariff from £74 per night single, £89 twin/double room.

All rates include use of leisure facilities. Hairdressing and beauty treatments are paid for as taken.

Travel Directions

Take motorway network to M69 and exit at junction 1, taking A5 to Milton Keynes for just 300 yards.

Nearest railway stations Hinckley (local) 1 mile, Nuneaton 5 miles, Leicester 12 miles.

Hoar Cross Hall Health Spa Resort
Hoar Cross Nr Yoxall Staffordshire DE13 8QS
Tel 028375 671   Fax 028375 652

| 86 | ☆ 2 3 4 5 6 7 8 11 12 13 14 16 17 C | £ B* |

Hoar Cross Hall Health Spa Resort is hidden away in the heart of the rural Staffordshire amid 45 acres of woodlands and gardens. The gracious residence was built in 1860 as a family home, and most of the interesting original features have been carefully restored including the oak-panelled long gallery and drawing room, banqueting hall and family chapel. Present owner Steve Joynes has lovingly transformed the Grade 11 listed building into one of Britain's finest health resorts and the first to offer a complete range of continental thalassotherapy treatments.

The luxurious spa is housed in a purpose built wing and includes a cruciform shaped swimming pool, five hydrotherapy massage baths, relaxation area, loatarium, whirlpool spa, sauna, solaria, 30 treatment rooms, hairdressing salon, supervised gym and exercise studio.

Accommodation is exceptional - all rooms have crown or half tester beds, many have four poster water beds and corner whirlpool baths. All have en suite bathroom, garden views, television, beverage tray, fruit basket and daily newspaper. Luxurious new penthouses have lounge, staircase to master bedroom, dressing room with walk-in wardrobes, whirlpool bath, private sauna and balcony.

Delicious healthy breakfasts and lunches are available in the Plantation Restaurant beside the pool. Dinner is served by candlelight in the splendid surrounding of the A La Carte Dining Room, complete with ornate gilded ceilings, crystal chandeliers and Louis style furniture. All food is colour coded to assist dieters, and menus include fresh fish, vegetarian dishes and prime cuts of beef, lamb and chicken carefully prepared and served with salad or lightly cooked vegetables. Wine is served with dinner - and for pre-dinner drinks, a discreetly hidden cocktail bar has been created in the former library.

Residents have unlimited use of the pool and whirlpool spa, steam room, sauna and the extensive leisure and sporting amenities. These include 9-hole golf improvement course, outdoor tennis and badminton, croquet, gym, exercise studio, boules, bicycles and many different types of exercise classes. Everyone is welcome to attend evening talks, videos and demonstrations on health, beauty and fitness topics.

Treatments

In addition to the treatments included in the tariff, a vast range of optional treatments can be reserved including complete thalassotherapy programme £65; aromatherapy massage £38; reflexology £28; floatation from £16; ladies' steam cabinet £6; full body seaweed wrap £30; blitz jet £17; G5 massage £15; facials from £22; eyelash tint £9; manicure from £14; pedicure from £14; high-intensity sunbed £13.50; relaxation therapy £15.50; fitness profiles from £19; stress management £30; hairdressing and Dead Sea mineral treatments.

Five non-residential day programmes are offered and all include lunch and complimentary beverages. *Special Relaxation Day* £38; *Body Treat Day* £78; *Relax & Rejuvenation Day* £98; *Beauty Treat Day* £78; *Top to Toe Day* £98.

Tariff

From £98 per person per night sharing double room or four poster water bed, suites from £135 per person per night, penthouses from £150 per person per night. Single supplement £20.

Rates include accommodation, all meals and complimentary beverages, allocated treatments (number depends on length of visit, from three treatments per two night stay to 14 treatments per seven night stay), use of all sports and leisure amenities, exercise classes, evening activities, tour and treatment consultation with blood pressure check (if required).

Travel Directions

Follow motorway network to A515. From the north, follow signs to Lichfield, turning right after Draycott in the Clay and onto unclassified road to Hoar Cross. From the south, follow A515 signed to Ashbourne and turn left after Yoxall onto unclassified road to Hoar Cross.

Nearest railway station Lichfield 10 miles.

The Lygon Arms
Broadway Hereford & Worcester WR12 7DU
Tel 0386 852255   Fax 0386 858611

| 63 | 2 3 4 6 13 14 15 17 C | £ B |

This former Elizabethan country inn stands in the middle of the pretty Cotswold village of Broadway. It has been offering hospitality for over 450 years, and is now a comfortable and welcoming hotel, combining modern luxury alongside historic reminders of its long history. There are wonderful inglenook fireplaces, cosy public rooms and some period bedrooms complete with four poster beds.

Luxurious accommodation is provided in either the period bedrooms of the original inn or the modern guest rooms of the Garden and Orchard wings. All rooms have en suite bathroom, bathrobes, hair drier, telephone and television.

The Great Hall Restaurant complete with minstrel's gallery, offers traditional high quality cuisine. In summer informal meals can be taken in the garden courtyard Patio Restaurant.

The newly opened leisure club is the last word in relaxation and rejuvenation, and offers guests a wide range of superb facilities. There is a luxurious swimming pool with adjacent spa bath, separate saunas with plunge pools, steam room, two modern solaria with compact disc systems, beauty salon, treatment rooms, fitness studio and billiards room. A spiral staircase from the pool leads to the upper lounge and adjoining roof garden, where drinks and light meals can be taken overlooking the pool.

An all-weather floodlit tennis court provides an opportunity for some outdoor exercise - rackets and balls provided. Informative jogging/walking maps of the area can be obtained from reception.

Treatments

Treatments are carried out in the pleasant surroundings of the Country Club which has treatment rooms and a beauty salon. Treatments include Decleor anti-cellulite treatment £20; Elemis aromatic body massage £27; Elemis aromatic back/shoulder massage £17; faradic toning £17 per session or 6 for £85; G5 massage £16 or 6 for £80; Decleor holistic facials £28; Elemis de-sensitising facial £28; manicure £12, pedicure £14, eyelash tinting £9; make-up £15; waxing from £6 and electrolysis from £10. *'For that Special Evening'* treatment package £40; lifestyle evaluation £10; fitness programme from £10.

Tariff

A *Cotswold Champagne* weekend break for two nights costs £210 per person and includes accommodation in luxury double or twin bedded room, bottle of champagne on ice; early morning tea, copy of *The Daily Telegraph*, continental breakfast each morning, table d'hôte dinner each evening, and full use of the leisure facilities (treatments extra). A two night mid-week break as above but minus the champagne from £195 per person.

Travel Directions

Take M40 to Oxford then A40 to Burford. At Burford turn onto A424 towards Stow-on-the-Wold for 15 miles, picking up A44 to Broadway.
Nearest railway stations Evesham 5 miles, Moreton-in-Marsh 8 miles.

Malvern Nature Cure Centre
5 College Grove Great Malvern Hereford & Worcester
WR14 3HP
Tel 0684 566818

| 8 | ☆ 2 3 4 7 9 10 12 | £ D* |

Malvern Nature Cure Centre is situated in a quiet cul de sac in the attractive town of Malvern. Panoramic views of the Severn Valley and Malvern Hills are enjoyed from the house, which is a short walk from the centre of the spa town and its many visitor attractions.

The Centre provides skilled and reasonably priced Nature Cure treatment for those wanting help and guidance in their search for good health or recovery from illness.

All bedrooms in the main house are centrally heated with comfortable Slumberland Orthofirm beds, electric blanket, wash-basin and television. Bathroom facilities are shared and no en suite rooms are available. Annexe rooms are similarly appointed but do not have electric blankets.

The Centre's cuisine is lacto-vegetarian whole food cuisine, following food-reform principle without being unduly austere. All water used in fasting and in conjunction with fruit or vegetable juice fasts is Malvern spring water.

Treatments

To take full advantage of the treatments offered, it is necessary to book in as a 'patient' rather than as a 'guest'. Treatments are taken usually in the mornings Monday to Saturday and include one hour initial consultation £20; daily massage £16; manipulation £18; relaxation class £3.50; discussion group £3.50; sunbed £3.50.

Tariff

Rates for accommodation vary slightly with the time of year and room location. Rooms in the annexe, a short distance from the main house are the least expensive.

Visitors booking in as 'patients' are expected to take the full board tariff, 'guests' are not offered treatments and can opt for bed/breakfast, half or full board. Daily terms are £14 - £19.75 bed/breakfast, £21.50 - £27.25 dinner/bed/breakfast, £26 - £31.75 for full board. Single supplement £3.50 daily.

Travel Directions

From M5 exit at junction 7 and take A449 to Great Malvern, from the east take A4103, B4219 and A449. Follow signs to Malvern College.

Nearest railways station Great Malvern less than 1 mile.

Norwich Sport Village and Hotel
Drayton High Road Norwich Norfolk NR6 5DU
Tel 0603 788898   Fax 0603 406845

55	2 3 4 6 13 14 16 17 18 C	£ D

Set close to the famous Norfolk Broads and the historic city of Norwich, the Norwich Sport Village and Hotel in Broadland offers sport and leisure facilities for all the family.

The attractive self-contained leisure and sporting complex offers over 60 different sports and comprises an hotel, three restaurants and bars, sports shop, and the Broadland Aquapark, one of the Britain's most spectacular swimming complexes. Its unique design incorporates both leisure and competition pools under the same roof. A tropical theme runs throughout with hanging trees, plants, sun loungers and soft music.

Set above the complex is the modern hotel. All rooms have en suite bath or shower, satellite television, 24 hour room service and tea/coffee making facilities.

The health and fitness centre provides a restful atmosphere with relaxation pool, spa bath, steam and sauna rooms, solariums and a beauty clinic offering

an extensive range of treatments. Hotel residents have free use (subject to availability) of aerobic classes, gym, sauna/steam rooms, relaxation pool, spa bath and snooker, plus one session in the Aquapark per day.

Treatments

The Beauty Salon uses a complete range of Dermalogica products which are non-allergenic, cruelty-free and suitable for use by both men and women. Treatments include 1 hour deep cleansing facial £16; full body massage £16.50; aromatherapy £20; waxing from £5.25; G5 massage and Slendertone £8.50 each per 30 minute session. *Top to Toe* treatment package £46.50.

Tariff

Mid-week bed/breakfast rates from £59 single, £69 twin/double room.

Weekend bed/breakfast rates (two nights minimum including a Saturday) from £40 single, £50 twin/double room per night. No charge for children under 15 sharing parents' room, meals charged for as taken.

Professional sport coaching weekends from £149 per person (sharing twin/double room).

Travel Directions

Complex is on A1067 Drayton High Road, north west of the city of Norwich. Nearest railway station Norwich approximately 2 miles.

Patshull Park Hotel
Pattingham Nr Wolverhampton Shropshire WV6 7HR
Tel 0902 700100 Fax 0902 700874

48 2 3 4 6 13 14 16 17 18 C £ D

Patshull Park Hotel is set in the peaceful Shropshire countryside in 280 acres of parklands and lakes. It offers good leisure facilities with attractive accommodation and a scenic golf course.

Many of the bedrooms overlook the lake and golf course and have a balcony or terrace. All rooms have en suite bathroom, television, radio and tea/coffee making facilities.

Patshull's Lakeside Restaurant offers good value table table d'hôte and à la carte menus and has an extensive wine list. Bunker's Coffee Shop serves all day snacks and drinks in comfortable surroundings.

Leisure facilities include a supervised gym and weight room, indoor swimming pool, jacuzzi, steam rooms and saunas and beauty salon. Golf and tennis are available on site and additional activities such as fishing, action vehicles, clay shooting, riding and archery can be arranged.

Treatments

TheBeauty Within salon offers a wide range of body and beauty treatments using Decleor products. The choice includes Decleor slimming and relaxation treatments from £19; bust care treatment £18; anti-cellulite treatment £15; leg care for poor circulation £11; Decleor 5 Vitamin facials from £20; Hollywood facial for maturing skin £30; Seborreor facial £23; waxing from £2.50; manicure £6.50; pedicure £6.50; eyelash tint £3.

Tariff

Bed/breakfast from £62.50 single, £75 twin/double room.

Two night Leisure Break £110 per person inclusive of shared double en suite room, full breakfast, snack lunch, table d'hote dinner and use of facilities.

Two night Golf Break £160 per person, details as above but including three rounds of golf. Additional rounds £10.

Travel Directions

Exit M54 at junction 3 taking A41 towards Wolverhampton. At junction of A464 continue to Tettenhall and then follow country road to Pattingham. Alternatively exit M54 at junction 4 and take A464 to Tettenhall then proceed as before.

Nearest railway station Wolverhampton approximtely 12 miles.

Puckrup Hall Hotel and Golf Club
Puckrup Tewkesbury Gloucestershire GL20 6EL
Tel 0684 296200   Fax 0684 850788

| 84 | 2 3 4 6 13 14 16 17 18 C | £ C |

Situated in over 140 acres of parkland between the Cotswolds and the Malvern Hills, the Puckrup Hotel has recently been extended with 68 new rooms and a luxurious new leisure club.

The 16 original bedrooms are all individually furnished and decorated to reflect the seasons of the year. Most accommodation is now in the new wing, where the en suite rooms are equally luxurious and comfortable, but more modern in style.

Lounges and public areas are pleasantly quiet and relaxing. The Restaurant is acclaimed for its imaginative cuisine and fine wines with less formal meals and drinks served in the Orangery.

The hotel boasts its own fishing lake and 18-hole par 72 golf course, as well as the superb new leisure club, Generations. Facilities include indoor swimming pool, solarium, spa bath, steam room, separage saunas, high tech gym with cardio-vascular equipment, aerobics studio with range of exercise classes, children's splash pool, creche, coffee bar and beauty salon.

Treatments

Generations Beauty Salon offers a range of Decleor body and beauty treatments including facials from £25 to £48; Affinoderm seaweed wrap £25; Vital Energy facial and body treatment £30; anti-cellulite treatment £20; 1 hour aromatherapy massage £35; eyelash tint £7; waxing from £4; cleanse and make-up £15; manicure from £9.50; pedicure from £12.50. *Decleor Top-to-Toe* (four hours) £70; *Aromatherapy Top-to-Toe* (three hours) £60.

Tariff

Weekend break (minimum stay two nights) from £64.50 per person per night inclusive of accommodation, dinner and breakfast. Regular nightly bed/breakfast tariff from £79.50per person.

All hotel residents have use of Generations leisure club and enjoy special rates on the golf course - details on application.

Travel Directions

Puckrup Hall is 2 miles north of Tewkesbury on A38, and a few minutes from junction 8 on M5, via junction 1 of the M50.
Nearest railway station Tewkesbury 2 miles.

Ragdale Hall Health Hydro
Ragdale Nr Melton Mowbray Leicestershire LE14 3PB
Tel 0664 434831/434411   Fax 0664 434587

| 64 | ☆ 2 3 4 5 6 7 10 11 12 14 16 17 C | £ B* |

Ragdale Hall is situated in a charming Victorian country manor amid the rolling Leicestershire countryside. Facilities and accommodation have been completely upgraded in recent years and Ragdale Hall is now one of Britain's most luxurious and sought after health resorts.

On arrival, guests have a health check and sports and beauty consultations to arrange treatments and activities. A health questionnaire is completed to ensure all treatments are individually safe. An extensive programme of optional body and beauty treatments and hairdressing is available and carried out in pleasant treatment rooms by friendly therapists. Innovative new therapies introduced include the Ragdale Multi-Method Massage - the ultimate relaxation treatment using warm oil and two skilled therapists.

The spa area is next to the swimming pool and has separate facilities for men and women. These include sauna and steam rooms, plunge pools and needle showers. The spa has a lovely whirlpool, floatation tank and hydrotherapy bath. After a spa session, enjoy resting in the quiet relaxation room, complete with lounger chairs, cushions and cosy duvets.

Bedrooms are attractively furnished and decorated with en suite bathroom, television, telephone, hair drier, tea/coffee making facilities and flasks of chilled mineral water. A choice of newspaper and breakfast in bed is served each morning around 8am.

Lunch and dinner are served on long tables in the dining room. All food is helpfully calorie counted, with an appetising 1100 calorie diet provided for slimmers. Lots of vegetarian options are always available. Meals are well prepared and plentiful - four course dinner in the evening, freshly baked rolls *and* jacket potatoes at lunch plus a substantial main course and unlimited helpings of salad. Guests can drink wine with their meals if they wish. Coffee, tea and other refreshments are served in the Garden Room and Conservatory, a pleasant area filled with exotic plants in enormous pottery tubs and comfortable cane furniture.

Outdoor exercise opportunities include swimming in the outside pool (summer only) tennis, cycling, organised walks, pitch and putt and croquet. Exercise classes, aquarobics. swimming and supervised use of gym equipment are provided indoors.

Treatments

The vast range of body and beauty treatments includes aromatherapy £40.50; body massage £22.50; Multi-Method Massage £65; Slendertone £12.50; G5 massage £15; Clarins body treatments £36; Decleor body wraps from £30; Ionithermie £38.50; Cellu M6 treatments from £20.50; facials from £15; eyelash tint £10.50; manicure £16.50; pedicure £18.50; waxing from £8.50; make-up £14.

Other services include Suncentre tanning from £10.50; fitness assessment £26; personal exercise programme £18.50; tennis and swimming coaching £12.50 per session;dietary advice from £15; floatation £30; reflexology £36; shiatsu £38; hairdressing from £9 for shampoo/set. Hairdressing consultations free.

Day Guest Packages from £52 per person.

Tariff

Prices include accommodation, meals, consultations, scheduled exercise classes, use of gym and spa area, swimming pools, sports facilities and evening talks. The number of treatments included in the tariff is based on the length of stay and varies from three treatments on a two night stay to 12 on a seven night visit.

Four types of accommodation range from single budget rooms with shower at £79 per night, £99 per person sharing twin bedded room, to £160 per night single suite, £135 per person sharing.

Packages and special offers are available during the year, apply for details.

Travel Directions

Exit M1 at junction 23 taking A512 to Loughborough, then take B676 to Melton Mowbray for 7 miles, passing under bridge carrying A46. Ragdale Hall is about 1/2 mile from the bridge on the right. From A1, turn off at Stamford (A606) or Grantham (A607) and drive to Melton Mowbray. Follow signs to Loughborough taking B676 for 7 miles then follow signs on left for Ragdale Hall.

Nearest railway station: Leicester 12 miles.

Center Parcs Sherwood Forest Holiday Village
Rufford Nottinghamshire NG22 9DN
Tel -274 244744 *(brochure)* **0623 411411** *(reservations)*

| 709 | **self-catering villas 2 3 4 5 6 7 13 14 15 16 17 C**

Sherwood Forest - the UK's first Center Parcs holiday village - is situated in 400 acres of woodlands and lakes in the heart of rural Nottinghamshire. It offers an exceptional range of sporting, health and leisure activitiesthat can be enjoyed throughout the year, even in inclement weather.

Accommodation is in groups of bright modern self-catering villas situated in woods and around the lakes, giving privacy without isolation. Villas vary in size from one to four bedrooms. All are spacious and well equipped with modern appliances, central heating and double glazing. The rental includes use of the villa and all its services (video films, electricity,gas, heating and bedlinen) plus free entry to the Subtropical Swimming Paradise. Charges are made for all other activities and services, including towel and equipment hire, so bringing your own saves time and expense.

After unpacking, cars are parked in special areas, ensuring a safe and traffic-free village for pedestrians and cyclists. Just about everyone - young and old - uses a bike and the wide safe roads make cycling a pleasure. Non-bikers should reserve villas near the village centre, so activities and shops are within walking distance. Adult bike hire is £3.75 daily, £7.45 weekend, £13.20 per week, a large BMX £3.80 daily, £6.90 weekend and £12.70 weekly.

The village has a well-stocked supermarket, gift shops, grill, bars, coffee shop, fast food outlet, a launderette and even a church. Shops stay open until late on visitor-arrival days.

An outstanding range of outdoor pursuits is offered - archery, pony riding, soccer and soccer coaching, tennis, canoeing, jogging, putting, golf driving range and volleyball - the choice is staggering. Facilities indoors are equally impressive with aerobics, fitness and weight training, rollerskating, tennis, snooker, squash, badminton, fencing and table tennis to name but a few!

Main focus of the village is the Subtropical Swimming Paradise, with its tropical landscape of palms and lush vegetation, tumbling cascades of water and bubbling whirlpool spas - all in a constant year round temperature of 84°F. A separate shallow water pool with wheeled playpens and buoyancy aids is provided for small children. The Jungle River and Wild Water Rapids are almost as popular as the wave machine, which periodically transforms the calm pool water into a surging swell. A warning sound precedes the wave, a signal to less confident bathers to move into the shallow end.

The only entrance to the Spa is from inside the main pool. Spa and sunbed bookings are taken at the reception desk also inside the pool and accessible only in swimsuit and bare feet. Despite this inconvenience, the facilities are excellent, with saunas and pools indoors and out, plunge bath, steam room, sunbeds (additional charge), foot spa, and a pleasant relaxation area.

Spa sessions include family, ladies' only and mixed. The entrance fee of £6.80 includes complimentary soft drinks and towel hire. Under 14s can use the Spa during family sessions only when the entrance charge is £3.30.

Treatments

The Aqua Sana health and beauty facility is situated next to the Sports Centre and offers a pampering range of treatments including some unique to Center Parcs such as Karwendel, a therapeutic bath with fossil oils, effective in skin disorders £21.50 per session. The Aqua Sana also features thalassotherapy and floatation - a session in one of the shallow warm pools costs £12.55. Other treatments include seaweed body wrap £27.60; aromatherapy £39.95 for 1 1/2 hour treatment; reflexology £27; thalasso facial from £13.50; Ionithermie body treatment £38; quick-tanner sunbed £6.75; manicure £9.60; pedicure £18; eyelash tint from £6.50. *Day Beauty Packages* from £22 - £76.70.

A full hairdressing service is available in the Aqua Sana's hair salon.

Tariff

Villas can be booked for whole weeks (start and finish on Fridays), mid-week breaks (start on Monday finish on Friday), or weekends (start on Friday finish on Monday). Rental costs vary with the size of villa and the time of year.

A weekend break in a three bedroom villa (four persons) in early January costs £214 and rises to £336 at the end of May. During July and August when rentals are on a weekly only basis, the rate is £673.

Reservations are made ONLY by telephone on the above number - no postal bookings.

Travel Directions

Sherwood Forest Holiday Village is located at Rufford, near Newark in Nottinghamshire, approximately 25 minutes drive from M1 and A1 on the B6034.
Nearest railway station (mainline) Newark approximately 12 miles.

Shrubland Hall Health Clinic
Coddenham Nr Ipswich Suffolk IP6 9QH
Tel 0473 830404   Fax 0473 832641

| 39 | ☆ 2 3 4 5 6 7 8 9 10 11 12 14 16 17 | £ B* |

Shrubland Hall, Lord de Saumarez's family home, was converted into an exclusive health clinic in 1966, and is still under family management. The impressive Georgian mansion is set in 50 acres of spectacular terraced gardens and surrounded by a private park with extensive views of the Suffolk countryside.

The efficient and up-to- date health clinic is run on serious nature cure lines under the supervision of physicians and nurses. The atmosphere is friendly and welcoming, and many guests (referred to as patients) return regularly each year.

A vegetarian 'Rohkost' (raw food) diet is served and considered to be a treatment in itself. It can be adapted to most needs and consists of imaginatively prepared, exotic and colourful salads, raw fruit, vegetable soups and broths, together with homemade yoghurt, wholegrain bread baked from the Estate's own wheat and barley, and a variety of cheeses.

No cooked meals, coffee or alcohol are available. Patients can undertake complete fasts on liquid or light diet and are supervised and well supported by a caring and attentive staff. A light breakfast is served in the bedrooms with the daily treatment plan and newspapers. Other meals are taken in the Light Diet Room or the main Dining Room.

A total of 51 visitors can be accommodated - 38 in the main house and the remainder in an interesting variety of locations. The main house has a lift to all floors and room prices vary according to size, location and amenities - there are two four poster rooms and 21 rooms with en suite facilities. Old Hall, half a mile from the main house is in the heart of the Park and has six attractive bedrooms; the Garden Rooms, 50 yards from the main house have en suite facilities and excellent views; Russian Lodge, a timber cottage in its own garden, is 200 yards from the main house, with two single rooms, sitting room, small kitchen and a bathroom all cheerfully furnished and well heated.

Sports facilities include tennis, gym, billiard room, table tennis, swimming pools (indoor and out) croquet, fishing, cycling and woodland walks.

Treatments

Shortly after arrival, all visitor have a thorough medical examination by one of the Clinic's doctors, and treatments and diet are recommended. The consultation and treatments prescribed by the doctor are included in the tariff, and might include massage, Kneipp water therapy, Turkish bath, sauna, steam cabinet, Sitz bath, blitz guss, aquarobics, exercise, yoga and exercise classes.

Optional extra beauty treatments and therapies are available on request, some use Clarins, RoC or Shrubland Hall's own herbal preparations. The choice includes Phytomer seaweed bath; wax, peat, balsan and herbal baths; aromatherapy; reflexology; shiatsu; floatation tank; Alexander Technique; vacusage; faradic treatments; manicure; pedicure; colonic irrigation; acupuncture; physiotherapy; chiropody; manipulation; hairdressing and specialised hair treatments; personalised exercise and relaxation therapies. Prices on application.

Tariff

Weekly £420 - £650 single room, £450 - £480 per person sharing double room. Arrivals on Sundays and Wednesdays. Shorter visits, Sunday to Wednesday (£320) and Wednesday to Sunday (£370) are sometimes possible. Prices **do not** include VAT which will be added to all accounts at the current rate.

Travel Directions

Via motorway network to Ipswich (north) on A45. Exit at B113 signed to Great Blakenham and drive through Claydon. Shrubland Hall is after the village.

Nearest railway station Ipswich 6 miles (1 hour 10 mins from London, Liverpool Street Station).

Springs Hydro
Packington Nr Ashby de la Zouch Leicestershire LE6 51TG
Tel 0530 273873   Fax 0530 270987

| 41 | ☆ 2 3 4 5 6 7 10 10 12 14 15 16 17 C | £ C* |

Springs opened in August 1990 and is Britain's first purpose built health hydro. Owned and managed by the Purdew family, owners of *Henlow Grange*, it enjoys a countryside setting in rural Leicestershire and is an ideal choice for a relaxing or active rejuvenating break.

Springs successfully combines modern luxury and convenience with natural decor and an extensive range of amenities - saunas, steam rooms, whirlpool spa, swimming pool, splash and plunge pools and a floatation room. The extensive choice of exercise oppportunities ensures a class or workout for every level of fitness. The fine gym boasts the latest cardio-vascular and toning equipment with friendly supervision always available.

Accommodation is in spacious, modern rooms with en suite facilities and either a patio or balcony. Many rooms have whirlpool bath, bidet and separate pulsar shower. All rooms are equipped with telephone, satellite television, in-house video channel, mini bar, ironing board and a personal safe.

Food is carefully prepared from quality ingredients. Wine is available and served with the table d'hôte lunch and dinner menus.

The comfortable lounges invite relaxation - curl up with a good book after dinner or attend one of the interesting evening talks or demonstrations. Sports lovers can play tennis on the floodlit tennis court, hit a basket of golf balls on the driving range, or hire a mountain bike to explore the surrounding country-side. Archery, squash and horse-riding can be arranged locally.

Treatments

Springs has over 30 treatment rooms including a hydrotherapy bath, dry floatation room and solarium. Treatments include aromatherapy £32.50; body massage £18.50; facials from £18.50; floatation session £25; hydrotherapy £35; Presciption body treatment £33.50; Paris method massage £37.50; Cathiodermie £36.50; G5 massage £10.; Slendertone £14.75; Frigo-Thalgo £32.50; manicure £14.85; pedicure £18.50; eyelash tint £8.75; waxing from £9.75; sunbed from £7.20; cut/blow dry £22.50.

Non-residential *Springs Day* from £42.95 *Hydro Day* from £27.95, *Top to Toe* from £59.95.

Tariff

The daily tariff includes accommodation, meals, initial consultation, daily body massage and inclusive treatments depending on length of stay, unlimited use of sauna and steam rooms, sports amenties, exercise classes, talks and demonstrations.

Standard Room £89.95 single, £69.95 per person sharing twin room; *Studio Room* with whirlpool bath £99.95 single, £79.95 per person sharing; *Superior Studio* with whirlpool bath, bidet, separate pulsar shower, use of towelling robe and fresh fruit basket £109.95 single, £89.95 per person sharing.

One to five night stays are available throughout the year and include various treaments eg *Five Night Stay* costs from £359.95 single, £299.95 sharing twin room, and includes 3 full body massages, facial or neck/shoulder massage, 1 gyratory massage, 1 UVA sunbed or 1 body exfoliation.

Travel Directions

From M1 exit at junction 22 and follow signs for A50 Burton-on-Trent. Take A42/M42 South and follow signs for Snarestone B4116.

From west, follow M42/A42 North then take B5006 Ashby exit, and follow signs for Snarestone B4116.

Nearest railway station Burton-on-Trent 12 miles, Loughborough 14 miles.

Sprowston Manor Hotel
Wroxham Road Norwich Norfolk NR7 8RP
Tel 0603 410871   Fax 0603 423911

| 117 | 2 3 4 6 13 14 15 17 C   £ D

An avenue lined with oak trees leads to historic Sprowston Manor, a fine 19th century country house with origins dating back over 400 years. Situated in ten acres of parkland adjoining a golf course, the hotel has been transformed by a new wing of 87 executive bedrooms and a state of the art leisure club. The new wing complements the 36 bedrooms in the main house, which have all been refurbished to a high standard.

All the luxurious bedrooms are double rooms and have en suite bathroom, bathrobes, satellite television, telephone, tea/coffee making facilities, trouser press and hair drier.

Traditional English and French cuisine is served at lunch and dinner in the Manor Restaurant and Orangery. Pre-dinner drinks can be taken by an open fire in the adjoining Gurney Bar, or on the garden terrace in fine weather.

The new Sprowston Manor Leisure Club is open to hotel residents and a selected club membership. Designed in tropical style, the club has a large indoor swimming pool, king size spa bath and children's lagoon with two steam rooms, sauna, solarium, gym, beauty salon and pool-side bar selling soft drinks and health food snacks. All areas of the hotel and the swimming pool are accessible to wheelchairs, by lift or ramp.

Sprowston Manor adjoins an 18-hole golf course, and residents can play a round of golf for £15.

Treatments

La Fontana beauty salon offers facial and body treatments including body massage £21 per hour; G5 massage £9 for 30 minutes or 6 for £50; Sisley Aromatique facial with massage and make-up £30; facials from £15; manicure and hand massage £6.50; pedicure with foot and leg massage £10; eyelash tint £6; waxing from £3.50; electrolysis from £6.75; solarium £5.

Two health and beauty packages are offered - the *Health & Slimming Day* and the *Health & Beauty Day* - both cost £95.

Tariff

Two night *Getaway Break* from £59 per person per night sharing a room, inclusive of dinner/bed and breakfast. Room only tariff from £85 per night (two persons), English breakfast £8.25, continental breakfast £6.25.

Travel Directions

From the Norwich northern ring road take A1151 Wroxham Road, the hotel is 11/2 miles on the right.
Nearest railway station Norwich 4 miles

NORTHERN ENGLAND

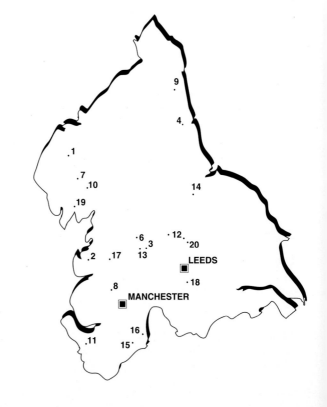

9
.

4
.

.1

.7
.10

5.

.19

14
.

.6 .12
.3   .20

.2 .17 13   **LEEDS** ■

.8   **MANCHESTER** ■   .18

16
.

.11   15.

NORTHERN ENGLAND

Armathwaite Hall Hotel
Bassenthwaite Lake Keswick Cumbria CA12 4RE
Tel 07687 76551   Fax 07687 76220

| 42 | 2 3 4 5 13 14 15 16 17 C | £ C |

Armathwaite Hall enjoys a secluded situation in 133 acres of deer park and woodlands overlooking Lake Bassenthwaite in the heart of the Lake District.

Public rooms are spacious with wonderful fireplaces and wood panelling. Comfortable bedrooms have lakeside or parkland views and modern amenities including en suite bathroom, television, in-house video, telephone, hair drier and tea/coffee tray.

The wood panelled restaurant overlooks Bassenthwaite Lake and provides a choice of table d'hôte and à la carte menus including some local 'Taste of Cumbria' dishes. Lighter meals and high teas are served daily in the leisure club, where amenities include indoor heated swimming pool, jacuzzi, sauna, solarium, trimnasium and beauty salon.

Sporting opportunities are many and varied; tennis, pitch and putt, croquet, snooker, boating on the lake and hill walking in the Skiddaw Mountains. Armathwaite Hall has its own equestrian centre and offers riding and jumping tuition, country hacking, carriage driving, livery and riding holidays - prices on application.

Treatments

Treatments are available in the leisure club's beauty salon including Decleor holistic facials £130 for 5 treatments or individually from £28.50; Triactive Aroma facial £40; men's facial £28.50; Seborreor facial £28.50; aromatherapy/reflexology £30; waxing from £3; manicure £10; pedicure £15; eyelash tint £6; shampoo/blow dry £7. *Full Day Relaxation* £85, *Half Day Relaxation* £25.

Tariff

Two night *Beauty Breaks* cost £275 per person. Price includes consultation with beauty therapist, optional walks, jogs, gym session and **six** treatments. Price is based on sharing executive twin/double room with fruit basket, mineral water and bathrobes. Tariff includes breakfast, light lunch, six course table d'hôte dinner on two nights, refreshments and use of swimming pool, spa pool and sauna.

Two night regular breaks from £63 per person per night including four course table d'hôte dinner, bed and full breakfast. Children stay free when sharing parents' room, with high tea, bed and breakfast provided.

Travel Directions

Take M6 and exit at junction 40 signed Penrith, then A66 to Keswick roundabout. Take A591 towards Carlisle for 8 miles, turning left at Castle Inn junction, 200 yards from Armathwaite Hall.

Nearest railway stations Carlisle or Penrith, both 20 miles.

Brooklands Health Farm

Calder House Lane Garstang Preston Lancashire PR3 1QB

Tel 0995 605162

| 12 | ✩ 2 3 4 5 6 9 10 14 16 17 | £ B* |

Brooklands is a well appointed small health farm, situated on the edge of the Lake District in five acres of gardens. Its rejuvenating health and beauty courses attract a mainly female clientele.

Amenities include a warm indoor swimming pool, spa bath, sauna, steam room, sunbathing pavilion, solarium, conservatory room for exercising, jogging trail and tennis court. The pool area has a disabled changing room, shower and toilet.

Bedrooms are appointed in Victorian style, mainly with en suite bathroom and all with television, telephone, electric blanket and tea/coffee making facilities. Six new en suite bedrooms and a lounge have been added recently, and the refurbished East Lodge now accommodates four guests.

A brief personal consultation is given initially so individual diet and treatments choices can be arranged. Detailed health and nutritional advice is not given.

Fresh local produce is used to create a variety of healthy low calorie menus. Meals in the dining room are usually served plated, eliminating any temptation to cheat on portion size. Menus amounting to 1,000, 750 and 500 calories per day are available for slimmers. Most special dietary needs can be catered for if advance notice is given.

No evening activities are arranged. Visitors can play tennis, go for a jog, read or watch television before taking an early night.

Treatments

Many optional treatments are available including body massage £15.50; facials from £17; G5 massage £12.50; sunbed £4; sauna £8.80; Turkish room £8.80; aromatherapy from £33; reflexology £15.50; Decleor facials from £25; Decleor body treatments £30 each; waxing from £6.50; manicure and pedicure £12.50 each; eyelash tint £10; hairdressing from £6.30 for trim, £31.50 perm.

Tariff

The tariff includes all meals, use of the facilities and a generous number of treatments. *Weekend Break* from Friday to Sunday afternoon costs from £206.25 single, £200.64 per person sharing a twin bedded room inclusive of exercises, sunbed, body massage, facial, manicure G5 massage and make-up. Residential rates **do not** include VAT which is added to all accounts at the current rate.

A non-residential day costs £80 with optional morning exercises, sauna and steam room, swim, solarium, body massage, lunch, manicure facial and make-up.

Travel Directions

Take the M6 and exit at junction 32, taking A6 for 9 miles towards Lancaster. Turn onto B6430 at the junction and turn into Calder House Lane.

Nearest railway stations Preston 12 miles, Lancaster 12 miles.

Devonshire Arms Hotel
Bolton Abbey   Skipton   North Yorkshire BD23 6AJ
Tel 0756 710441   Fax 0756 710564

| 40 | 2 3 4 5 6 13 14 15 16 17 C | £ B |

Situated at Bolton Abbey in the Yorkshire Dales National Park, the Devonshire Arms is one of Yorkshire's most charming and traditional hotels. The original coaching inn has been carefully restored and enlarged to create a hotel of great character and style.

A stone-flagged reception hall with an open log fire leads into comfortable lounges furnished with antiques and portraits from Chatsworth, the Derbyshire home of the hotel's owners, the Duke and Duchess of Devonshire.

The Burlington restaurant, famous throughout Yorkshire for its outstanding cusine, has recently been refurbished and serves outstanding English and continental dishes, complemented by an extensive wine list. The dining room is non-smoking.

Bedrooms are luxuriously appointed and seven rooms in the old inn have four poster beds. The more modern accommodation in the new wing is equally comfortable and pleasant. All rooms have en suite bathroom, television, radio, telephone, tea/coffee making facilities, iron and ironing board, trouser press and hair drier.

The hotel's superb new health and fitness facility The Devonshire Club opened in January 1994. Amenities include indoor swimming pool with swim-flow machine, spa bath, Turkish steam room, sauna and plunge pool, sunbed, fully equipped gym with toning and cardio-vascular equipment, relaxation and refreshment area, hairdressing salon and beauty treatment room with Matis trained therapists.

Treatments

Full range of Matis body and beauty treatments, aromatherapy, full and part body massage, manicure, pedicure and hairdressing. Details and prices on application.

Tariff

Nightly bed and breakfast rate from £120 for Wharfedale wing double room (two persons), £145 for a deluxe double in old inn. Single occupancy from £90 to £95 in Wharfedale room, £100 in deluxe old inn.

Getaway Breaks (minimum two nights) £150 per Wharfedale room accommodating two persons inclusive of dinner, bed and breakfast, £165 in deluxe old inn.

Travel Directions

The Devonshire is on the B6160 to Bolton Abbey, 250 yards north from its junction with the A59 Skipton to Harrogate road.

Nearest railway stations Ilkley 5 miles, Skipton 5 miles.

Gosforth Park Swallow Hotel
High Gosforth Park Newcastle-upon-Tyne Tyne & Wear NE3 5HN
Tel 091 236 4111   Fax 091 236 8192

178	2 3 4 5 6 13 14 16 17 C	£ D

The Swallow is a comfortable modern hotel on the outskirts of Newcastle and set in 12 acres of wooded parkland. It boasts an impressive range of sporting and leisure facilities and makes a great base for a weekend exploring the unspoiled villages and coast of Northumberland.

The Leisure Club's facilitis are open to all hotel residents and include an indoor swimming pool, sauna, steam room, plunge pool, whirlpool spa bath, solaria, games room and gym with computerised fitness assessment equipment. There are two squash courts, three floodlit all weather tennis courts, children's adventure playground and a 'trim trail' with specially designed obstacles. Nominal charges are made for the squash courts and sunbeds, but all other facilities are free.

Bedrooms are on three floors and are comfortably furnished with private bathroom, hair drier, telephone, satellite television, mini-bar and bathrobes.

The hotel has two restaurants - the Brandling overlooking floodlit gardens and the informal Conservatory, a non-smoking restaurant open throughout the day for informal meals and snacks.

Treatments

The Bodyworks Salon is based in the Leisure Club and offers a full range of body and beauty treatments using Italian RVB products. Complimentary

147

consultations are available, and where possible appointments should be booked prior to arrival.

Basic facials from £14; aromatherapy body massage £23; G5 massage £10; faradic treatment £15; make-up £9.50; manicure with varnish £8; pedicure with varnish £10; waxing from £3.50; electrolysis from £7; eyelash tinting £4. Hairdressing services for men and women are available in the Hair Salon.

Tariff

Bed and breakfast from £45 per person per night based on two people sharing a double room. Two night *Conservatory Breakaway* (with dinner in the Conservatory restaurant) £125 per person, *Brandling Breakaway* (with dinner in the Brandling restaurant) £145 per person. The price is inclusive of dinner/ bed and breakfast and one lunch, plus use of the leisure facilities. Children aged 14 years and under sharing a room with two adults are accommodated and served with a full breakfast free of charge.

Travel Directions

Follow A1 until 5 miles north of Newcastle then turn onto A1056 to Wide Open. Nearest railway station Newcastle Central 5 miles.

The Grand Island Hotel
Ramsey Isle of Man
Tel 0624 812455   Fax 0624 815291

54	2 3 4 5 6 13 14 16 17 C	£ C

Overlooking palm fringed lawns sweeping down to the sea and with panoramic views of the mountains, the Grand Island Hotel has an unrivalled setting. A former Georgian manor house, the hotel is situated in a quiet part of the island, a short drive from the bustle of Douglas, the island's capital. The Isle of Man has much to offer the visitor, with many beautiful quiet beaches, mountains and glens - all within a day's drive and well worth exploring.

Comfortable bedrooms are individually designed in country house style with co-ordinating chintz furnishings. All rooms have en suite bathroom and a generous supply of quality toiletries. Baby listening devices enable parents to enjoy an evening meal with peace of mind.

Residents have a choice of restaurants - the elegant Bay Room overlooking the sea and serving varied à la carte and table d'hôte menus including freshly caught fish, or the cheerful and informal Bistro offering snacks and refreshments.

This is the headquarters of the Isle of Man Croquet Association and the hotel has five croquet lawns and a putting green. Access to golf courses on the island can be arranged on request.

Hotel residents have use of Grand Island's magnificent Henley leisure spa with wave-swimming pool, jacuzzi, solarium, sauna, steam room, gym, snooker, hair and beauty salons. Refreshments are available from the poolside bar.

Treatments

A varied range of treatments is available in the Henley's beauty salon including 1 hour body massage £22; aromatherapy £27; facials from £12; G5 massage £13; faradic slimming treatments £10; vacuum suction massage £13; manicure from £8.50; pedicure from £12.50; Sixtus foot treatment £14. *Top to Toe* day package £53 includes use of swimming pool, sauna or steam room, full body massage, cleanse and make up, manicure, shampoo and set or blow dry, morning coffee, salad lunch and afternoon tea.

Tariff

Three night bed and breakfast tariff from £29.50 per person per night sharing a standard twin/double room. Weekend dinner/bed/breakfast from £44.45 per person per night sharing standard twin/double room. A seven night bed and breakfast package costs from £206.50 per person.

Travel Directions

Ferries to Douglas from Heysham, Liverpool and Stranraer. or flights from various UK airports. From Douglas take the A2 road to Ramsey; the Grand Island Hotel is 1 mile north of Ramsey centre.

Hartrigg Country House
Buckden Skipton North Yorkshire BD23 5HA
Tel 0756 760246

9	2 3 4 15	£ D

Hartrigg is a Victorian country house hotel situated in the heart of the Yorkshire Dales and the idyllic setting for *Ladies' Pamper Breaks*. These great value short breaks are designed for women of all ages wanting a change of routine, relaxation and a bit of well deserved cossetting.

The programmes are arranged from Friday to Sunday, or from Tuesday to Thursday, with afternoon arrival and departure after lunch on the Sunday or Thursday. Ladies are served early morning tea in bed, farmhouse breakfasts, 'help yourself' lunches, home cooked evening meals with generous portions, candle-lit dinners and tea/coffee at any time. A team of beauty therapists is on hand with a wide range of pampering body and beauty treatments.

Ladies are accommodated in twin-bedded rooms and one triple bedded room. Eight of the nine bedrooms have en suite showers and all have wash-basins. All rooms enjoy stunning views of this remote and beautiful part of upper Wharfedale.

Full central heating and open fires in the two lounges (one with well-stocked bar) ensure warmth and a cosy atmosphere even in the depths of a Yorkshire winter (the B6160 road is accessible at all times even in bad weather.)

During the break, healthy optional pursuits are organised: Guided walks in this most picturesque part of the Yorkshire dales; swimming, sauna and jacuzzi at nearby luxury pool; use of exercise bike and rowing machine; musical relaxation hour and informal evening talks by various speakers on a range of different topics.

Treatments

The extensive choice of reasonably priced body and beauty treatments includes aroma-massage £15.95; facials from £9.95 to £17.50; eyelash tint £5.50; manicure £5.95; pedicure £8.95; exfoliating massage £19.50; back massage £10.95. A special *pregnancy package* incorporating gentle and revitalising treatments costs £35.

Tariff

A two night *Pamper Break* at this friendly establishment costs £110 per person, and includes accommodation, food and activities, with only drinks at the bar and beauty treatments charged extra.

Travel Directions

From Skipton follow B6265 to Grassington for approx 5 miles, turning onto B6160 at Thresfield. Hartrigg Country House is just before the village of Buckden.

Nearest railway station Skipton approx 12 miles (free collection).

Langdale Hotel, Lodges & Country Club
Langdale Estate Great Langdale Ambleside Cumbria LA22 9JD
Tel 05394 37302   Fax 05394 37694

| 65 | 2 3 4 5 6 13 14 15 16 17 C | £ C |

Nestling in woodlands beneath the mysterious Langdale Pikes, the Langdale Hotel, Country Club and award winning timeshare development enjoy an exceptional setting in the heart of the English Lake District.

All visitors staying at the hotel or in the self catering lodges enjoy membership of the exclusive Country Club, acclaimed as one of the most imaginative year round social, sports and leisure facilities in the area. There is a regular and varied programme of entertainment which changes weekly.

Club amenities include indoor swimming pool, spa baths, jet stream exercise pool, sauna, steam room, plunge pool, fitness and aquatone exercises; table tennis, supervised gym, snooker, games room and two squash courts. Outside are nature and trim trails, badminton, volley ball and an all weather tennis court. Some facilities and activities have nominal charges. Visitors are welcome to join in organised barbeques, discos, quiz nights and talks organised at the Club on a regular basis.

Challenging outdoor activities with expert supervision are possible - water skiing, orienteering, mountain biking, rock climbing and fell walking to name but a few. Children's fun activities and sports coaching are also available.

Hotel bedrooms (all en suite twin or double) are clustered village fashion in small groups near the main facilities. Rooms are either modern in style or elegant Edwardian, furnished with four poster or half tester canopied beds. Luxurious self-catering lodges and apartments are available for weekly rental and sleep four to eight people.

International dishes and local cuisine are served in Purdey's, the hotel's main restaurant. Informal meals, drinks, themed evening menus and weekend carvery are available on the Tamarind Terrace overlooking the pool.

Treatments

The Health and Beauty Salon provides a range of hair and beauty treatments including aromatherapy massage £28; Clarins facial from £17.50; make-up lesson and full make-up £15.50; body scrub and massage £23.50; G5 massage £14.75; eyelash tint £5.50; manicure and pedicure from £9 each; waxing from £4.25; wash/blow dry £7.75; wash/cut/blow dry £13.95. *Top to Toe* package £47.50, *Holiday Top Up* £29.

Tariff

Two night leisure breaks from £77 per person per night mid-week, £86 per person per night on Friday and Saturday, based on two sharing a twin/double room and inclusive of dinner bed and breakfast. Children under 3 free of charge; under 14 years and sharing with 2 adults £20 per night including full breakfast.

Weekly lodge rental from £525 - £935 for two bedroom lodge, £640 - £1,060 for three bedrooms. Full rental details and dates on application.

Travel Directions

Take M6 and exit at junction 36 onto A591 by-passing Kendal. At Ambleside turn left onto A593. At Skelworth Bridge turn right onto B5343 to Langdale. Nearest railway station Oxenholme (Kendal) approx 20 miles.

The Last Drop Village Hotel
Hospital Road Bromley Cross Bolton Lancashire BL7 9PZ
Tel 0204 591131   Fax 0204 54122

83	2 3 4 13 14 17 C	£ C

The Last Drop Village is an imaginatively restored collection of 18th century moorland farm buildings used to create a new village in olde world style, with a pub, village bakery tea-shop and weekly antique fair. Central focus of the village is the comfortable hotel with its unusual cobbled street leading from reception to the cocktail bar and restaurants.

The hotel has an outstanding health and leisure club with kidney-shaped swimming pool and wave pool, jacuzzi, separate saunas, four sunbeds, multi-gym and a health and beauty clinic. Squash and snooker are also available.

Pleasant bedrooms overlook the village courtyard or the open countryside, and have en suite bathroom, television, telephone tea/coffee making facilities, hair drier and trouser press. Luxury suites, some with four poster bed are also available.

Meals are served in the Stocks Restaurant or the unique Last Drop Restaurant, converted from the original cattle-shed and complete with original cow stalls and tables made from glass covered cartwheels.

Treatments

Finishing Touch, the leisure club's innovative health and beauty salon specialises in remedial massage treatments using infra red heat. Massage is varied to suit the need - vigorous sports massage or gentler movements for muscle, joint or circulation problems. Body treatments include aromatherapy £30; full body massage £20; back, neck and shoulder massage £9.50; infra red and back massage £14; infra red and shoulder massage £9.50; Slendertone £6.50 or six sessions for £32.50; body peel £8.50; waxing from £4.50. Facials, nail and make-up treatments also available and bookable in advance or at Reception. Special offers on treatment packages - *Day of Beauty* £60, *Holiday Special* £45; *Evening Preparation* £27.50.

Hairdressing services are available in the Last Drop Village.

Tariff

A two night weekend break including use of the leisure facilities (treatments and sunbeds extra) costs £99 per person sharing a double/twin bedded room with en suite bathroom. This includes accommodation and dinner Friday, full breakfast and dinner dance on Saturday, and full breakfast on Sunday.

Travel Directions

From Motorways 61/62/63 and the M6, follow A666 towards Bolton and Blackburn turning right at the end of the motorway link. Turn onto B6472 signed Bromley Cross and the Last Drop Village is just a couple of minutes away and signposted.

Nearest railway stations Bromley Cross 1 miles, Bolton 5 miles.

Linden Hall Hotel & Spa
Longhorsley Morpeth Northumberland NE65 8XF
Tel 0670 516611   Fax 0670 788544

55	2 3 4 5 6 7 13 14 15 16 17 C	£ B

Linden Hall is situated in 450 acres of wooded parkland in the lovely county of Northumberland. The ivy-clad Georgian manor has been transformed into a gracious traditional hotel with fine cuisine and excellent leisure facilities including a health and beauty spa offering good value residential programmes.

Bedrooms are furnished in individual styles and all have en suite bathroom, television, radio, telephone, hair drier, baby listening service, trouser press and mini bar. Most have spectacular views of the mid-Northumbrian countryside. Inter-communicating bedrooms for families and a specially designed room for the disabled are available on request.

Antique furnishings grace the pleasant drawing room where traditional afternoon tea is served beside a blazing log fire. Dinner is taken in the award winning Dobson restaurant where diners have a choice of table d'hôte, à la carte or healthy options menus complemented by fine wines. Alternatively, the Granary restaurant in the Linden Pub serves a tasty selection of informal meals and snacks including calorie controlled dishes.

The new health and beauty spa's amenities include an indoor swimming pool, spa bath, steam room, solarium, fitness room, treatment rooms and hairdressing salon. There is a billiards room on the lower ground floor and a sun terrace adjacent to the pool with relaxing loungers. Leisurewear, gifts and cosmetics can be purchased in the boutique.

The extensive grounds include a croquet lawn, putting green and tennis court (equipment can be borrowed) as well as jogging routes with maps provided. Other outdoor pursuits include mountain biking (bikes available for hire on daily or hourly basis), coarse fishing on the hotel lake, giant chess, clay pigeon shooting and sightseeing over three heritage trails. Discounted green fees are available on several local golf courses with transport provided by hotel courtesy car.

Treatments

Health and beauty treatments include aromatherapy massage with infra red (90 mins) £27; aromatherapy without infra red (60 mins) £24; reflexology £21; facials from £22; Cathiodermie from £22; Ultratone or Slendertone £12 per session; G5 massage (30 mins) £15; sunbed £3; manicure £10.50 (men's £9.50); pedicure £12.50 (men's £11.50); eyelash tint £7; waxing from £4.50; electrolysis from £7. Deluxe full day treatment package £85.

A full range of hairdressing services is also available.

Tariff

Spa Residential Plan two night stay £265 single, £215 per person in twin/double room, includes **eight** inclusive treatments.

Three night stay £380 single, £305 sharing twin/double room, includes **fourteen** inclusive treatments.

Price includes Garden room with fresh fruit and bathrobes, room service breakfast, morning coffee, buffet lunch in the Old Granary Restaurant, afternoon tea and selection from the Dobson Restaurant's Health Options dinner menu.

Regular bed and breakfast from £88.50 per night single room, £118.50 double or twin room. Two night breaks inclusive of dinner, bed and breakfast from £77.50 per person per night sharing a double room. Rates include use of all facilities and two daily aquarobic classes (optional).

Travel Directions

From south:Take A1 out of Newcastle for 15 miles and then A697 signed Coldsteam and Wooler. Hotel is a mile north of Longhorsley. From north:Turn off A1 10 miles south of Alnwick turning right at junction signed Weldon Bridge, then right again after 1 1/2 miles. Turn left at next junction onto A697. After a mile Linden Hall is signed on the left.

Nearest railway station Newcastle approximately 20 miles.

The Low Wood Hotel
Windermere Cumbria LA23 1LP
Tel 05394 33338   Fax 05394 34072

96	2 3 4 5 13 14 17 C	£ D

The Low Wood Hotel is situated on the northern end of Lake Windermere, a short drive from the little town of Ambleside.

Bedrooms are comfortable furnished with en suite bathroom, television, telephone and tea/coffee making facilities. Some rooms have lakeside views and four poster beds.

Traditional English cuisine is served in the Windermere restaurant, with morning coffee and afternoon tea taken in the lounge. Drinks and refreshments are available in four friendly hotel bars.

The Low Wood Club is one of Lakeland's most active leisure clubs and hotel residents enjoy full use of the extensive facilities. The pool area is imaginatively designed with cascading waterfalls, bubble bursts and tropical rain showers. An 18 metre stretch of clear water is reserved for serious exercising. Toddlers have a separate pool with fountains, shallow steps and a beach! Other features include a large jacuzzi, 'Roman Baths', sauna and steam rooms, power showers and a plunge pool. The club also boasts two solaria, two squash courts, table tennis, snooker, well equipped gym and a health and beauty salon

Supervised activities are arranged for under-fives and older children have a games room with electronic and computer games. Club activities such as circuit training, aerobics, exercise to music and aquarobics are all open to hotel guests - details and timetable at Reception.

Excellent on-site water-sports opportunities are provided with a water-ski school, tuition and equipment hire. Visitors who prefer a less strenuous way of enjoying Windermere can sail in *Leander*, the hotel's 32 foot steam yacht.

Treatments

Treatments include Aroma massage £25.55; exfoliating treatment £18.40; Decleor facials £20.50; Slendertone £7; G5 massage £16.95 for 40 mins; body massage £19.75; aromatherapy body and facial massage £26.50; waxing from £4.50; electrolysis from £3.95; manicure £8; pedicure £12; eyelash tint £5.50.

Tariff

From £45 per person per night for bed and breakfast sharing twin/double room. Dinner from £19.50. Children under 15 sharing parents' room pay only for breakfast and dinner.

Travel Directions

From M6 exit at junction 36 and take A591 signed to Windermere; Low Wood is 2 miles beyond the village.

Nearest railway station Windermere 3 miles.

Mollington Banastre Hotel
Parkgate Road Chester Cheshire CH1 6NN

Tel 0244 851471   Fax 0244 851165

64	**2 3 4 5 6 13 14 17 C**	**£ C**

Mollington Banastre is a friendly country house hotel set in attractive grounds, a mile from the historic city of Chester.

The hotel offers an innovative range of short break holidays combining appetising cuisine with comfortable accommodation and excellent leisure facilities. *Ladies' Indulgence Breaks* are especially good value and include a generous number of inclusive treatments.

Bedrooms have en suite bathroom, television, mini bar, telephone and tea/coffee making facilities. Adjoining family bedrooms for children are available, some with bunk beds, as well as a number of four poster rooms and suites.

Meals are served in a choice of restaurants; the Garden Room for formal dining with à la carte and fixed price menus, the Grill Room overlooking the swimming pool; the Terrace Bar for smorgasbord lunches and also in The Good Intent - the hotel's own olde worlde pub in the grounds.

The Sportif Leisure Club has a chlorine-free indoor swimming pool surrounded by palm trees and exotic plants, special children's pool, jacuzzi, pulsating showers, sauna, squash courts, solarium, fully equipped and supervised gym with personalised health programmes, hairdressing and body/beauty therapies.

Treatments
The Hair and Beauty Club is open Tuesday to Saturday with a huge choice of

pampering treatments and hairdressing including massage £10; aromatherapy £25; reflexology £15; faradic treatment £10 or £80 for 10; G5 massage £10; waxing from £4; René Guinot facials £17.50; Cathiodermie £19.50; Bio-peel £17.50; eye treatment £15; eyelash tint £5; eyelash tint £5; cleanse, tone and make-up £9.50; manicure £7.50; pedicure £8; electrolysis from £8.50.

Top to Toe £58 (full body massage, Cathiodermie, half leg wax, manicure, pedicure, eyelash tint and eyebrow shape); *Hair and Beauty Special* £50 (swim/jacuzzi, heat treatment or fast tan sunbed, full body massage, 1 hour facial, hairdressing consultation followed by a cut/ blow dry).

Tariff

Two Night Indulgence Break costs £195 per person and includes accommodation for two nights in twin/double room, full breakfast, £18.50 per day towards dinner in either main restaurant.

Inclusive activities and treatments include exercises, sauna and sunbed on both days; body massage, facial, manicure, G5 massage, make-up and cut/ blow dry.

Three Night Indulgence Break costs £335 and includes **17** inclusive treatments: Sauna, two body massages, sunbed, two G5 massages, two facials, manicure, two wash/blow dry or set, pedicure, electrolysis or eyelash tint, make-up, hairdressing, half leg waxing, aromatherapy.

Partners and friends sharing the accommodation but pursuing their own interests will find activities such as golf, shooting, local football, four-wheel driving and racing within easy reach of the hotel. Regular tariff from £56 per person per night for dinner/bed and breakfast in twin/double room.

Details of other themed breaks including *Shopping Weekends* and *Golfing Breaks* on application.

Travel Directions

From M56 motorway exit at junction 16 and take A540 for 11/2 miles to Mollington.

Nearest railway station Chester approximately 2 miles

Nidd Hall Country House Hotel
Nidd Harrogate North Yorkshire HG3 3BN
Tel 0423 771598   Fax 0423 770931

| 58 | 2 3 4 6 13 14 15 16 17 C | £ B |

This imposing 19th century manor house nestles in 45 acres of parkland a few miles from the spa town of Harrogate. The extensive grounds include many rosebeds, winding pathways and covered arbours as well as a three acre lake stocked with mature rainbow trout.

Nidd Hall provides relaxing breaks in tranquil surroundings, combining historic elegance with modern comforts. Residents have full use of the Leisure Club's many facilities including an indoor heated pool, squash court, all weather tennis courts, trimnasium, sauna, sunbeds, full size snooker table, games room with table tennis, beauty salon, poolside snack bar and boutique. Croquet, trout fishing and punting on the lake are also available.

Bedrooms are individually designed with colour co-ordinated furnishings and fine antiques. All rooms have en suite bathroom, television, telephone, trouser press, hair drier, private bar and tea/coffee making facilities.

The elegant Lancaster Restaurant offers wonderful views of the gardens across the terrace and a delicious range of menus. Vegetarian options are always available, and given advanced notice, most special dietary needs can be catered for. No smoking in the dining-room. Informal meals and refreshments are also served in the vaulted Cellar restaurant.

Treatments

Ttreatments offered in the Aromatique beauty salon include Decleor facials from £20; Decleor body treatments £25; Decleor exfoliate massage £15; Aroma body massage £20; manicure and hand massage £10; pedicure and leg massage £12; eyelash tinting £5; waxing from £4; anti-cellulite treatments £15.

A Day of Luxury from £30 includes use of leisure facilities, Decleor facial or body treatment and lunch. *A Residential Day of Luxury* costs £120 and includes treatment choice, dinner, overnight stay and breakfast.

Selected treatments and products recommended for men.

Tariff

Two night weekend breaks £85 per person per night sharing a double room. This includes table d'hôte dinner (or equivalent from à la carte menu), full cooked breakfast, newspaper and membership of the leisure club.

Travel Directions

From A1 take A59 to Knaresborough then B6165 to Ripley. The tiny hamlet of Nidd is about a mile from Ripley village. Travellers from Harrogate take A61 Ripon road for approximately 5 miles.

Nearest railway station Harrogate 5 miles.

Randell's Hotel

Keighley Road Snaygill Skipton North Yorkshire BD23 2TA
Tel 0756 700100   Fax 0756 700107

| 61 | 2 3 4 5 6 13 14 17 C | £ D |

Randells is situated next to the historic Leeds and Liverpool Canal, a mile from the north Yorkshire town of Skipton. Visitors are offered a high standard of accommodation and excellent leisure facilities.

All rooms have en suite bath and shower, satellite television, iron, board, trouser press, hair drier and tea/coffee making facilities. Family rooms and suites, disabled and specially planned ladies' rooms available on request. A laundry service and 24 room service are also provided.

Table d'hôte dinner (£15.95) is served in the Waterside Restaurant, and refreshments and snacks are available throughout the day in the Mallard Bar.

The health and leisure centre's excellent faciities are open to hotel residents and include indoor swimming pool, poolside whirlpool spa, family sauna, individual male/female saunas, poolside steam room, sunbeds, fully equipped gym, snooker and pool tables, two squash courts with spring floors, club room with bar, unisex hair salon and a health and beauty suite. Well run creche and nursery facilities for under sevens are provided for parents using the leisure centre.

Treatments
Harriet's health and beauty suite provides a range of treatments using mainly Clarins products. Facials from £17; body massage £10.50 for 30 mins, £16 for an hour; back massage £8.50; eyelash tint £4.50; make-up £6.50; waxing from £3; manicure £7; pedicure £8; *Day of Beauty* £44 (including 30 minute body massage, facial, manicure, pedicure and make-up).

Tariff
Mid week bed and breakfast rate from £72.50 single, £82.50 twin/double room.
    Weekend bed and breakfast rate from £45 single, £60 twin/double room.

Travel Directions
Randells is 1 mile out of Skipton town on A629 Bradford road.
    Nearest railway station Skipton 1 mile.

Redworth Hall Hotel & Country Club
Redworth Nr Newton Aycliffe County Durham DL5 6NL
Tel 0388 772442 Fax 0388 775112

100 2 3 4 5 6 13 14 15 16 17 C £ C

Redworth Hall is an imposing Elizabethan manor standing in 25 acres of parklands and woods in rural County Durham. Tastefully converted into a luxurious hotel, its modern comforts and amenities pleasingly combine with such interesting historic features as stained glass windows, a Jacobean tower and a galleried hall.

The lovely bedrooms are spacious and individually designed with co-ordinating fabrics and furnishings. All rooms have en suite bathroom, fax point, teletext television, radio, telephone, hair drier, trouser press and tea/coffee making facilities. Non-smoking, disabled, hard of hearing and ladies' rooms provided on request. Three superb four poster rooms are also available.

Both restaurants at Redworth Hall have a unique ambience - the elegant Crozier Blue Room serves innovative modern cuisine in quiet and intimate surroundings, the Crozier Conservatory offers a traditional carvery and contemporary à la carte menus throughout the day.

Hotel residents have use of the many facilities of the Health Club, which include indoor swimming pool, mixed sauna and steam rooms, sunbeds, spa pool, two squash courts, fully equipped gym, snooker room, hair and beauty salon. Outside are jogging trails, children's adventure land, and two all weather tennis courts. Exercise classes, coaching and equipment hire are also offered. Nominal charges levied for squash and tennis court fees, snooker, exercise classes and coaching.

Disabled visitors have access to all areas, and are provided with specialist facilities including a minivator swimming pool lift, wheelchair hoists, toilets and showers.

Treatments

The excellent range of treatments includes facials from £15 - £39.95; toning body wrap £28; Frigi-Thalgo £25; body massage £25; G5 massage £15; aromatherapy £35; reflexology £15; make-up £12.50; eyelash tint £8; manicure from £7.50; pedicure from £10; waxing from £4.

Colour analysis £50 (two hours) with colour swatch, skin care advice and make-up application £50.

Various day packages are offered, all include use of the swimming pool, spa, sauna, steam room and gym. *Health & Beauty Taster* £25 lasts four hours and includes consultation, sunbed, G5 massage or facial, cut and blow dry in Saks hair Salon; *Pamper Day* £49 includes consultation, G5 massage or facial, manicure, sunbed, lunch in Conservatory Restaurant, cut and blow dry in Saks Hair Salon. Aromatherapy and Thalgo treatments available for a supplement. *Pamper Day* with overnight stay costs £149 and includes dinner for two with wine in the Blue Restaurant, free spouse accommodation and breakfast in room the following morning.

Tariff

Two night *Leisure & Health Break* £175 per person. This half board package commences with arrival on Friday afternoon (blow dry in Saks Hair Salon) and dinner in the Conservatory Restaurant, on Saturday, breakfast in room, consultation and four treatments, dinner with wine in the Blue Room Restaurant, Sunday, consultation and colour analysis (to include wardrobe problems, confidence building and colour advice), traditional Sunday lunch before departure.

Mid week bed and breakfast rate from £105 per double room accommodating two people. Weekend rates £48.50 per person bed and breakfast, £64.50 per person half board.

Travel Directions

From A1(M) exit at junction 58 taking A68 to Corbridge for 2 miles. At roundabout turn onto A6072 (signed to Bishop Auckland) hotel is 2 miles hotel down road on the left.

Nearest railway station Darlington 7 miles.

Shrigley Hall

Shirigley Park Pott Shrigley Nr Macclesfield Cheshire SK10 5SB
Tel 0625 575757   Fax 0625 573323

| 156 | 2 3 4 5 13 14 16 17 18 C | £ C |

Shrigley Hall is situated on a 262 acre estate in the pretty hamlet of Pott Shrigley on the Cheshire/Peak District borders. Restored to its former grandeur as an English country house after 60 years as a Salesian monastery and college, the hotel was extensively enlarged with 100 new rooms in 1991. Exceptional health, leisure and sporting facilities include an 18-hole golf course and a driving range.

The hotel's comfortably furnished en suite bedrooms have television, telephone, radio alarm and tea/coffee making facilities. Many rooms have extensive views over the estate, and four poster beds are available.

The elegant Oakridge restaurant and The Orangery serve a great choice of à la carte and table d'hôte menus with a dinner dance on Saturday nights. Informal meals and drinks are also available from the Poolside Bar.

The Leisure Club is sited in the former church, and has swimming and spa pools, sauna and steam room, solarium, hairdresser, beauty treatment room, snooker, two squash and two tennis courts and a fully equipped gym. Leisure Club amenities are free to residents with the exception of golf. Green fees are £16 per round during the week and £23 at weekends.

Treatments

A limited treatment range is offered in the beauty salon at reasonable rates. Body massage £18; spa body scrub £13.50. G5 massage £8; back massage £10; facials £13.50 to £22.50; manicure from £7.50; pedicure from £7.50; eyelash tint £4.75; waxing from £2.25. *Full Day Programme* with snack lunch and refreshments £75 - includes facial, eyelash tint, body massage, pedicure, sunbed and body firming treatment. *Half-day Package* £50 - includes massage, facial, manicure, pedicure and eyelash tint.

Tariff

Two night weekend break from £130 per person for dinner, bed and breakfast with Saturday night dinner dance.

Mid-week bed and breakfast tariff from £80 single, £100 double room for two persons; weekend tariff £50 single room, £90 double room. Four poster rooms and suites available. Children occupying parents' room £10 including breakfast.

Travel Directions

Via motorway network to mid-point on A523 midway between Stockport and Macclesfield. Village of Pott Shrigley and Shrigley Hall are reached by an unclassified road 2 miles off A523.

Nearest railway station Macclesfield 6 miles.

Staden Grange

Buxton Derbyshire SK17 9RZ

Tel 0298 24965   Fax 0298 72067

| 14 | 2 3 4 15 C   £ E

Staden Grange enjoys a peaceful setting in the heart of the Peak District, just two miles from the spa town of Buxton. Owners Duncan and Mary Mackenzie have renovated the original farmhouse and farm buildings, creating an establishment of character and charm.

The farmhouse bedrooms offer twin or double rooms, while the connecting old buildings house a number of self-catering studios, easily converted to family apartments or two-roomed suites. All rooms are tastefully furnished and have en suite bathroom, satellite television, radio, hair drier and tea/coffee making facilities. Some rooms have a mini-kitchen and fridge and one room has a four poster bed.

One of the highlights of a visit is the abundance of wonderful food. Hearty breakfasts and a four course dinner created from fresh local produce, beautifully cooked and served in generous portions.

Staden Grange has a sauna and spa pool which can be used privately. A wide range of body and beauty treatments using French GM Collin products are offered in the beauty treatment centre.

Treatments

Sunbed session £2.50, course of six £12.50; sauna session £4; spa pool £4; sauna with spa pool £7, two persons together £10. Sauna and spa pool can be reserved for private use on request.

Body and beauty treatments include back massage £7.50; full body masage £13; body massage with aromatherapy oils £16; G5 body massage £10.50, course of six £52.50; aromatherapy treatment £25; facials from £8; manicure £5.50; pedicure £8.50; make-up lesson £9.75; eyelash tint £4.50; electrolysis from £5.50; waxing from £2.

Tariff

Room and full English breakfast £59 per room per night for two persons, £55 per room per night for two nights, £50 per room per night for stays of more than two nights. Four poster room £75 per night for two persons.

£15 reduction for single occupancy of double room.

Four course dinner £15.50 per person, including coffee.

Self-catering apartments from £130 to £150 per week in low season to £175 to £300 per week in high season. Bank holiday weeks from £245 to £315.

Travel Directions
Take A515 road out of Buxton for approximately 2 miles.
Nearest railway station Buxton 2 miles.

Thorneyholme Hall Health Spa
Dunsop Bridge Nr Clitheroe Lancashire BB7 3BB
Tel 0200 448271   Fax 0200 448271

9 | 1 2 3 4 5 6 7 11 12 14 15 16 C   £ A*

Thornyholme Hall Health Spa stands in its own grounds on the banks of the River Hodder in the lovely Vale of Bowland. This delightful country house was converted into an exclusive health spa in 1991 by the resident proprietors, Wendy and Bill Whitwell. Catering for only 16 resident guests at any one time, the emphasis is very much on looking after individual needs.

All bedrooms have en suite bath or shower rooms and are equipped with television, telephone and tea/coffee making facilities. Bathrobes are provided for use in the health spa.

Shortly after arrival, visitors have a private treatment consultation when their personal wishes and requirements are incorporated into a suggested programme. Qualified staff lead guests through exercise routines suited to their levels of ability and particular needs. Otherwise, pure relaxation is the order of the day, taking in whatever treatments and therapies appeal.

Thorneyholme Hall is equipped with a beautifully appointed swimming pool and treatment complex, whirlpool, sauna, steam room, sunbeds, hair salon and a variety of the latest toning tables.

Outdoor activities include all weather tennis court, bicycles, croquet and a putting green. The surrounding countryside is ideal for walking, cycling and hill climbing - horse-riding, fishing and golf can also be arranged.

The Spa offers the finest cuisine, and even calorie counters can enjoy a satisfying and attractive meal. Healthy eating, not starvation is the goal. A small cocktail bar is provided for non-dieters.

Treatments

Optional treatments include facials from £14; cleanse, tone and make-up £15; manicure including hand and arm massage £12.50; Sixtus pedicure £15; waxing from £3.50; aromatherapy £35 initial treatment, £30 subsequently; exfoliation and skin softening treatment £17.50; slimming and firming treatment £17; firming and toning bust treatment £11; body massage £25; G5 massage £15; shampoo and blow dry £12.50.

Other treatments and therapies: Lifestyle and stress management £25; reflexology £25; colour analysis (half day course) £50; ladies' image day £75; men's image day £95.

Non-residential *Spa Day* £50 - includes buffet lunch, and use of swimming pool and whirlpool, reviving facial, body massage, toning salon session, exercise class, sauna and steam.

Tariff

£300 for a three night stay in a single or double room.

Rate includes all meals, use of amenities (swimming pool, whirlpool, tennis, bicyles, evening talks and demonstrations) and the following treatments: Consultation on arrival, 3 toning salon sessions, 3 exercise classes, 3 daily body massages, 3 sauna and steam sessions, 1 facial, 1 manicure, 1 cleanse, tone and make-up.

Details of rates for different lengths of stay and special offers available on application.

Travel Directions

From M6 exit at junction 31, taking A59 to Clitheroe, then B6478 to Newton. Turn left to Dunsop Bridge and along narrow road, Thorneyholme Hall is on left before entering village.

Nearest railway station Preston approximately 15 miles (transport to meet trains can be arranged).

Waterton Park Hotel
Walton Hall Walton Wakefield West Yorkshire WF2 6PW
Tel 0924 257911   Fax 0924 240082

| **31** | **2 3 4 13 14 16 17 C** | **£D** |

Waterton Park Hotel is a Georgian mansion situated on an island in the middle of an 26 acre lake and accessed by a picturesque iron bridge. The lake and surrounding parkland is a nature reserve and bird sanctuary.

Bedrooms have lovely views over the lake and West Yorkshire countryside. All have en suite bathroom, telephone, television, hair drier, trouser press, fresh fruit and tea/coffee making facilities. Some rooms have four poster beds.

The dining room serves an extensive choice of traditional English menus complemented by a comprehensive wine list.

The excellent leisure complex includes indoor swimming pool, spa bath, sauna, steam room, solarium and treatment room.There are also five squash courts and a full sized snooker table. Trout fishing is available on the lake and other water activities can be arranged.

Treatments
The treatment room adjoins the pool and treatments offered include deep facial cleanse £9; treatment facial £18; G5 masage £9; eyelash tint £5; waxing from £4.50; manicure £6; pedicure £8. Specialised aromatherapy treatments are available and must be booked in advance. These include two hour *Top to Toe* relaxation £39; body massage £18.50; back massage £11; facial £22.80; facial, neck, shoulder and scalp massage £18; consultation and reflexology diagnosis £10.

Tariff
Weekend rates from £99 per person for two night stay inclusive of dinner, bed and breakfast - three night weekend rate from £130 per person. Weekend bed/breakfast from £55 single, £80 double room.

Regular mid-week bed/breakfast tariff from £68 single, £88 double room. Children under 10 years of age sharing room with parents stay free of charge.

All rates include complimentary use of facilities and a daily newspaper.

Travel Directions
Take M1 and exit at junction 39 following signs to A61 Wakefield road. Turn right into Chevel Lane then first left into Station Lane, right into Greenside, left into Shay Lane and follow signs to the hotel.

Nearest railway station Wakefield 4 miles.

Whitewater Hotel

The Lakeland Village Newby Bridge Ulverston Cumbria LA12 8PX

Tel 05385 31133 Fax 05395 31881

| 35 | 2 3 4 5 6 13 14 15 17 C | £ C |

Formerly a centuries-old mill, Whitewater Hotel and the adjoining Cascades Health and Leisure Club, occupy an imposing site on the banks of the fast flowing River Leven, the southern outlet of Lake Windermere. The complex forms the focal point of the Lakeland Village - an award winning timeshare leisure resort of luxury lodges, located on both sides of the river. The village enjoys the driest and mildest climate in the Lake District.

Cascades' many amenities are available to hotel and lodge residents and include indoor swimming pool, whirlpool, fully equipped exercise studio, sunbeds, sauna, steam cabinets, beauty salon, hairdressing, two squash courts and a children's games room. Outdoors are all-weather tennis courts and putting course, golf driving net, trim trail and children's adventure playground.

The hotel offers comfortable accommodation in single, double, twin, triple, or king-sized rooms (one with four poster bed). All rooms have a bathroom and shower en suite, and some have balconies overlooking the river.

Treatments

Aromatherapy £24 (£34.50 with bath and body oils for home use); steam cabinet £4.95; moor peat bath £6.25; seaweed or pine spa bath £4.95; body massage from £9.50 to £17; G5 massage £9.50; aromatic full body paraffin wax with heat treatment £16; facials from £15.50; manicure £6.60; pedicure £7.65.

Tariff

Two night *Health and Leisure Breaks* cost £86.50 per night single room, £146 per night twin/double, and include dinner/bed and breakfast, lunch in Cascades, daily heat treatment (steam cabinet, spa bath or sauna), daily aquarobics and fitness classes, unlimited use of swimming pool, whirlpool and exercise studio throughout the visit.

Regular bed and breakfast rate from £60 single, £90 double room (two persons); half board rate (minimum two nights) £67.50 single, £52.50 per person per night sharing double room.

Luxury lodges (one to three bedrooms) in the Lakeland Village available to rent on various dates from £450 per week - full price details and dates on 05395 31144.

Travel Directions

From the M6 motorway exit at junction 36 and follow the A590 to Barrow. Follow through to Newby Bridge and dual carriageway, after which there is a sharp bend and the sign for the Lakeland Village - then turn right.

Nearest railway station Ulverston 8 miles.

Wood Hall Hotel
Trip Lane Linton Nr Wetherby West Yorkshire LS22 4JA
Tel 0937 587271   Fax 0937 584353

44 **2 3 4 6 13 14 15 17 C**   **£ C**

 Set in over 100 acres of rolling parkland, and bounded by a mile of the River Wharfe, this former ecumenical college was lovingly transformed into one of England's finest country house hotels in 1989. The gracious Georgian mansion is reached by a winding one-and-a-half mile drive through the grounds. Many of the Yorkshire greatest attractions are within a pleasurable day's drive including the York, Harrogate, the Dales and the spectacular coast.

 All bedrooms are tastefully furnished and decorated to the highest standard of comfort and luxury with private bathroom, bathrobes, hair drier, tea/coffee making facilities, complimentary sherry, fruit and mineral water. Many rooms have extensive views over the Yorkshire countryside. A four poster room and two suites are also available.

 Three main public rooms lead off the stone-flagged grand entrance hall - the renowned dining room complete with with chandeliers and elegant drapes, the oak-panelled bar and the welcoming drawing room with cosy log fire, sumptuous sofas and relaxing armchairs. The many superb floral displays, fine art and antiques throughout the hotel create a luxurious and relaxing ambience.

 Many guests come to Wood Hall solely for the spendid food served in the Georgian Restaurant. Menus skilfully combine the highest culinary standards with the best of Yorkshire's plentiful ingredients and traditions. Imaginative à la cartedinners are complemented by an extensive wine list and served in a non-smoking environment.

 The Wood Hall Leisure Club opened at the end of 1992, and further enhances any stay at this delightful hotel. Hotel residents have full use of the Club's facilities including an indoor swimming pool, spa bath, treatment room, fully equipped gym, steam room, high powered sunbed, jogging track, relaxation and refreshment areas.

Trout fishing is available on a two mile stretch of the Wharfe, and golf and horse riding can be arranged locally.

Treatments

Beauty treatments using Clarins products and holistic massage are available in the Club. The range includes holistic yin/yang massage incorporating aromatherapy body massage working on specific pressure points throughout the body £27.50; aromatherapy back massage £14.95; aromatherapy facial £15.50; reflexology £12.50 per treatment, course of six £62.50; back massage £10.50; body massage (ladies only) £19.95; self-tanning treatment £24; Clarins facials from £15.50 to £21; manicure £7.50; pedicure £12.50; eyelash and brow tint £7; waxing from £2.50 to £21.50.

Tariff

All bedrooms at Wood Hall are double or twin rooms.

Two night stays from £67.50 per person per night in shared room, are inclusive of dinner, bed and breakfast, newspaper and use of Leisure Club's amenities.

Regular bed and breakfast rates from £85 single occupancy, £95 double occupancy with English breakfast, newspaper and use of Leisure Club.

Deluxe room with a view and four poster room £125 per night single occupancy, £135 double occupancy. Suites £250 per night single or double occupancy.

Travel Directions

Travel to Wetherby by M1 (Leeds) or A1 (Wetherby). From Wetherby take A661 Harrogate road north from market place for 1/2 mile. Turn left to Sicklinghall and Linton. Cross the bridge and follow signs to Linton and Wood Hall on left. Turn right opposite the Windmill pub and follow estate road for approximately 11/2 miles.

Nearest railway station York or Leeds, both 12 miles.

WALES

.7

5 .

.4

.2

.1   .6

.8

CARDIFF .3

WALES

Cwrt Bleddyn Hotel
Tredunnock Near Usk Gwent NP5 1PG
Tel 0633 450521   Fax 0633 450220

36	2 3 4 13 14 16 17 C	£ C

Cwrt Bleddyn is a classic country house hotel situated betwen the historic towns on Caerleon and Usk. The lovely old house has been sympathetically refurbished and all rooms are en suite with television, radio, trouser press, hair drier and tea/coffee making facilities.

Cwrt Bledden's premier restaurant is Nicholls, a period dining room furnished in the elegant style of bygone days, and serving French and Welsh cuisine. The Oak Room is available for smaller parties, and the restaurant in the Country Club serves a good choice of three course meals and snacks.

The Country Club's leisure facilities are extensive and include an indoor swimming pool, steam room, sauna, spa bath, solarium, hairdressing and beauty salons. Sports amenities include a snooker room, gym, squash and floodlit tennis courts.

Treatments

A wide choice of body and beauty treatments and hairdressing is offered in the two Finishing Touches Salons

Facials start from £8.50; aromatherapy body massage £27.50; faradic treatments £6.60 per session; eyelash tint £5.20; manicure £6.05; pedicure £7.45; shampoo/set or blow dry from £5; perms from £24.50; hair colouring from £12; highlights from £25.

Tariff

Two night weekend from £57.50 per person per night sharing a double/twin room on half board basis (breakfast and dinner inclusive).

Room only nightly tariff from £65 single, £82.50 double room.

All hotel residents have unlimited use of all leisure facilities during their stay (treatments and hairdressing charged as taken).

Travel Directions

From M4 exit at junction 25 and take road to Caerleon, then follow signs to Usk. From West Midlands take M5 and M50 to Ross on Wye junction 4, then A40 to Monmouth and A449 to Usk.

Nearest railway station Newport approximately 3 miles.

Metropole Hotel
Temple Street Llandrindod Wells Powys LD1 5DY
Tel 0597 822881   Fax 0597 824828

| 121 | ☆ 2 3 4 6 13 14 15 C | £ C |

Revitalising two day breaks are offered at this family owned hotel in the charming spa town of Llandrindod Wells, where the town's Victorian pump room has been restored to its former glory, enabling visitors to sample the healing, mineral rich waters.

Surrounded by the beautiful Welsh countryside, the Metropole offers residents the extensive facilities of the Francis Leisure Complex which include a heated swimming pool, jacuzzi, sauna, steam room, solarium, bicycle and rowing machines - all housed in an attractive Victorian conservatory, in a constant temperature of 84^0F.

Accommodation is on four floors serviced by two lifts. Bedrooms are decorated in soft pastel shades and have en suite bathroom, television, hair drier, trouser press, telephone and tea/coffee making facilities.

The Metropole has comfortable lounges and bars plus a first class dining room where salmon and trout from the Wye, Powys beef and Welsh lamb feature on menus complemented by fine wines.

Treatments

Reasonably priced body and beauty treatments are available in the Beauty Suite - the choice includes 1 hour full body massage £13; faradic massage £8.50; beauty-peeling facial £17; revitalising facial £12; manicure with massage £5.50; pedicure with massage £8.50; eyelash tint £4.50; cleanse and make-up £6.50; waxing from £3; electrolysis from £4.50 for 15 minutes.

A *Top to Toe* treatment package is available for £30, and includes a choice of treatments.

Tariff

Two night *Revitalising Breaks* cost £125 per person on a dinner /bed and breakfast basis and include one full body massage and one facial. Other treatments arranged on request.

For partners not wanting beauty therapies, the two night *Golf Break* is a good alternative. This costs £130 per person on a dinner/bed and breakfast basis and includes two rounds of golf on nearby courses.

Travel Directions

Easily reached from M4, M5, M6, M50 and M54, Llandrindod Wells is situated on A483, 3 miles south of A44.

Nearest railway station Llandrindod Wells (Swansea to Shrewsbury line) is just 350 yards from the hotel.

Miskin Manor
Miskin Mid Glamorgan CF7 8ND
Tel 0443 224204   Fax 0443 234706

32	2 3 4 6 13 14 15 16 17 C	£ C

Although this lovely old manor house dates back to the 11th century, its amenities and comforts are decidedly modern and have won various prestigious awards. Built of local stone and sited in 20 acres of gardens and woodlands on the banks of the River Ely, Miskin Manor is now a romantic and elegant Welsh country house hotel.

All bedrooms have en suite bathroom, television, trouser press, hair drier and telephone, in addition to pleasant little extras like mineral water, fresh fruit and magazines. High quality cuisine prepared from fresh local produce is served in the wood-panelled dining room, complemented by an extensive wine list.

During their stay residents enjoy membership of Fredericks Health and Leisure Club situated within the hotel grounds, and have free use of the swimming pool, gym and snooker table. Other facilities have nominal charges including three squash courts £1 or £2 per 1/2 hour, badminton court £2 per 1/2 hour, solarium £2 per session, sauna, steam and spa bath £1.50 per session each. Gym tuition, aerobics classes, swimming lessons and yoga sessions are held on a regular basis and hotel residents are welcome to join in.

Treatments

Fredericks offers a wide variety of body and beauty treatments at competitive rates including aromatherapy body massage £25; G5 massage £8 and £10.50; Decleor facials from £18 to £28; pre-make up facial £15; body massage £20; anti-cellulite treatment £21; bust care treatment £21; pregnancy treatment £26; eyelash tinting £5.50; manicure from £5.75; pedicure £8.95; waxing from

£2.95; electrolysis from £4 with free consultation; *Top to Toe* package £32.

Non-residential health days from £43.50 include lunch, choice of treatments, exercise classes and use of facilities in Fredericks Leisure Club.

Tariff

Healthy Venues short breaks from £195 per person sharing accommodation for two nights and include a range of treatments and exercise classes, health breakfast, lunch, refreshments during the day and dinner in Meisgyn Restaurant (with optional healthy/calorie controlled menus) and full use of leisure facilities.

Two night weekend breaks £199 per couple inclusive of accommodation, table d'hôte dinner and Welsh or continental breakfast, daily newspaper and use of Fredericks Leisure Club.

Short breaks are available any weekend except Christmas and New Year.

Regular bed and breakfast tariff from £80 single room, £95 double/twin room include daily newspaper and use of Fredericks Leisure Club.

Travel Directions

Miskin Manor is easily accessible just 1/2 mile from Junction 34 of the M4, 8 miles from Cardiff.

Nearest mainline railway station Cardiff 8 miles.

Plas Talgarth Health & Leisure Club
Plas Talgarth Estate   Pennal   Nr Machynlleth   Powys   SY20 9JY
Tel   0654 791631   Fax 0654 791640

12 apartments, 63 lodges and villas

Self-catering basis

2 3 4 5 6 7 13 14 17 C

Plas Talgarth enjoys a superb situation in a corner of the Snowdonia National Park. This family health resort offers a wide range of health, beauty and sporting facilities centred around an ivy-covered Georgian mansion in 50 acres of beautifully landscaped gardens.

Accommodation is in self-catering luxury holiday bungalows, villas, studios and garden apartments, all centrally heated and fully equipped with modern appliances such as dishwashers, microwaves, food processors, crockery and cutlery. There is television with satellite stations, family games table, leather furniture, cocktail cabinet and selection of best-selling books. Each villa has a private patio balcony or patio garden with wonderful views over the surrounding hills and mountains.

Off the 'Village Square' is the leisure centre, the bar and restaurant. The leisure centre includes an indoor swimming pool and a Champneys-designed health and beauty suite providing body and beauty treatments and hairdressing. Other facilities include spa bath, sauna, steam room, solarium, squash and tennis courts, snooker tables, pitch and putt, children's play area and a coffee shop. Plas Talgarth has many bars and restaurants in which to enjoy good food in Welsh style - the 16th century farmhouse for lunch and the Dyfi View for dinner is recommended.

Treatments

Aromatherapy £29 first treatment and consultation; reflexology or 'zone therapy' £18; steam cabinet £7; spa bath £7; full body paraffin wax £18; facials from £16; high-intensity sunbed £5, 3 for £12; G5 massage £9.95; Cathiodermie £23; manicure £6; pedicure from £9; eyelash tinting £6. Hairdressing for all the family is also available.

Tariff

Apartments and lodges sleep two, four, six or eight persons and start at £195 per week in January for a studio sleeping two, rising to £445 per week for the same accommodation in mid-summer.

A lodge sleeping eight persons costs £445 per week in January rising to £895 per week in mid-summer.

Two night short breaks are also offered throughout the year from as little as £49 per property in low season - phone for current availability on 0479 811810.

Travel Directions

Take M6 and exit at junction 11, then take M54 and A5 bypassing Shrewsbury. Turn onto A458 to Welshpool, then A470 and A48 to Machynlleth. Cross Bridge and turn left onto road to Aberdyfi A493, continuing through Pennal - Plas Talgarth is on left.

Nearest railway station Machynlleth (London Paddington 4 1/2 hours).

St David's Park Hotel
St David's Park Ewloe Clwyd CH5 3YB
Tel 0244 520800   Fax 0244 520930

| 121 | 2 3 4 13 14 17 C | £ C |

Situated just over the Welsh border seven miles from the historic city of Chester, St David's Park Hotel is a luxurious new hotel designed around an inner courtyard and set in landscaped gardens.

All rooms have en suite bathroom, trouser press, hair drier, mini-bar and satellite television. A great choice of accommodation is available - suites and studio rooms, rooms designed for the disabled, adjoining family rooms, non-smoking and ladies' executive rooms.

The Fountains Restaurant serves an international choice of dishes with a la carte menus and a buffet table. Less formal meals and snacks are available in The Orangery.

The leisure club is open to all residents and has an indoor swimming pool, spa bath, steam and sauna rooms, solarium, gym, treatment room, snooker, American pool room and a children's games room. In May 1994 the hotel opened the superb Northop Country Park Golf Club, just five minutes from the hotel with transport provided for hotel guests. The Clubhouse will feature a restaurant and a full range of leisure activities including tennis, saunas and a gym.

Treatments

The choice of treatments at St David's Park is impressive. Body massage £20, aromatherapy £22; back and shoulder massage £13; Cathiodermie facial £20; Geloide Prescription facial £13.50; revitalising mini facial £11; aromatherapy facial £12; cleanse and make-up £10; waxing from £3.50; electrolysis from £7; eyelash tint £4.50; manicure and massage £9.50; pedicure and massage £10.50.

Tariff

Weekend rates from £56 single, £70 double or twin room per night; mid-week rate from £79 single, £89 double or twin room per night.

Rates are for room only. Full Welsh breakfast costs £8.95, continental breakfast £5.95.

Travel Directions

Take M6 and exit at junction 20 signed M56 North Wales. At conclusion of M56 take A5117 to N Wales for 2 miles. At traffic lights follow A550 to N Wales for 1 mile, then A494 to Queensferry for 4 miles, then left slip road B5127 to Buckley.

(Estimated drive time from M56 10 minutes).
Nearest railway station Chester approximately 7 miles.

St Pierre Hotel Golf & Country Club
St Pierre Park   Chepstow   Gwent   NP6 6YA
Tel 0291 625261   Fax 0291 629975

| 147 | 2 3 4 6 13 14 16 17 18 C | £ C |

Situated three miles from the Severn Bridge in over 400 acres of beautiful parkland complete with lake and championship golf courses, St Pierre offers an outstanding range of leisure facilities and short break holidays.

Major improvements to the hotel have recently been completed, including the building of a covered walkway from the 14th century manor to the refurbished accommodation wing where all rooms offer en suite bathroom, television, trouser press, hair drier and tea/coffee making facilities. Meals are served in the elegant Park Restaurant, while the Poolside Bar and Grill remain open throughout the day for informal meals and drinks.

St Pierre's outstanding range of leisure facilities includes two 18-hole golf courses, practice ground and golf shop, indoor heated swimming pool, jacuzzi, sauna, steam room, two sunbeds, health and beauty salon, gym, squash and tennis courts, snooker tables, badminton, bowling green and children's play area.

Treatments

The Health & Beauty Clinic is open every day and offers treatment packages including the *Two Hour Relaxation* £36, and the *Half Day Package* £42. Clarins facials from £15; aromatherapy facial £12; body massage from £10; aromatherapy body massage £24.95; G5 massage £9; body firming treatments £19.50; manicure £7; pedicure £8; eyelash tint £5; waxing from £3; vacuum suction £9 per session; make-up and manicure £12.50.

Tariff

All hotel residents enjoy free use of leisure facilities (golf, sunbeds, snooker and beauty treatments have additional charges).

Weekend Break £75 per person per night in shared double/twin room includes dinner, bed and breakfast and full use of leisure facilities (golf, sunbed, snooker and beauty treatments extra).

Two day *Golf Break* £98 per person per night in shared double/twin room on above basis includes one round of golf per day.

Room only weekend rate £105 per night (two persons).

Travel Directions

Exit at junction 22 on M4 and follow signs to Chepstow. At first roundabout turn left onto A48 and proceed for approximately 3 miles.

Nearest railway stations Newport 12 miles and Chepstow 1 mile.

Seiont Manor Hotel
Llanrug   Caernarfon   Gwynedd   LL55 2AQ
Tel   0286 673366   Fax 0286 2840

28	2 3 6 13 14 15 17 C	£ C

Seiont Manor is set amid 80 acres of parkland, close to Snowdonia and the Isle of Anglesey. It offers peaceful relaxation with country house style ambience.

Leisure facilities include a heated swimming pool in a Victorian-style bath-house, sauna, solarium, spa bath and invigorating needle shower, well-equipped gym with weights to promote fitness and toning.

Every room at Seiont Manor is created around a different decorative theme, and all have en suite bathroom, tea/coffee making facilities, hair drier, trouser press, mini-bar, television and telephone.

Classic French cuisine as well as local Welsh dishes feature on the menus. The hotel prides itself on using only the finest fresh ingredients and has its own extensive herb garden and a salmon-filled river running through the grounds.

Treatments

Natural body treatments include aromatherapy body massage £30, neck and shoulder aromatherapy £17.50; reflexology £30 per hour; body massage and facial £40; combined aromatherapy/reflexology £50.

Tariff

Special rate of £59.50 per person per night applies to stays of two/three nights sharing double or twin room and includes breakfast and dinner. Single supplement £17.50.

Bed and breakfast tariff £72.50 single, £96.50 double room per night.

Travel Directions

Take A5 to Betws-y-Coed and Capel Curig and turn onto A4086 to Caernarfon, Llanrug is a few miles before Caernarfon.

Nearest railway station Bangor 9 miles.

West Usk Lighthouse
Lighthouse Road St Brides Wentlooge Nr Newport Gwent NP1 9SF
Tel 0633 810126/815860 Fax 0633 815582

6	2 7 10 11 15 C	£ E

This must be the most unusual entry in Healthy Breaks - a delightfully restored real lighthouse with panoramic views, offering unique revitalising breaks.

The West Usk Lighthouse is a circular building standing in its own grounds and offering comfortable accommodation on two floors, with a roof patio, lamp room (without the light) and central spiral staircase. One of the attractions of a stay here is sleeping in the unsually-shaped rooms which are well furnished and have satellite television. All rooms are non-smoking and most are en suite including the four poster and waterbed rooms. Breakfast and lunch are served in the dining room, and there is a cosy open fire in the lounge.

Treatments

The Lighthouse boasts the only floatation tank in Wales, and offers a variety of unusual therapies promoting relaxation, lifestyle improvement and stress management. The choice includes floatation £16 per session; aromatherapy £25; colour healing £25; past life regression £30; esoteric astrology £25; biorhythm charts £6; session in energy box £3; transformation game hire £5; self-development tape hire £3.

Tariff

Revitalising Break £165 - comprises a two night stay with breakfast and lunch (vegetarian optional) in luxurious accommodation,two floatarium sessions, guided meditation, aromatherapy/reflexology massage; and an esoteric astrology consultation.

Regular bed and breakfast tariff from £20 single, £36 twin room; en suite double £40; en suite water bed room £56; four-poster en suite £50.

Travel Directions
Leave M4 at junction 28 (Tredegar House) and take roundabout exit A48 towards Newport. At next roundabout take B4239 to St Bridges and follow road for 2 miles and watch for B&B sign on the right.

Nearest railway station Newport 3 miles.

SCOTLAND

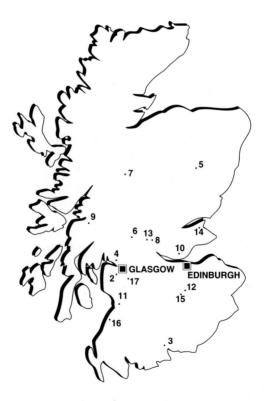

SCOTLAND

Auchrannie Hotel
Brodick Isle of Arran Strathclyde KA27 8BZ
Tel 0770 302234   Fax 0770 302812

| 28 | 2 3 4 5 13 14 15 16 17 C | £ D |

Situated in six acres of woodlands and gardens on this most lovely of Scottish islands, Auchrannie was once the home of the Dowager Duchess of Hamilton. The historic mansion is now Arran's most prestigious hotel, and has been tastefully refurbished and extended with a splendid leisure centre and new luxurious accommodation.

Bedrooms are elegantly furnished and well equipped with en suite bathrom, television, radio, telephone, hair drier, personal safe, mini bar and tea/coffee making facilities. Ground floor rooms reserved on request. Executive rooms and suites are available for a supplementary charge.

Enjoy a pre-dinner drink in one of the hotel's three bars before tucking into the delicious Scottish fare provided in the two restaurants - the formal Garden Restaurant, housed in an airy conservatory and the more casual Brambles Bistro serving a selection of informal meals and snacks throughout the day.

Hotel residents have unlimited use of the facilities of the leisure centre, which include a large heated indoor pool, turbo spa bath, sauna and steam rooms, sunbed, fitness suite, snooker room (£1 per 20 minutes), beauty salon and a boutique. Hairdressing, sunbed and treatments are charged for as taken.

Treatments
A limited range of treatments and hairdressing are available most days, but check availability as the salon is not open all day every day. Aromatherapy massage costs £20 for a 90 minute session, sunbed £2.95 for 25 minutes.

Facials, manicures and pedicures are also available with prices on application.

Tariff

Prices vary according to season and length of stay, starting at £84 per person for a two night stay in low season (£94 per person weekends) on a dinner/bed and breakfast basis. From May to September this rises to £64 per person per night on the same basis, or £46 per person per night for bed and breakfast. Rates are lower for longer stays. 50% discount for children under 16 sharing parents' room.

Travel Directions

Easily accessible from Glasgow via motorway network to Ardrossan in Ayrshire from where car ferry to Brodick takes approximately 55 minutes. Several daily crossings but advance booking essential. Frequent crossings in summer between Claonaig on the Mull of Kintyre and Lochranza in the north of Arran. Twice weekly ferry service in 1994 between Brodick and Rothesay on the Isle of Bute.

On leaving Brodick Pier turn right through the village, taking the second left road after Brodick Golf Clubhouse.

Nearest railway station Ardrossan. A through train/boat service operates from Glasgow Central.

Bowfield Hotel and Country Club of Bowfield
Howwood Renfewshire PA9 1DB
Tel 0505 705225   Fax 0505 705230

| 12 | 2 3 4 6 13 14 17 C | £ D |

The Bowfield Hotel and Country club is situated in pleasant countryside a short distance from Glasgow airport.

Bedrooms are decorated in country cottage style and located in a quiet wing of the intriguing 18th century building, which was once a country mill. All have en suite bathroom, television, radio alarm, telephone, trouser press, hair drier and tea/coffee making facilities. The restaurant serves a delicious range of a la carte meals. Drinks and snacks can also be purchased in the bar.

The Bowfield Country Club is Scotland's most established leisure facility and boasts an indoor swimming pool, saunas, steam room, plunge pool, jacuzzi, fitness rooms, squash courts, snooker, games room and health and beauty studio.

Treatments

Aromatherapy £25; reflexology £12; cellulite treatment £15.50; massage £7.50 for 20 minutes, £10.50 for 30 minutes, £18.75 for 1 hour; G5 massage £7.50;

facials from £8.50; eyelash tint £6.25; manicure and pedicure £6.50 each, or £11.50 with paraffin wax; sunbed £4.50; waxing from £3.25; electrolysis from £4.25. Ladies' day course of treatments lasting six hours £48; mini-day course £25.

Tariff

Weekend rate for dinner/bed and breakfast £75 single, £58 per person sharing double or twin room.

Regular bed and breakfast tariff from £65 single, £90 double room weekday night, £55 single, £76 double room per weekend night.

Travel Directions

From Glasgow exit M8 at junction 29 and follow signs to A740, then A737 (Irvine). Turn off A737 at Howwood and take B776 uphill towards Caldwell for 1 mile.

Nearest railway stations Johnstone and Millikenpark both approximately 3 miles.

Cairndale Hotel & Leisure Club
English Street Dumfries   Dumfries & Galloway DG1 2DF
Tel 0387 54111   Fax 0387 50555

76	2 3 4 6 13 14 17 C	£ C

Situated in the centre of the market town of Dumfries, the Cairndale Hotel is an ideal base for touring the many attractions of southern Scotland.

All rooms have en suite bathroom, television, radio, telephone, hair drier and coffee making facilities. Executive rooms and suites have queen-sized beds, mini-bar, trouser press and jacuzzi spa bath. Three restaurants offer diners a choice of menus, traditional Scottish fare in the main dining room; roasts, pies and casseroles from the carvery in Sawney Bean's bar and grill; light meals, snacks and drinks alongside the pool in the Forum cafe bar.

Hotel residents have use of the hotel's leisure club, the Barracuda during their stay. Facilities include an indoor swimming pool, sauna, steam room, spa bath, gym and health and beauty salon.

Treatments

The Cloud Nine hair and beauty salon offers an excellent range of services and treatments including body massage £20; back, neck and shoulder massage £9; bust treatment £15; slimming body treatment £17.50; G5 massage £7 or five treatments for £30; deep brush cleansing facial £21; mini-facial £9.50; Dermatone facial £25; eyelash tint £4.50; waxing from £3; electrolysis from £5.95; manicure £10; pedicure £15; sunbed £3; toning tables session £3; thread vein therapy from £10.

Tariff

Weekend Breaks (minimum two nights) cost £55 per person per night for dinner, bed and breakfast.

Saturday night dinner dances are held throughout the summer months. On Sunday evenings, the popular Cairndale Ceilidh gives visitors a chance to experience Scottish culture. This professional entertainment includes Scottish music, dancing and singing and is an event not to be missed.

The Cairndale also offers a *Golf Break* inclusive of dinner/bed and breakfast and one round of golf per day on local courses from £60 to £75 per person per day, depending on choice of course.

Regular bed and breakfast tariff from £75 single, £85 double or twin room per night. Four-course table d'hôte dinner £15.

Travel Directions

From the south take motorway network (M1 then M6) and exit at junction 44 (end of motorway) and continue on A74 to Gretna Green. From Gretna there is a choice of routes, either A74 to Lockerbie then A709 to Dumfries, or A75 to Dumfies via Annan.

Nearest railway station Dumfries 200 yards.

Cameron House & Country Estate
Loch Lomond Alexandria Dunbartonshire G83 8QZ
Tel 0389 55565   Fax 0389 59522

| 68 | 2 3 4 5 6 13 14 15 16 17 18 C | £ B |

With 108 acres of lawns, woodlands and gardens sweeping down to the bonnie banks of Loch Lomond, Cameron House has one of the most romantic locations possible. Formerly an ancestral family home, the lovely mansion has been transformed into a distinguished country house hotel with excellent health and leisure facilities.

The Country Club's many amenities include swimming pools (one, a fun pool with chute, the other a lagoon with waterfalls and rock pools), jacuzzi, sauna, steam rooms, high and low intensity sunbeds, fully equipped gym with professional instruction and treatment rooms. Aerobic classes are held in the dance studio, which is also used for badminton.

Even in inclement weather there are lots of sporting opportunities (equipment can be borrowed) - two glass-walled squash courts, games room with table tennis and pool/snooker room. Outdoors are tennis courts (coaching available), a challenging 9-hole golf course (nominal charge), sailing, cruising and windsurfing on Loch Lomond. Cameron House has its own marina and clubhouse on the lochside.

All bedrooms at Cameron House are tastefully furnished and decorated in soft colours, well equipped with en suite bathroom, television, telephone, tea/coffee making facilities, hair drier, complimentary sherry and fresh flowers.

Some specially designed family rooms have separate sleeping alcoves for children.

Three restaurants serve an excellent choice of fresh Scottish produce including seafood from the west coast fishing villages, quality Scottish meats and locally grown vegetables and herbs.

The Japanese water garden and acres of beautiful grounds alongside the loch are an inspiration to all garden enthusiasts, while those looking for a challenge will find the climb to the top of Ben Lomond (973 metres) exhilarating and rewarding - the views from the summit are outstanding.

Treatments

Aromatherapy body massage £30; body scrub and massage £28; relaxing body masssage £24; Prescription treatment £23; firming body treatment £18; make-up including cleanse tone and colour analysis £16; Clarins facial £15; manicure £13; pedicure £17; waxing from £4.50. A full range of hairdressing services is available, prices on application.

Tariff

The nightly tariff of £125 single room, £150 double/twin room includes full Scottish breakfast, complimentary newspaper and use of the leisure club.

Three luxury suites at Cameron House feature four poster beds large sitting room and spa bath. These cost £299 per night (single or double occupancy) - extra adult £35 nightly, extra child £25 nightly.

Standard suites £225 per night (single or double occupancy) with the same additional adult and child rates.

Travel Directions

From central Glasgow take A82 to Loch Lomond - a 30 minute drive. Cameron House is on the south west shore of the loch, 7 miles south of Luss. Turn right off the A82 at the sign for Duck Bay and the entrance is on the right.

Nearest railway station Balloch approximately 2 1/2 miles.

Craigendarroch Hotel and Country Club
Braemar Road Ballater Royal Deeside AB3 5XA
Tel 03397 55858 Fax 03397 55447

| 50 | 2 3 4 5 6 13 14 15 16 17 C | £ C |

Once the Highland mansion of the Keiller 'marmalade' family of Dundee, this lovely old country house hotel is set on a hillside in 29 acres of woodlands. It provides high class accommodation and excellent leisure activities amid picturesque highland scenery - Balmoral Castle is just a short drive away.

All the bedrooms at this delightful hotel offer a high degree of comfort with en suite facilities, television, telephone, tea/coffee making facilities, hair drier and trouser press. Extra touches like fresh flowers, books on local interest, a trinket box with playing cards, sewing kit and other useful small items are also thoughtfully provided.

Three fine restaurants - the Oaks Gourmet and Lochnagar restaurants in the hotel, and the Cafe Jardin in the Country Club, offer the very best of Scottish cuisine, with local game, beef salmon and trout featuring on the menus. For vegetarians and those watching calorie intake, local vegetables and wholesome light meals are available.

Hotel residents have temporary membership of the Craigendarroch Country Club with its comprehensive range of leisure and sporting amenities (enjoyed by Princess Diana during stays at Balmoral). There are two spectacular indoor pools, one an exotic lagoon with rock pool and waterfall, the other a children's fun pool. Entry to the indoor pools complex is free to hotel residents, but some amenities and sports facilities have nominal charges: Squash £2 per 40 minutes; tennis £3.20 per hour; skiing £8.50 per 90 minutes including instruction and equipment hire; solarium £6 per 20 minutes; snooker £3.20 per hour.

The Club has a spa pool, sauna, steam room, solarium, two squash courts, snooker room and fully equipped trimnasium. A pleasant crèche has been provided to enable parents with young children to enjoy a carefree visit to the Country Club.

Outdoor sports amenities include an all weather tennis court and a dry ski slope (with instruction) as well as countless walks and trails through the estate.

Treatments

A luxurious health and beauty salon offers an extensive range of body, beauty and hair treatments for men and women including aromatherapy £30; back massage £30; Clarins Paris Method facial £30; Clarins relaxing facial £20; manicure £13; pedicure £17; shampoo/set £9.50; wash/blow dry £14.50.

Tariff

The tariff includes full Scottish breakfast, newspaper and temporary membership of the Country Club and starts at £99 per night for a single room, £125 for a double/twin room accommodating two persons.

Four poster rooms and suites are also available on request.

Travel Directions

From Perth or Aberdeen take the A93 to Ballater. Craigendarroch is north of the village and signposted.

Nearest railway station: Ballater 2 miles or Aberdeen 40 miles.

Crieff Hydro Hotel
Crieff Perthshire PH7 3LQ
Tel 0764 655555   Fax 0764 653087

| **200** | **2 3 4 5 13 14 16 17 18 C** | **£ E** |

Set in extensive grounds amid the beautiful Perthshire hills, the Crieff Hydro has welcomed visitors for over 125 years. The modernised hydro is a self-contained resort, offering a unique combination of old-fashioned style and quality with an unrivalled range of activities for visitors of all ages to enjoy - many free of charge.

Indoors is the spacious Lagoon Pool Leisure Complex with a 20 metre swimming pool and separate children's pool, spa bath, steam room, sauna, fitness room and sunbeds. The purpose built Sports Hall offers indoor tennis, badminton, squash, volleyball, five-a-side football, pool and basketball. Other enjoyable diversions include a cinema, discos and regular dances in the ballroom. Shopping facilities are provided with a boutique and gift shop and small newsagents.

Outdoors, the range of things to do is equally impressive with a golfing centre and club house, driving range, golf practice area and 9-hole par 32 course, krazy golf course, five tennis courts, croquet and football pitches, riding school, pitch and putt, 18-hole putting green, children's adventure playground, jogging and nature trails. Children of all ages are kept happily occupied with a plethora of events, competitions and activities, giving parents some carefree time to themselves. In the evenings, the playroom is supervised by nursery staff enabling parents to eat a peaceful dinner together.

The Hydro has a varied range of accommodation - family bedrooms and suites, single rooms, executive 'rooms with a view', spacious studio suites, self-catering chalets and cottages, even a secluded honeymoon suite complete with four poster bed and spa bath. All accommodation has en suite bath or shower, telephone, television, baby listening service and tea/coffee making facilities. Executive rooms have hair drier, trouser press, mini bar, fresh fruit and complimentary newspaper. The needs of disabled visitors have been carefully considered with ground floor bedrooms, a specially fitted therapy bath and lifts to all floors and amenities. The Hydro's wide corridors and entrances are easily negotiable by wheelchairs.

Meals are served in the comfortable 450-seater dining room. Special diets provided by prior arrangement. Snacks and refreshments can be purchased in the Winter Garden Coffee Shop, Lagoon Leisure Complex and the Golf Centre's licensed Clubhouse. A limited room service is offered 8am till 11pm.

Treatments

The First Class Hair and Beauty Salon is located near the Lagoon and offers treatments and hairdressing seven days a week. The choice includes aromatherapy £25 per 75 minute session; 30 minute massage £8.80; Slendertone £6.60 per session; Cathiodermie £25; other facials from £13; manicure from £5.50; pedicure from £8.80; waxing from £3.30; eyelash tint £4.95; shampoo/ blow dry from £7.15; perms from £27.50; highlights from £28.65.

The Full Treatment Package provides nine treatments for £48.80; *The Soothing Experience* offers five treatments for £38.50.

Tariff

Hotel prices range from £44 per person for dinner/bed and breakfast in a standard room January to March, rising to £55.50 per person on the same basis in high season. Children stay free or at reduced rates according to age and time of year.

Good value *Bargain Breaks* are offered at certain times of the year from £157.50 for a five night winter break on a dinner/bed and breakfast basis. *Golden Age Breaks* for over 60s cost from £32 per person per night for dinner/ bed and breakfast.

Special interest weeks are organised throughout the year - *Tennis, Golf, Teenage Activities* and others - details on application.

Self-catering chalets (sleeping four) cost from £120 - £244 for two nights, £300- £658 for seven nights. New three-bedroom cottages overlooking the golf course cost from £145 - £273 for two nights, £365 - £684 for seven nights.

Travel Directions

From M9 motorway exit at junction 11 onto the A9 and take A822 to Crieff.
Nearest railway stations Gleneagles 11 miles (limited sleeper service from London), Perth approximately 15 miles.

Dalfaber Golf & Country Club
Aviemore Inverness-shire PH22 1YB
Tel   0479 811244   Fax 0479 811168

80 self-catering units   2 3 5 13 14 15 16 17 18 C

The Dalfaber Resort nestles in a sheltered valley beside the River Spey close to the town of Aviemore and the Cairngorm Mountains. Excellent leisure facilities and luxury accommodation provide an enjoyable holiday for all the family. Aviemore is a winter ski resort and during the season ski-hire can be arranged.

Accommodation, for two to eight persons, is in cosy Finnish-style pine chalets, apartments or luxury lodges sleeping from four and eight persons. All are fully equipped down to the last teaspoon, have one or two bedrooms, bathroom, television, patio or balcony, barbecue and fully fitted kitchen. Bedding and towel hire are included in the rental. Luxury lodges have leather furniture, a dishwasher and a telephone, larger units have two bathrooms and some have individual sauna.

On site activities include a heated indoor swimming pool, spa bath, solarium, sauna and steam room, gym, indoor tennis, table tennis, badminton and squash courts, snooker and games room, pool, bowls and a hairdressing salon. Ourdoor facilities include tennis, Australian half tennis, river fishing, children's play park and 9-hole golf course, free to residents. Most activities have nominal charges - prices on application.

The Country Club cafe-bar is open all day for drinks and light meals, and has regular evening entertainment. The restaurant grill serves an interesting range of à la carte and table d'hôte menus.

Treatments
The choice of individual 'hands on' treatments is limited to aromatherapy massage from £9 to £30 and reflexology from £10 per session. Hairdressing is also available, prices on application.

Tariff
Seven night holidays cost from £260 to £445 per unit in low season rising to between £495 and £895 in mid-summer.

Late availability and bargain weekend rates occasionally available, details on application.

Travel Directions
Travel by motorway network to Perth, then A9 road to Aviemore.
Nearest railway station Aviemore approximately 1 mile.

Gleneagles Hotel
Auchterarder Perthshire PH3 1NF
Tel 0764 662231 Fax 0764 662134

| 236 | ☆ 2 3 4 5 6 7 13 14 15 16 17 18 C | £ B |

Gleneagles is one of Scotland's most prestigious resort hotels and offers unrivalled sporting and leisure facilities against the backdrop of the rolling Perthshire hills. It attracts wealthy visitors from all over the world who come to sample its unique ambience and play over the renowned golf courses.

All bedrooms and suites at this famous Scottish institution are lavishly furnished and equipped to the highest standard. Stately public rooms include a drawing room and ballroom with dancing to a resident orchestra most evenings. Guest services include a bank, hairdresser and shopping arcade.

The elegant Strathearn Restaurant serves an appetising choice of international and Scottish cuisine prepared from fresh local produce. Informal meals and refreshments are also available in the Dormy House Grill, the Country Club Brasserie and Silks at the Equestrian Centre.

Golfing facilities amid Gleneagles 830 acre estate are legendary and include the famous King's and Queen's courses and the popular 9-hole Wee course. In 1993, the new Monarch course opened. Designed by Jack Nicklaus, it plays a variable length with five optional tees at each hole. Gleneagles also offers visitors the opportunity to try some unique country sports such as shooting, riding, offroad driving, falconery and salmon and trout fishing. More conventional forms of exercise and relaxation are available at the Gleneagles Country Club. The excellent facilities include a lovely lagoon shaped pool, jacuzzi, hot tubs, sauna, Turkish baths, gym, squash, snooker, croquet, bowls, putting, pitch and putt, tennis and mountain bikes. Within the Country Club is the Spa, where pampering treatments can be enjoyed in luxurious surroundings.

Treatments

The Spa offers a wide range of treatments for men and women including steam cabinet and spa bath £8 or free for those taking a further treatment; body massage £34 and £20; G5 massage £25; aromatherapy with spa bath £44; manicure £14; pedicure £18; Clarins facials from £30 - £52; Cathiodermie £36; Christian Dior pre-make-up facial £18; high intensity sunbed £12.50 and £16.50; waxing from £8; eyelash tinting £10; cleanse and make-up £26.

Tariff

A two-day *Health Break* costs from £300 per person and includes dinner/bed and breakfast, a personal consulation and three hours of spa treatments.

Regular single room rate from £115 per night or £165 per night double/twin room with full Scottish breakfast.

Reduced rates sometimes offered in low season - details on application.

Travel Directions

Gleneagles is easily reached on A9 Glasgow/Edinburgh to Perth road. Turn onto A823 after Blackford.

Nearest railway stations Gleneagles 1/2 mile, Perth approximately 10 miles.

Isles of Glencoe Hotel
Ballachulish Argyll PA39 4HL
Tel 08552 603   Fax 08552 629

| 39 | 2 3 4 5 6 7 13 14 C | £ D |

The Isles of Glencoe Hotel seems almost afloat, lying alongside a peninsula reaching into the waters of Loch Leven. The futuristic style of this modern and well designed hotel blends perfectly with the lovely surroundings.

The hotel's spacious and comfortable en suite bedrooms enjoy magnificent views and are equipped with television, telephone and tea/coffee making facilities.

Seafood is the speciality of *McPhersons*, the hotel's lively Brasserie Restaurant which serves delicious à la carte and table d'hôte dishes. Coffee and light meals are provided in the Lochside Bar throughout the day.

During their stay, hotel residents have use of the Isles Club leisure facilities which include a lovely indoor swimming pool, spa bath, steam room and sauna.

The Isles of Glencoe Hotel is one of three *Freedom of the Glen Hotels* situated around Loch Leven. Guests staying on inclusive terms can 'dine around the loch' at no extra charge, enjoying table d'hôte dinners at *The Ballachulish Hotel* and *The Lodge on the Loch.*

Treatments

Hairdressing and beauty treatments arranged on request - ask for details. A limited range of therapies is available in the leisure centre including physiotherapy and sports medicine - initial assessment £18, subsequent treatments £12; acupuncture and shiatsu £18; body massage £18.

Lessons in water confidence and aquarobics are held regularly and cost £2 per session.

Tariff

The nightly rate per person sharing a double or twin room is £42.50 bed/breakfast or £59 for dinner/bed and breakfast.

Children occupying parents' room pay a standard charge of £11 (ages 2- 7) or £18.25 (ages 8 - 16) to cover breakfast and dinner.

Discounted rates offered at various times of the year, ask for a quote for specific dates.

Travel Directions

Take A82 Glasgow to Fort William road to Glencoe. The hotel is 1 miles to the west of Glencoe village.

Nearest railway station Fort William approximately 15 miles.

Keavil House Hotel
Crossford Dunfermline Fife KY12 8QW
Tel 0383 736258   Fax 0383 621600

30	2 3 4 13 14 15 17 C	£ C

Keavil House Hotel is situated close to the historic town of Dunfermline, five miles from the Forth Road Bridge. This Scottish country house hotel with its acres of gardens and woods makes an ideal retreat for a restful break, and is well placed for viewing the many interesting sights in the locality.

En suite bedrooms are furnished to a high standard and equipped with trouser press, hair drier, television and in-house movies, telephone and tea/coffee making facilities. Rooms can be adapted for family parties with interlocking doors. Some rooms have direct access to the gardens.

Two excellent restaurants serve Scottish food at its best, the Keavil restaurant offers buffet lunches, à la carte and table d'hôte dinners in a pleasant and airy conservatory, while the Armoury Steak House serves the finest Scottish beef expertly cooked and delivered to the table by friendly staff.

Hotel residents are invited to make full use of the lovely leisure centre and 14 metre swimming pool, children's pool, steam room, sauna, solarium, spa bath, treatment room and fully equipped gym.

Treatments

Fitness profiles arranged on request, details on application. Beautician Helen Swan offers a limited range of body and beauty treatments including full body aromatherapy massage £18; half-body massage £14.50; eyelash tint £3.50; eyebrow tint £3.50; waxing from £3.50 to £13.

Tariff

Two night *Getaway Breaks* cost £54.50 per person for dinner/bed and breakfast.

Activity Breaks including *Fitness, Motor Racing* or *Golf* from £130 per person for two nights, inclusive of dinner, bed and breakfast and chosen activity.

Regular bed and breakfast tariff £65 per night single, £85 double room.

Travel Directions

From Edinburgh take M9 over Forth Road Bridge and exit at junction 3. Take A994 following signs to Crossford and Dunfermline.

Nearest railway station Inverkeithing 6 miles.

Marine Highland Hotel
Troon Ayrshire KA10 6HE
Tel 0292 314444   Fax 0292 316922

| 72 | 2 3 4 13 14 17 C | £ C |

Breathtaking views across the Firth of Clyde towards the Arran mountains are enjoyed by visitors to this friendly Victorian hotel, situated on the 18th fairway of the Royal Troon championship golf course.

The hotel has been substantially modernised and refurbished in recent years, and a splendid new leisure facility built. The Marine Club's amenities are available to hotel residents and include heated indoor swimming pool with jacuzzi, separate saunas, steam room, solaria, snooker room, two squash courts, beauty therapy room and a fully equipped gym with personal fitness assessments.

Comfortable bedrooms are well furnished and decorated and all have en suite bathroom, television and free video system, hair drier, trouser press, telephone and tea/coffee making facilities.

Meals are served in either the elegant Fairways restaurant or the more informal Crosbie's, which is open all day and until late at night with a good choice of food and a well-stocked bar.

Treatments
Barbara's Beauty Room offers a varied choice of beauty treatments including aromatherapy £21 per hour; body massage £21; mini-facial £10; deep cleansing facial £15; aromatherapy facial £21; eyelash tint £6.50; manicure £7; pedicure £9.50. A *Top to Toe* package of treatments costs £40.

Tariff
Weekend Break £150 per person inclusive of dinner, bed and breakfast and Sunday lunch before departure.

Regular bed and breakfast tariff £88 per night single, £138 double or twin room.

Travel Directions
Easily reached via motorway network and A78 (follow signs to Prestwick airport), and turn onto A759 into the town of Troon.

Nearest railway station Troon less than 1 mile.

Peebles Hotel Hydro
Innerleithen Road Peebles Peeblesshire EH45 8LX
Tel   0721 720602   Fax 0721 722999

| 135 | 2 3 4 5 6 13 14 16 17 C | £ C |

Nestling in the heart of the beautiful Scottish Borders in 30 acres of grounds, the Peebles Hydro Hotel is a complete resort in its own right, offering an extensive range of holiday packages all year round. Privately owned, the Hydro opened in 1907 and still retains a comfortable Edwardian atmosphere alongside modern day amenities.

A wide range of accommodation is available - family rooms, suites and superior twin rooms with balconies. Rooms are well furnished with en suite bathroom, trouser press, hair drier, television and tea/coffee making facilities.

The dining room overlooks the Tweed valley and offers a varied menu of haute cuisine and traditional Scottish fare prepared with fresh local produce. 'Healthier eating' dishes are available daily for slimmers and vegetarians.

This is an ideal hotel for family holidays and caters well for children of all ages. A great choice of leisure amenities is provided, with weekly sports and games programmes organised during the summer months. Dances and discos are held at weekends in the hotel ballroom, with occasional fancy dress parties and teenage discos.

As a 'resort' hotel, the Hydro provides a full range of indoor recreational facilities with badminton, squash courts, table tennis and snooker tables, as well as the Bubbles leisure complex with heated swimming pool, sauna, solarium, steam bath and gym.

Outdoors are tennis courts, croquet, putting, pitch and putt, pony-trekking, and an adventure playground. A 20% discount on rounds of golf played over the Peebles Course is offered to hotel residents, tickets available from reception.

Treatments

A wide range of body and beauty treatments can be enjoyed in the beauty salon. The choice includes aromatherapy body massage £21; faradic muscle toning machine course of 3 sessions £22.50, 6 sessions £37.50, 10 sessions £60; G5 massage £7.50 per 1/2 hour, 6 for £37.50; waxing and electrolysis from £4 to £19; deep cleansing facials with face and shoulder massage £15; face mask and ozone steaming £15; aromatherapy facial with pressure points, facial and shoulder massage £15; manicure £9; pedicure £10; eyelash tint £7; make-up lesson £15. *A Soothing Experience* costs £35 and includes full body massage, facial with massage, face mask and ozone cleansing, manicure and pedicure.

Tariff

Prices vary according to the time of year, number of nights stayed and type of room required.

The nightly rate starts at £59.50 (£55.75 when staying three nights or more) for a standard double or twin-bedded room. Prices are per person per night and include accommodation, full breakfast and table d'hôte dinner. A superior twin bedroom with balcony costs from £70 per person per night or £66.25 per person per night for stays of three nights or more.

A complicated table of modest charges for children applies, calculated on age, length of stay and time of year, full details on application.

Pamper Yourself Breaks are available throughout the year at various prices inclusive of half board accommodation and use of health facilities (nominal charges for solarium, snooker and squash).

Travel Directions

Peebles is in the Scottish Borders, 22 miles from Edinburgh and 55 miles from Glasgow. It is on A72 approximately 16 miles from Galashiels.

Nearest railway station Edinburgh Waverley 22 miles

Roundelwood
Drummond Terrace   Crieff   Perthshire PH7 4AN
Tel 0764 653806   Fax 0764 655659

7 ☆ 2 3 4 5 6 9 10 11 12 13 15 C   £ C*

Roundelwood has the advantage of being situated amid some of Scotland's loveliest scenery, with many famous beauty spots close at hand. It overlooks the charming town of Crieff, popularly known as the 'Gateway to the Highlands'.

This small and friendly health spa offers health, fitness and slimming courses throughout the year. These are tailored to individual needs and include weight control, stress management and smoking cessation programmes as well as health/fitness improvement and physiotherapy for back, joint and muscular problems. On arrival, weight and fitness are assessed, goals discussed and the most appropriate treatments arranged by a course supervisor.

The spa is entirely self-contained and the pleasant sun lounge, sun deck and rooftop dining area have stunning views of the river valley and Grampian mountains. Single and double accommodation is available in warm and comfortable en suite rooms. A lift operates to all floors.

Facilities on the premises include a small hydrotherapy pool, sauna, solarium, sunbed, spa bath and a well equipped gym. Treatments and activities include specialised physiotherapy, hydrotherapy, aromatherapy, massage, hairdressing, facials, chiropody, relaxation and exercise classes.

During the first days of the course, only fruit and salad meals are served, followed by a balanced wholefood vegetarian diet. No alcohol is served, and in the interests of good health, no smoking permitted on the premises.

All treatments included in the tariff are carried out in the mornings.

Afternoons and evenings are free for optional extra treatments, organised walks and sightseeing. Roundelwood's own minibus operates according to demand, taking guests to such lovely spots as Loch Earn, Glen Lednock and the Sma' Glen, so visitors should pack appropriate clothing and suitable walking shoes for these excursions.

Treatments

The *Health and Fitness Course* offers a complete package of treatments from Monday to Friday, including massage, facials, manicures, sauna, solarium, spa bath, sunbed, Slendertone, G5 massage and thermal wraps. The tariff does not include hairdressing which is available as an optional extra. No weekend treatments.

Optional extra treatments include facials £12; eyelash tinting £4; waxing from £3.50 to £11; manicure £6; pedicure £6.50; G5 massage £4; Slendertone session £3; aromatherapy massage £15.

Tariff

Rates include accommodation, all meals, classes, evening talks, use of facilities and treatment package.

Single room with en suite bathroom £369 for five nights, £738 for a twelve night stay.

Twin-bedded room with en suite bathroom £355 per person sharing accommodation for five nights, £710 per person sharing for twelve nights.

All courses start late Sunday afternoon and finish after lunch on Friday. No treatments available on Saturdays or Sundays.

Visitors staying for the twelve night course stay free of charge over the middle weekend.

Roundelwood also offers nursing facilities and respite care.

Travel Directions

Take M9 and exit at junction 9, taking A9 and then either A822 or A823 into Crieff. On reaching the town take the road to Comrie, Lochearnhead or Crianlarich (A85) and at the edge of the town. follow signs to Roundelwood.

Nearest railway station Gleneagles 11 miles.

St Andrews Old Course Hotel
St Andrews Fife   KY16 9SP
Tel 0334 74371   Fax 0334 77668

125   ☆ 2 3 4 5 6 7 13 14 15 16 17 18 C   **£ A**

Overlooking the 17th green of the Old Course and close to the sea, this famous hotel's austere exterior belies the luxury and comfort within its solid walls. More than £15 million has been spent refurbishing the entire hotel in recent years, and it is now one of Europe's most luxurious establishments.

All 125 renovated guest rooms and suites offer sumptuous accommodation, marble bathrooms and every comfort and facility. Many rooms have balconies and French doors with views over the Old Course to the sea or towards the old town and the distant Scottish Highlands.

Lower calorie and vegetarian food choices are available in all four hotel restaurants for the health conscious guest. Diners can choose from the Road Hole Grill with its open kitchen and rotisserie, the formal Old Course restaurant, the Conservatory serving light meals throughout the day, or the Jigger Inn with real ale and wholesome food.

This is the birthplace of the modern game of golf, and there are about 30 more courses in the area, which is a delight to explore, with art and antique shops in the old town of St Andrews, local castles, and picturesque fishing villages.

Hotel residents have free access to the lovely Spa. Facilities include a warm swimming pool and spa bath housed in an airy conservatory, exercise room, separate ladies' and gents' steam rooms, sun tanning room, hair salon, juice bar and treatment rooms.

Treatments
The range of treatments includes aromatherapy £37; reflexology £20; seaweed wrap £26; mud wrap £26; facials from £27; eyelash tint £8; manicure £13; pedicure £15.50; make-over £16. A *Day at the Spa* costs £79 and includes several treatments and lunch, a *Spa Half Day* is £42.

Tariff
Body & Soul short breaks start at £152 per person per night (minimum two nights) sharing a twin/double room and includes full breakfast and dinner.

Regular bed/breakfast tariff from £210 per room (single or double occupancy)

Low season rates are a bargain by comparison! From £83.50 per person per night for dinner/bed and breakfast in double room for a minimum of two nights.

Travel Directions
St Andrews is reached by the Forth Bridge and M90 from Edinburgh. Exit the motorway at junction 8 and take A91 to St Andrews. From Glasgow take M80 exiting at junction 9 and taking A91 to St Andrews.

Nearest railway station Leuchars 5 miles.

Stobo Castle Health Spa
Stobo Castle Peeblesshire EH45 8NY
Tel 0721 760249   Fax 0721 760294

| 22 | ☆ 2 3 4 5 6 10 12 14 15 16 17 C | £ A |

If being thoroughly pampered in a magnificent Scottish castle sounds the ultimate relaxing break, then Stobo Castle Health Spa in the lovely Borders countryside is the perfect choice.

Purchased by the Winyard family in 1978 and skilfully transformed into a modern health resort, Stobo Castle has a warm and friendly atmosphere despite the grandeur of its palatial decor and furnishings.

In 1993, Stobo was closed for a short period and a major refurbishment carried out, upgrading bedrooms and creating new en suite rooms on the second floor. The Spa area, tucked cosily away in the basement of the Castle, has been transformed with additional treatment and changing rooms, sunbed studio and a new gym equipped with the latest high-tech apparatus. Even the swimming pool has been improved and enlarged with new tiling, underwater lighting and a modern filtration system. A new whirlpool bath has been installed beside a classically inspired wall mural.

Stobo's bedrooms are all individually designed in bright fresh colour schemes and furnished with elegant period furniture. All have en suite facilities, telephone and television. Although the Castle is beautifully warm and centrally heated, all beds are provided with electric overblankets for extra comfort.

A blazing log fire creates a homely and cheerful atmosphere in the lounge, and is especially welcoming on chilly evenings.

The quality of the food at Stobo is excellent - imaginative menus beautifully presented, satisfying the heartiest of appetites. Vegetarian options are always available and all dishes are calorie counted. Most produce - beef, lamb, trout, Scottish salmon game, fresh vegetables and fruit - comes from local farms. Even the water supply is special, and is piped, pure and sparkling from Stobo's own spring.

Breakfast is served buffet style in the wood-panelled dining room (or in bed if preferred), followed by a three course lunch and a satisfying dinner in the evening. Complimentary teas and coffee are available at all times.

Recreational activities are many and include exercise, dance, relaxation and self-defence classes, swimming, aquarobics, mountain bikes, organised walks and tennis. Golf, fishing and riding can be arranged locally. The Japanese Water Gardens in the Castle grounds are exquisite and well worth a visit.

Treatments

A generous number of treatments are included in the tariff, for instance 10 treatments on the three night *Health & Beauty Plan.*

Optional extra treatments include sauna or steam cabinet £8.50; hydrotherapy bath £8.50; Ultratone £16; aromatherapy from £36; reflexology £24; Ionithermie £42; heavy legs treatment with Thalgo plasma gel £16; sunbed £8.50; acumassage £14.75; facials from £26; collagen treatments from £22; eyelash tint £11.50; waxing from £6.50; manicure £17 or £13 (men's); pedicure £18 or £15 (men's); make-up lesson £26; shampoo/blow dry £16; men's blow dry £11; ladies' trim £18; men's trim £13.

Tariff

Health & Beauty Plan and *Health & Fitness Plan* (includes treatments and activities) from £155 - £165 per night single room, £132 to £152 per person per night sharing a twin-bedded room.

Holiday Plan (includes sauna, steam cabinet or hydrotherapy bath and daily body massage except on day of arrival) from £140 - £150 per night single room, £112 - £132 per person per night sharing twin-bedded room.

Rates include accommodation, food and amenities but **NOT VAT** which is added to all accounts at current rate.

Discounted prices (up to 25%) are occasionally offered on shared accommodation - details on application.

Travel Directions

From Glasgow and Edinburgh head for the A72 to Peebles then B712 directly to the village of Stobo. Travellers from the south take either A74, A68 or A1 into the Borders, then A72 and B712.

Nearest railway station Edinburgh Waverley 27 miles.

Turnberry Hotel, Golf Courses and Spa
Ayrshire KA26 9LT
Tel 0655 31000   Fax 0655 31706

| 132 | ☆ 2 3 4 5 6 7 13 14 15 16 17 18 C | £ A |

Turnberry Hotel is set on a 360 acre estate, close to a deserted sandy beach with extensive sea views across the fairways of the Arran and Ailsa golf courses. The world famous links are named after the two islands in the Firth of Clyde that provide the hotel with its spectacular views. The Ailsa course is ranked among the world's top twenty courses and was the 1994 venue for the British Open Championship.

Recent additions at this splendid hotel include one of Britain's finest spas and a luxurious new golf clubhouse. The Spa incorporates Scotland's first hydrotherapy suite with innovative treatments for men and women. The outstanding facilities comprise a stunning 20 metre swimming pool with sea views, spa bath, separate saunas and steam rooms, bio-sauna with enclosed garden, relaxation areas and a superbly equipped gym. There is also a restaurant and bar, solarium, two squash courts, six treatment rooms and a hair and beauty salon. The complex is accessible from the main hotel building.

The stylish guest rooms are individually designed with lovely colour schemes and furnishings, many have sea views. All have have satellite television and telephone and are matched by luxurious bathrooms with bathrobes, hair driers and baskets brimming with toiletries.

Turnberry also offers putting greens, pitch and putt course, tennis courts and billiards on site and other activities by arrangement. There are many interesting places to visit in the area, and the islands of Arran, Millport and Ailsa Craig can be reached in a day's outing.

Treatments

Aromatherapy £38; body massage £30; hydrotherapy massage bath £30; total body mask £30; body blitz £16; Turnberry facial £30; manicure £20; pedicure £20; holistic treatment £50; fitness evaluation £30; cholesterol check £8.

Hydrotherapy, Top to Toe and *Anti-Stress* programmes cost £85 and include various treatments, use of spa amenities and a light lunch.

Tariff

Room and Scottish breakfast high season from £170 single, £200 twin/double room; low season from £135 single, £155 twin/double room. *Golf* and *Spa Break* details and prices on application.

Green fees for hotel residents from £15 to £20 per round Arran course, £30 to £50 Ailsa course (includes optional same day round on Arran).

Travel Directions

The A77 Glasgow to Stranraer road passes within half a mile of the hotel. Glasgow airport is 55 miles from Turnberry.

Nearest railway station Girvan 6 miles.

Westpoint Hotel
Stewartfield Way   East Kilbride G74 5LA
Tel 03552 36300   Fax 03552 33552

74	2 3 4 6 13 14 17 C	£ D

Situated in attractive landscaped gardens on the outskirts of East Kilbride, 20 minutes from central Glasgow, this beautifully designed modern hotel opened in 1991. Like sister Scottish resort hotels Craigendarroch and Cameron House, it boasts luxurious accommodation and outstanding leisure facilities.

The spacious and welcoming bedrooms are equipped with full en suite bathroom, bathrobes, satellite television, telephone, tea/coffee making facilities and welcoming sherry.

All the public rooms in this contemporary hotel are situated on the ground floor and have generous picture windows overlooking the gardens. Breakfast, lunch and dinner are served in the informal setting of the Point Grill, where daily vegetarian choices are included on table d'hôte and à la carte menus. In the evenings, guests can dine in Simpson's, the hotel's gourmet restaurant, well known for its formal cuisine.

Residents have temporary membership of the hotel's superb private country club and its splendid facilities. These comprise indoor pool complex with large heated pool, children's fun pool, poolside spa bath, sauna, steam room and plunge pool. 'Dry' amenities include a dance studio, solarium, supervised crèche, snooker room with two full-sized championship tables, and a Clarins health and beauty salon.

Treatments

Body massage (60 minutes) £20; back massage £15; sunbed from £5 for 15 minutes; aromatherapy massage £28; aromatherapy facial £16; aromatherapy back massage £18; Paris Method body treatments from £25; facials £20; men's facial £20; make-up (with cleanse, tone and colour analysis) £15; eyebrow and eyelash tinting from £4.50; manicure £12 (men's £8); pedicure £16 (men's £12); exfoliation and self-tanning treatment £36.

Tariff

Weekend bed and breakfast rates from £38 per person per night sharing accommodation for two nights on Friday, Saturday or Sunday. Single supplement £18 per night. Dinner/bed and breakfast rates on application.

Regular bed and breakfast tariff Monday to Thursday from £95 single, £115 twin/double room for two persons per night.

Travel Directions

From M74 take exit 6 and follow signs to Hamilton and East Kilbride.
Nearest railway station Glasgow Central approximately 6 miles.

IRELAND

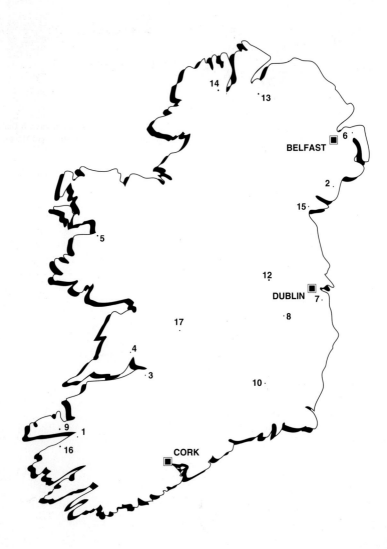

IRELAND

Aghadoe Heights Hotel
Killarney Co Kerry Ireland
Tel 064 31766   Fax 064 31345

| 60 | 2 3 4 13 14 15 16 17 C | £ B |

The Aghadoe Heights is a luxurious modern hotel renowned for its breathtaking views of the lakes and mountains of Killarney. It overlooks two championship golf courses and combines luxurious accommodation and gourmet cuisine with excellent leisure facilities and personalised service.

The beautiful bedrooms and suites are fitted with quality wood furniture and have co-ordinated fabrics, furnishings and drapes. All rooms have private bath and shower, telephone, hairdrier, satellite television, mini bar and trouser press.

The lounges and reception area are richly furnished with chandeliers, paintings, fine tapestries and antiques and on cooler days the warmth of a real log fire enhances the enjoyment of afternoon tea and pre-dinner drinks. The rooftop restaurant has panoramic views and outstanding Irish cuisine made from fresh local produce and served with a choice of fine wines.

Health and fitness facilities have recently been added and include a lovely indoor swimming pool with cascading waterfall, jacuzzi, pool bar, sauna, plunge pool, solarium, fitness and beauty treatment rooms.

Golf on Kerry's premier courses can be arranged, as well as other activities such as fishing, pony trekking, shooting or guided walking tours. There is also a tennis court within the grounds.

Treatments
A limited range of body and beauty treatments is offered including aromatherapy massage IR£25; body massage IR£18.50; Clarins facials from IR£14; Matis facial from IR£20; make-up from IR£8; pedicure IR£10; electrolysis from IR£9; waxing from IR£3; hairdressing wash & set/blow dry IR£15.

Tariff
Low season rates from IR£68 single room, IR£99 double room per night. High season (1 May to 31 October) IR£95 single room, IR£136 double room.

Rates include full Irish or continental breakfast, daily newspaper, early morning tea or coffee. No service charge.

Travel Directions
Hotel is 3 miles north of Killarney on N22 Tralee road, 10 miles from Kerry Airport (Farranfore).

Nearest railway station Killarney 3 miles.

Burrendale Hotel

51 Castlewellan Road Newcastle Co Down BT33 OJY

Tel 03967 22599   Fax 03967 22328

| 50 | 2 3 4 13 14 16 17 C | £ D |

This stylish hotel nestles in the shadow of the Mourne Mountains near the popular County Down resort of Newcastle, with its many attractions and long srtretch of golden sands.

Visitors enjoy en suite bedrooms, restaurant with carvery and a luxurious country club with indoor swimming pool, saunas, steam rooms and spa baths. Serious exercisers will appreciate the well-equipped gym and organised aerobics classes, as well as health bar, sunbeds and a beauty salon.

Treatments

Choice includes aromatherapy body massage £21; 6 slimming treatments £40; G5 massage £50 for 6 treatments; facials from £11.50; eye mask £7.50; manicure £8; pedicure £10; eyelash tint £4.50; cleanse and make-up £12.

Tariff

£90 per person for a two night *Weekender Break* including dinner/bed/breakfast for two nights and dance on Saturday night. Three-nights from £120.

Regular nightly tariff from £52 bed/breakfast in standard single room or £40 per person sharing twin/double room.

Travel Directions

Take A24 road from Belfast towards Newcastle, then A50 Castlewellan Road. Nearest railway station Newry approximately 15 miles.

Castle Oaks Hotel,   Holiday Village & Country Club

Castleconnell   Co Limerick   Ireland

Tel 061 377666   Fax 061 377717

| 24 | villas | 11 | hotel rooms | 2 3 4 5 13 14 16 17 | £ E |

This attractive complex is located amid 26 acres of grounds in the picturesque village of Castleconnell six miles north of Limerick City. Visitors can stay in the well-appointed en suite rooms of the hotel, or in one of the self-catering executive homes equipped with every modern convenience and luxury. All visitors are welcome to wine and dine in the elegant hotel restaurant which serves a varied range of table d'hôte and à la carte dishes and has an extensive wine list.

All visitors have use of the exclusive Castle Oaks Country Club with its many amenities including indoor swimming pool, sauna, steam room, spa bath, tennis courts, aerobics room, gym and sunbed. Golf, fishing and horseriding can be arranged on request - the Country Club has its own fully stocked angling centre and can provide expert advice on all types of fishing.

Treatments

Therapeutic body massage lasting an hour is currently available on Thursdays and Saturdays and costs IR£20. Fitness assessments can be arranged. Hairdressing and beauty therapy details on application.

Tariff

Accommodation in the Castle Oaks Hotel costs from IR£42 single IR£54 double/twin - October to March, or IR£54 single, IR£66 double/twin April to September. All rooms are en suite and prices include a full Irish breakfast. Rates for superior double rooms and suites available on application.

Villa rental from IR£150 per week in the low season to IR£380 per week in July and August. Three-night bank holiday weekends IR£195.

All villas consist of three bedrooms (one double, one twin, one single) with bed linen, bathroom with shower (towels supplied), hot press; sitting room; dining area; kitchen with cooker, fridge, microwave, dishwasher, washing-machine, tumble drier and all necessary equipment and utensils.

Travel Directions
Take N7 from Dublin to Limerick and follow signs to Castleconnell (north).
Nearest railway station Limerick 6 miles

Claureen Health Farm
Ennis   Co Clare   Ireland
Tel   065   28969

| 6 | ☆ 2 3 4 5 6 16 17   £ E*

This busy little health farm is on the site of an 80 acre farm, adjacent to Ennis town in the county of Clare, not far from the majestic cliffs of Moher, made famous in the epic film Ryan's Daughter.

It aims to help guests improve their general state of health in a relaxed and holiday-like atmosphere. The programme is planned for a stay of at least a week, with arrival on Sunday evening and departure the following Saturday morning. Following an initial consultation, a de-toxification cleansing diet is offered to encourage weight loss and give the digestive system a complete break Most treatments take place in the morning. The afternoons are left free for walks through the lovely countryside, trips to the coast or other scenic areas (transport by Claureen's own mini-bus at no extra cost) or other activities such as swimming or horse-riding.

Accommodation is mainly in twin-bedded rooms with shared bathroom facilities, although single accommodation is available on request. One room has an en suite bathroom.

Treatments
One body massage is included in the tariff which also covers all aerobics classes and supervised exercising in the new gym, use of the two squash courts, spa baths, sauna, Slendertone and toning tables. Extra beauty treatments such as facials IR£14 and hairdressing arranged on request.

Tariff
Inclusive weekly tariff IR£200 in single room or IR£175 sharing double room.

Travel Directions
From the town of Ennis take the N85 road to Lahinch for approximately a mile.
  Collection arranged from Shannon Airport 14 miles away.
  Nearest railway station Limerick approximately 24 miles.

Cloona Health Centre
Westport   Co Mayo   Ireland
Tel   098 25251

| 10 | ☆ 2 3 7 9 10 12   £ E*

Formerly an old Irish mill, Cloona was restored in 1973 and is Ireland's longest established residential health centre.

Situated three miles from Westport, County Mayo, and just a mile from the coast, Cloona boasts panoramic views over Clew Bay and its islands and is an idyllic spot to relax and regenerate.

The programme runs from Sunday to Saturday, February to November, and is primarily a cleansing course with a strong emphasis on relaxation and exercise. Actual weight loss is not the most important consideration.

Free time is allowed during the week to explore the beautiful countryside, and bikes are provided.

Every evening and following a sauna, a short massage is given to help the cleansing process and stimulate circulation. Brisk daily walks are an integral part of the weekly programme, and provide an opportunity to enjoy the outstanding scenery surrounding Cloona. Talks on nutrition and herbal remedies in the home are also given during the week. Prospective visitors are advised to wean themselves off tea, coffee and sugar during the week prior to their visit, and to avoid heavy meals on the days leading up to the course.

A week at Cloona is designed to be a complete break from the stresses of modern life - there is no television and use of radios is not encouraged - everyone is expected to participate fully in the week's activities. Be prepared to enjoy the rugged beauty of Ireland's west coast, and pack essentials such as walking shoes and rain wear, along with track suit and swimsuit.

Treatments

Daily treatments included in the overall weekly charge include yoga class, brisk organised daily walk, sauna and twenty minute massage.

Optional therapeutic full body massage or reflexology treatments are available for IR£12 each.

Tariff

Price of a week's course including accommodation for six nights, all meals, treatments, classes and talks is IR£198 for a single room and IR£363 for two persons sharing a double/twin-bedded room.

Fees are payable at the commencement of the course, and a booking deposit of IR£50 per person is required.

Travel Directions

Cloona is 1 mile from the main Louisburgh Road in Westport, County Mayo. It is within driving distance of both Knock and Galway airports.

Nearest railway station Westport 3 miles.

Culloden Hotel
Bangor Road Craigavad Co Down Northern Ireland BT18 OEX
Tel 0232 425223   Fax 0232 426777

| 94 | 2 3 4 5 13 14 16 17 C | £ D |

This historic hotel stands in 12 acres of gardens on the wooded slopes of the Holywood Hills overlooking Belfast Lough and the Antrim coast.

The palatial surroundings successfully combine 19th century charm with modern day amenities - luxurious accommodation, spacious antique-filled lounges and the renowned Mitre restaurant serving fine cuisine and wines.

Leisure amenities include squash courts, all-weather tennis court, putting green and lawn croquet. The spendid Elysium health and leisure club boasts swimming pool, steam room, spa bath, gym, poolside snack bar, hair salon and body and beauty clinic.

Treatments
Aromatherapy £25 initially £20 subsequently; Swedish body massage £18; tension massage £10.50; Swiss cellular treatment £37; Swiss cellular facials from £21; Clarins facials from £10.95; aromatherapy facial £16.85; make-up £10.50; manicure with massage £9; pedicure with massage £10; waxing from £2.50; eyelash tinting £3.25.

Tariff
Two night weekend rate from £45 per person per night in double/twin room (includes full Irish breakfast) midweek bed/breakfast tariff from £106 single, £140 double/twin room.

Travel Directions
Take Bangor road from Belfast for appoximately 8 miles.

Nearest railway station Belfast Central 8 miles or Holywood (request stop only approximately 1 mile.

Fitzpatrick Castle Hotel
Killiney Co Dublin Ireland
Tel 01 2840700   Fax 01 2850207

| 88 | 2 3 4 5 13 14 16 17 C | £ D |

Standing in landscaped gardens overlooking the sea and Wicklow mountains, this luxury castle hotel is nine miles from Dublin city centre.

All bedrooms have private facilities, direct phones and television. The Castle Grill and Truffles restaurants cater to all tastes with international and Irish dishes.

Sunday brunches and Jesters Nightclub are popular weekend attractions.

Leisure amenities include indoor swimming pool, sauna, steam room, squash courts, tennis, gym, hairdressing and beauty clinic.

Treatments

The beauty clinic offers a wide range of body and beauty treatments including aromatherapy /body massage IR£24; back massage IR£11; back mask IR£12; reflexology IR£18; sunbed IR£12 per session; Cathiodermie IR£22; Sothys facials from IR£20; make-up IR£10; manicure IR£8; pedicure IR£12.50; eyelash tint IR£5.75; waxing from IR£3; electrolysis from IR£6.

Tariff

Weekend Break - two nights' accommodation with breakfasts and one dinner IR£90 per person sharing double room (single supplement IR£15).

Rates include use of the leisure facilities, treatments extra charge.

Travel Directions

From Dublin take N1 south for approximately 8 miles then follow signs to Killiney.

Nearest railway station Dublin 9 miles.

The Kildare Hotel & Country Club
Straffan Co Kildare Ireland
Tel 01 627 3333   Fax 01 627 3312

| 45 | P 2 3 4 5 13 14 15 16 17 18 C | £ A |

The Kildare Hotel and Country Club nestles in 330 acres of wooded country-side scattered with lakes alongside a mile of the River Liffey. Designed to appeal to the most discerning of clientele, this is undoubtedly Ireland's foremost resort. The idyllic countryside setting is only 17 miles from the centre of Dublin and 23 miles from the city's international airport.

No expense has been spared transforming stately Straffan House into a magnificent hotel, which despite its breathtaking opulence has a friendly informality. The spacious public rooms have open fires, original oil paintings and superb furnishings. An intimate cocktail bar leads into the Byerley Turk restaurant, named after the great Arab stallion and a reminder that this is Irish horse country. Table d'hôte and à la carte menus feature the finest of Irish and international cuisine using organic home-grown produce and fish from the estate in season.

The Kildare's 45 bedrooms are designed in restful harmonious colours and have marble bathrooms, bathrobes, satellite television, video, hair drier, phone, minibar, and electronic safe. Exquisitely appointed self-contained apartments and a three-bedroomed lodge in the grounds are also available.

Residents have use of the superb country club (known as The K Club) with 18-hole championship golf course, river and lake fishing, indoor and outdoor tennis, squash, fully equipped gym, separate saunas and indoor swimming pool. Snooker, croquet and bicycles are also available. Exercise classes, fitness assessments, hairdressing and beauty treatments can be booked in the pool and health centre. The clubhouse has its own restaurant and Legends bar.

Treatments

Two therapy rooms offer a limited range of body and beauty treatments. Facials IR£40; manicure IR£15; pedicure IR£25; aromatherapy massage IR£55; 30 minute body massage IR£30; 60 minute body massage IR£55; ladies and gents hairdressing from IR£12 for wash and blow dry.

Tariff

Two night weekend leisure breaks from IR£195 per person sharing a double room are offered at various times during the year. This price includes accommodation, table d'hôte dinners and full Irish breakfasts, one day's golf or fishing (equipment and clothing provided free for fishing) as well as complimentary use of the leisure club and sports centre. Extra nights are available at IR£97.50 per person (including dinner and breakfast).

Regular nightly tariff for room only is from IR£150 single, IR£230 per night in double or twin room. Suites cost from IR£320, Courtyard suites from IR£200 (two persons) to IR£350 (three/four persons). The Lodge (sleeps six persons) and costs IR£450 per night.

Rates include VAT but not service charge of 15%.

Travel Directions

From Dublin city centre take N7 south for 17 miles.
  Nearest railway station Heuston Station, Dublin, 23 miles.

Lios Dana Natural Living Centre
Inch-Annascaul Co Kerry Ireland
Tel 066 58189

| 8 | 2 7 9 10 12 | £ E* |

If you long to get away from it all completely, spending time recovering vitality and energy with others of the same mind, then Lios Dana Natural Living Centre is an ideal choice.

Anne Hyland and Michael Travers acquired the Centre in 1985 and renovated it for residential courses and retreat holidays for people of all ages from all walks of life.

Lios Dana is essentially a holistic retreat, located on the side of a hill with magnificent views of the Dingle Peninsula, the beautiful Inch Strand and the Atlantic Ocean. Here you can take a walk along four miles of deserted sandy beaches and dunes, and watch (or even swim alongside!) dolphins frolicking in an ocean warmed by the Gulf Stream. There are many wonderful sights to be seen - the views of the mountains around Dingle are forever changing with the light and atmosphere of the mild Kerry climate.

The ambience is inspirational and supportive, promoting vitality and recovery of energy. Stays can be restful or active, with good food, clean air, interesting company and participation in activities such as yoga, meditation, cooking, art, aidido, shiatsu-acupressure, walking, swimming, fishing, birdwatching and seaweed gathering.

The Centre is purpose built - with eight guest bedrooms all with wash-hand basins, a large recreation room, library/drawing room, dining room and kitchen. Macrobiotic, vegetarian and seafood meals are prepared at the Centre, the aim being to provide balanced nutrition by choosing varied ingredients for individual needs. The food is wholesome Irish cooking at its best with home-made breads, jams, soups, spreads, fresh fruit and organic vegetables.

Discussion of diet, nutrition and natural health care may be included in weekend or weekly programmes when requested.

No beauty treatments are available, just lots of healthy outdoor activities and excursions.

Tariff
Weekend rate for a three night say is IR£96 per person, and IR£185 for a weekly stay (six nights). Rates include accommodation, activities and meals.

Travel Directions
From Cork (2 hours drive) take N22 to Castlemaine and then R561 to Inch. From Dublin (5 hours drive) use N7, N21 and R561 to Inch. Kerry airport is 20 miles away (direct flights from Luton and Heathrow).

Nearest railway station Tralee 18 miles - collection can be arranged.

Mount Juliet
Thomastown Co Kilkenny Ireland
Tel 056 24455   Fax 056 24522

| 53 | 2 3 4 13 14 15 16 18 C | £ B |

Mount Juliet is situated on a 1500 acre estate 75 miles from Dublin, and is one of Ireland's most exclusive hotels. The grandeur and ambience of the 200 years old house has been carefully preserved and enhanced in its conversion to luxury hotel.

32 individually designed and spacious rooms are available in Mount Juliet House, with a further 21 en suite courtyard rooms available in the Hunters Yard and Rose Garden Suites, a two minute walk from the main house. Larger parties can be accommodated in secluded Ballylinch House, which has four bedrooms and its own personal daily housekeeper.

Visitors enjoy the best of Irish cuisine and fine wines in the elegant Lady Helen Dining Room, while The Tetrarch and Mr Jinks Bars are popular with guests and local people alike.

Many sporting activities and outdoor pursuits are possible, including archery, salmon and trout fishing, clay target shooting, horse-riding and hunting, tennis, croquet, cricket and golf. The 18-hole par 72 Jack Nicklaus Signature golf course is playable all year and home to the Irish Open in 1993 and 1994. The 3-hole Golf Academy is designed to offer all players a chance to improve their game.

The Spa at The Hunters Yard has recently opened and offers a full range of body and beauty treatments, as well as sauna and steam rooms, exercise room and a lovely heated swimming pool with whirlpool spa.

Treatments

A luxurious range of body and beauty treatments is available in the Spa and includes tension massage IR£15; full body Swedish massage IR£40; cellulite massage with vacuum suction IR£20; aromatherapy IR£50; abdomen massage IR£10; Matis facial treatments from IR£22; eyelash tint IR£10; manicure IR£15; pedicure IR£15; cleanse and make-up IR£15; camouflage make-up from IR£25; waxing from IR£8.

Tariff

Nightly rates vary according to time of year from IR£80 to IR£144 single, IR£80 to IR£190 twin/double room. Suites from IR£200 to IR£360.

Short Break tariff from IR£150 per person sharing a twin or double room for two nights including dinner, bed and breakfast.

Travel Directions

From Kilkenny in southeast Ireland take R700 to Thomastown and follow signs to Mount Juliet.

Nearest railway station Thomastown approximately 2 miles.

Nuremore Hotel
Carrickmacross, Co Monaghan, Ireland
Tel 042 61438   Fax 042 61853

| 69 | 2 3 7 13 14 15 16 17 18 C | £ C |

Surrounded by acres of glorious countryside 50 miles from Dublin and Belfast, the Nuremore Hotel is ideally situated for a relaxing break. The hotel and grounds have been newly re-created to offer luxurious accommodation and a huge range of sporting and leisure facilities.

Originally a Victorian country house, the Nuremore has spacious lounges with open fires, comfortable chairs and sofas. On summer evenings, pre-dinner drinks can be taken on the terrace overlooking a pretty lake.

The elegant hotel restaurant serves classical European cuisine with a good choice of French and Irish dishes, all complemented by a wide range of fine wines.

The bedrooms are light and welcoming, furnished in co-ordinating fabrics and colour schemes in country-house style. All rooms are well equipped with en suite bathroom, television and direct dial telephones.

The Nuremore Country Club provides hotel residents with a range of top facilities including an 18 metre indoor heated swimming pool, whirlpool, steam room, sauna, gym, tennis courts, squash courts and a snooker room.

Trout fishing on the privately stocked lake within the grounds and local coarse fishing are also available.

The Nuremore boasts its own 18-hole championship golf course, with a resident PGA Professional on hand to offer advice and coaching.

Treatments
Although conventional body and beauty treatments are not available, a specialist aromatherapy salon in the leisure centre is open on weekends.

The treatments available include one hour aromatherapy massage IR£25 initial treatment, IR£20 subsequently; 30 minute aromatherapy massage IR£15; face, scalp, neck and upper chest aromatherapy massage with optional face mask £IR£15; reflexology IR£15; Swiss reflex technique £20 (reflexology using personalised essential oils to massage reflex points of the feet, with oils for home use).

Tariff
Weekend break includes two nights' bed/breakfast, dinner on Saturday evening and lunch on Sunday IR£134.50 per person sharing a double room. (Total green fees IR£15 extra).

Three day midweek breaks IR£165 per person, inclusive of dinner/bed/breakfast for three days. (Total green fees IR£20 extra).

Regular nighly tariff from IR£65-IR£75 single, IR£90-IR£120 double/twin.

Children sharing parents' room IR£5 per night (under 2) or 25% reduction (under 12). Special children's rates for July and August on application.

Travel Directions

Take the main N2 road from Dublin to Monaghan, a drive of approximately 90 minutes.

Nearest railway station Dundalk 12 miles.

The Old Glebe Health Farm
Kinnegad Killucan Co Westmeath Ireland
Tel 044 74263   Fax 044 74429

| 6 | ☆ 2 3 4 5 6 9 10 11 14 15 16 17 C | £ C* |

Old Glebe Health Farm is peacefully situated amid mature parkland in Westmeath countryside, an hour's drive from Dublin. This is a small and friendly establishment with good facilities, ideal for a short rejuvenating break.

All programmes at Old Glebe are tailored to suit specific requirements, usually losing weight, getting fit or simply relaxing and unwinding, and these are planned with a consultation on arrival.

Rooms are comfortable with private facilities, and in winter there is a cosy open fire in the lounge. Delicious Irish cuisine is served using organic fruit and vegetables from Old Glebe's own gardens, and lean steaks, poultry and eggs from its own farm. Calorie controlled diets are available for slimmers and short fasts supervised.

Treatments

Many optional body and beauty treatments are offered at Old Glebe, including facials from IR£10; aromatherapy IR£20; algae bath and body wrap IR£16; Slendertone IR£8; sunbed treatment IR£4; waxing from IR£3.

Tariff
The daily tariff includes accommodation and all meals, daily G5 massage, exercise class, organised walks, pre-dinner 'mocktails', use of fitness equipment in gym, indoor pool, tennis and squash courts, sauna and jacuzzi.
   Single room with bath IR£75 per night, IR£375 for five nights.
   Sharing twin room with bath IR£60 per person per night, IR£300 for five nights.
   Single room with shower IR£65 per night, IR£325 for five nights.
   A five night stay is recommended to achieve optimum benefit, from Sunday evening until after lunch on Friday.

Travel Directions
From Dublin take N4 west for 40 miles. After Kinnegad turn onto Killucan road for 4 miles. Old Glebe is on the left, at the 'stop' sign in the village.
   Nearest railway station Mullingar approximately 9 miles.

Raspberry Hill Health Farm
29 Bonds Glen Road   Londonderry   Northern Ireland   BT47 3ST
Tel 0504 398259 & 398000

| 6 | ☆ 2 3 4 5 6 7 11 12 15 16 17 | £ E* |

Raspberry Hill Health Farm is situated in the scenic Bond's Glen in the picturesque foothills of the Sperrin Mountains. It takes its unusual name from the wild fruit growing in profusion in this lovely area on the County Tyrone/Derry borders of Northern Ireland.
   The health farm is the residential expansion of a highly successful weight reducing clinic established over 15 years ago, and is personally supervised and managed by Claire and Alfie Danton. It caters for dieters wanting to lose weight and learn sensible eating habits and attitudes to food, as well as those just wanting a stress-free break in delightful rural surroundings.
   All accommodation is in tastefully decorated single, double and twin-bedded rooms with en suite shower and toilet. Some three and four bedded rooms are also available with en suite facilities.
   The day's routine is relaxed and informal - starting with fruit juice plus multivitamin tablet at 9.00am and some optional exercise such as brisk walking.
   A light but adequate breakfast is then taken, followed by the treatments and classes of the day with a break for a healthy, low calorie lunch. Dinner is usually a hearty salad with fish or lean meat, and a low calorie dessert with fruit, tea or coffee. A drink and fruit are served before bedtime.

Treatments

A week's stay includes daily counselling at weight reducing clinic, Slendertone treatment, sauna, steam cabinets, hydro-bath and full use of the gym. Sunbeds and solarium are coin-operated at £4 per hour. Optional alternative health treatments can be arranged on request - full body massage £20, reflexology £12, aromatherapy £20.

Other activities available include 9-hole putting green, tennis, indoor bowls, table tennis and badminton. Bicycles may be hired free of charge to explore the many local places of interest and swimming and horse-riding can be arranged.

Tariff

Weekly rate £180 per person sharing accommodation or £225 in a single room, from 7.00pm Sunday until after midday the following Saturday.

The ideal length of stay is a week (six nighs) as weight loss and stress programmes are not effective in a lesser period.

Travel Directions

From Eglington village (1/2 mile from airport, 8 miles from city of Londonderry) turn left onto Claudy road and head for A6 (south). Continue on A6 for 4 miles turning right onto B74 - Bond's Glen Road is 1/4 mile from this point.

Nearest railway station Londonderry approximately 10 miles.

Rathmullan House

Lough Swilly Rathmullan Letterkenny Co Donegal Ireland
Tel 074 58188   Fax 074 58200

| 18 | 2 3 7 13 14 15 16 C | £ D |

This gracious early 19th century house enjoys an outstanding situation in glorious north Donegal countryside. Its beautiful gardens slope down to the sandy shores of Lough Swilly, with views across the water to the Inishowen Peninsula.

Privately owned by Rob and Robin Wheeler, Rathmullan House has won many awards and praise over the years. Light filled rooms reflect the beauty of their surroundings, especially the Arabian style silky drapes in the dining room overlooking the lake. Log fires, crystal chandeliers, antiques and charming staff ensure an enjoyable stay.

Guests seeking a healthy holiday will be attracted to the Egyptian Baths, which house a large heated salt water swimming pool, with a sauna and steam room and separate changing areas. Nominal charges are made for private sessions in the steam room or sauna. Swimming lessons can be arranged during the summer.

Treatments

No beauty treatments are available, but qualified masseuse and reflexologist Caitlin Gallagher gives a variety of therapeutic body treatments. Head and face massage IR£7.50; back massage IR12.50; head, face and back massage IR£15; whole body massage lasting 11/4 hours IR£35. Reflexology treatments last an hour and more than one treatment is required for a healing response.

Tariff

Rathmullan House offers a variety of accommodation at different prices. Most rooms have en suite facilities - rates for budget rooms with private bathroom start at IR£27 per person bed/breakfast rising to IR£52.50 for a mini suite. Several rooms are large enought to accommodate families. Children sharing with parents have 50% discount.

Weekend or two night half board rates from IR£80 to IR£140.

All rates include use of the Egyptian Baths and tennis courts.

Travel Directions

From Letterkenny take the R245 road to Rathmelton, then follow the signs and the R247 road to Rathmullan.

Sheen Falls Lodge Hotel
Kenmare   Co Kerry   Ireland
Tel   064 41600   Fax 064 41386

| **49** | **2 3 13 15 16 17 19** | **£ A** |

This exquisitely restored 17th century lodge is situated a mile from the little town of Kenmare amid 300 acres of lawns, semi-tropical gardens and woodland walks. It epitomises the perfect country house hotel with elegance, comfort and friendly service.

Bedrooms are decorated in soothing pastels and have contemporary furnishings and marble bathrooms. Superb Irish cuisine is enjoyed by diners in La Cascade Restaurant.Lounges with blazing log fires are welcoming during the day and invite relaxation with drinks and cofee in the evening.

Leisure amenities include a health and fitness centre with spa bath, sauna, steam room, table tennis and gym, as well as billiards, croquet, horse-riding, tennis, woodland walks and free fishing along 15 miles of the Sheen River.

Treatments
Aromatherapy, reflexology and massages from IR£20 per half hour.

Tariff
IR£195 per person sharing double room for two nights bed/breakfast and one dinner. Single supplement IR£45 per room per night.

Regular tariff from IR£110 per person sharing per night for dinner/bed/breakfast.

Travel directions
Take N71 Glengariff road to Kenmare, almost a mile from Sheen Falls Lodge.
Nearest railway station Killarney approximately 12 miles.

The Signal Box Health Farm
Glenbeigh Co Kerry Ireland
Tel   066 68240   Fax   066 6843

| 6 | ☆ 2 3 6 7 11 12 15 17 | £ D* |

A unique health retreat has been created in Glenbeigh's former railway station at the foot of the Seefin mountin, close to a wonderful four mile sweep of clean sands with excellent bathing.

The Signal Box has been lovingly modernised by German owners Johanna and Helmuth Lopau, and has comfortable centrally heated rooms with colour television and spacious lounges and dining room with cosy open fires.

It is the only establishment within Ireland and Great Britain currently offering the Schroth and Kneipp natural detoxification and healing programmes. Both treatments have been running successfully for over 150 years in centres in German speaking countries and in Canada and the USA.

Treatments

No conventional body and beauty treatments are available, as The Signal Box specialises only in continental natural health programmes.

Programme 1 - Schroth treatment

This unique treatment comprises packs, dieting and a system of alternating 'dry' and 'drinking' days, resulting in the detoxification of the whole body which is relieved of excess water and fat. The whole process is carried out under medical supervision (one examination per week), and is reputed to be especially helpful in cases of fluid retention, rheumatoid arthritis, catarrh and chronic skin conditions.

A period of three weeks is recommended for this 'cure', but a modified version based on the same principles is available for clients with only a week to spare.

Programme 2 - Kneipp Hydro treatment

This treatments is based on water treatments to stimulate blood circulation and the body's ability to fight ill-health. Yoga and Callanetics accompany the programme. A healthy diet can be specially adopted to suit individual needs.

Tariff

The tariff is based on a week's stay commencing on a Sunday and finishing the following Saturday.

Programme 1 One week IR£295, two weeks IR£570, three weeks IR£845.

Programme 2 IR£329 inclusive of reduction diet - additional charge for special diet IR£18 per week.

Medical examinations IR£15 initially, IR£12 subsequently.

Prices cover accommodation, 'cure' diet, health treatments, massage, yoga, Callanetic classes and sauna bath. Brush-massage (IR£12.50) and chiropody (IR£15) are included in Programme 2.

Travel Directions

Glenbeigh is in the far south west of Ireland, on the N70 approximately 26 miles from Tralee.

Nearest railway station Killarney approximately 21 miles.

(Collection from Farranfore airport or Killarney railway station can be arranged.)

Temple

Horseleap Moate Co Westmeath Ireland

Tel 0506 35118   Fax 0506 35118

5   ☆ **2 4 7 11 15**   **£ D***

Temple is a lovely 200 year old farmhouse set in mature trees and gardens less than a two hour drive from Dublin. Temple's owners, Bernadette and Declan Fagan have won several prestigious tourism awards for their hospitality and excellent Irish cooking.

Spacious en suite rooms, great food, log fires and lovely gardens provide an ideal environment for the mid-week and weekend *Relaxation Programmes.* These short breaks are suited to both men and women and combine a healthy diet with yoga exercises, Ki-massage and aromatherapy. Meditation for self-healing, the significance of colour on physical and emotional well-being, and use of essential oils in treating stress and depresssion are explored. *Shiatsu Weekends* incorporating a vegetarian menu are also offered.

Participants can also enjoy walking, cycling, horse riding and golf locally during their stay. Declan organises guided walking and cycling tours of this often overlooked part of Ireland, taking in the famous monastic site of Clonmacnois with its Celtic high crosses and Westmeath's beautiful lakes.

Treatments

Optional treatments include individual aromatherapy consultation and blend of oils IR£10; aromatherapy baths and beauty treatments by prior arrangement.

Tariff

Midweek Relaxation Programme IR£160 per person sharing or IR£175 single room - includes full board from dinner Monday to lunch Thursday, with yoga class each day and two Ki-massage treatments

Weekend Relaxation Programme IR£105 per person sharing or IR£120 single room - includes full board from dinner Friday to lunch Sunday with yoga class each day and one Ki-massage.

Holistic and Shiatsu Weekends IR£105 per person sharing with full board from dinner Friday to lunch Sunday.

Vegetarian, gluten-free and calorie controlled diets catered for on request.

Bed/breakfast tariff IR£20 per person, dinner IR£14, weekend (2 bed/breakfasts, 1 dinner) IR£52 per person. Prices include service and VAT.

Outdoor activities in the area include horseriding at Mullingar Equestrian Centre from IR£9 per hour, all-year-round golf at Mount Temple Golf Club, Moate, green fees IR£7 weekdays, IR£10 weekends. Play on other local courses can be arranged.

Guided walk/cycle, including picnic lunch and bicycle hire IR£15 per day.

Travel Directions

From Dublin take N4 to Kinnegad (approximately 40 miles) then turn onto N6 for a further 20 miles to Horseleap, between Kilbeggan and Moate.

Nearest railway station Clara 3 miles.

THERAPEUTIC SPAS

Europe's world renowned mineral spring spas are popular with people of all ages and used regularly for health and recreation. Europeans consider the pleasure of bathing in warm curative waters and receiving health restorative treatments a natural part of everyday life. Spa use is encouraged by governments, trade unions and the medical profession, and health insurance schemes cover the cost of prescribed spa treatments. Balneotherapy (treatment with spa water) is seen as a safe, enjoyable and effective alternative to drug therapy, especially for those with problems of mobility, such as elderly people and those recovering from accidents or surgery.

European spas are properous, vibrant resorts attracting visitors all year round with their beautiful surroundings, pleasant shopping areas, sporting facilities and busy cultural calendars. Visitors are welcomed with affordable treatment centres and a choice of accommodation ranging from luxurious hotels to well-run campsites. In many resorts, the thermal spring water is tapped to wash streets and heat schools, hospitals and domestic water supplies.

By comparison, mineral and thermal spas in Britain are almost extinct, and therapeutic use of spa water severely limited. A few years ago, plans were drawn up to restore facilities in some of Britain's attractive spa towns, but lack of investment and a long recession, caused these plans to be seriously delayed or abandoned. The aim was to turn British spa waters back on for tasting and bathing and provide exciting 21st century health hydros on continental lines, offering the latest health and beauty treatments.

The most ambitious British project was at Matlock Bath in Derbyshire, and involved developing a £100 million health and leisure spa using hot and cold spa waters and volcanic muds. Although planning permission was granted, the whole project was abandoned when the site was sold for mineral mining. In Harrogate, the proposed spa development at the Old Swan Hotel has been 'put on hold' indefinitely, and in Malvern plans for a new spa treatment and leisure centre have been cancelled.

Fortunately, there is some good news! After a closure of nearly 13 years, Bath's public spa baths are to be redeveloped into a full modern health and leisure spa using the city's natural hot spring. When this goes ahead, Britain will have two authentic spas with bathing and treatment facilities,

the other being at Droitwich, where the brine baths have been very successfully developed for therapeutic and recreational use.

British spas originated in pre-Roman times, developing from mineral springs in holy wells. 'Taking the waters' was a standard medical practice in Tudor times, and continued into the hey day of the spa, the late Georgian and Victorian eras. Established resorts like Bath, Leamington Spa and Harrogate became part of the social calendar for royalty and rich society, seeking relief from problems caused by the excesses of their over-indulgent lifestyles. Huge hotels and health hydros were built to accommodate these rich visitors in style, together with bath houses and pump rooms designed on classical Roman lines.

The advent of the railways brought many more visitors flocking to the spas, creating wealth and prosperity for these attractive inland resorts. Elegant houses were built for wealthy families and landowners, and the distinctive architecture, parks and gardens gave the towns much of the character and beauty they retain today. The boom lasted until the onset of the First World War, when the spas' popularity began to wane. The development of new drugs and the creation of the National Health Service in 1948 caused further decline.

As the pharmaceutical industry grew, British doctors began treating patients with new drugs promising quicker relief from pain than the gentler, more gradual cures afforded by spa treatments. NHS use of theapeutic spas was gradually phased out. Today, the only spa water used for treatments on the NHS is in Buxton's Royal Devonshire Hospital.

Continental spas fared differently, becoming medically orientated with attractive new hydrotherapy facilities and modern treatment clinics. European doctors continued prescribing traditional spa treatments, but now had the option of combining them with effective drug therapy, giving patients the best of both types of care.

European health insurance (the equivalent of schemes like *BUPA* and taken out by most of the population) was designed to include the cost of spa treatments like fango, hydotherapy and thalassotherapy, when medically prescribed. With clinical use guaranteed, continental spas were able to extend their range of services and offer the latest fitness facilities and beauty treatments in addition to balneotherapy. The pharmaceutical industry sounded the death knell for the British spa; how ironic that today our search for natural remedies rekindles interest in one of our oldest assets. As the saying goes - the wheel has turned full circle.

SPA WATER PROPERTIES

There are three main categories of spa water, some spas having more than one type of spring:

1) Chalybeate water contains iron salts including ferrous sulphite, and is taken medicinally for blood disorders such as anaemia. Royal Tunbridge Wells and Trefriw Wells Spa have chalybeate spring water rich in minerals especially iron.

   The water has no smell but tastes metallic.

2) Sulphur waters (containing hydrogen sulphur) are immediately recognised by their 'bad egg' smell - they taste equally foul, but are said to 'purify' the blood if consumed, and to treat skin disorders when bathing. Harrogate, Llandrindod Wells and Strathpeffer have sulphur water, as do many continental spas, where effective filtration removes the unpleasant smell.

3) Saline water is known for its purgative properties, and contains various dissolved salts. Although it can be taken internally as a purifier and laxative, its most therapeutic use is for bathing.

   Bath, Leamington Spa and Droitwich have saline water. The Droitwich brine contains 30 per cent natural salts, and like the Dead Sea is ten times more concentrated than normal sea water. The huge measure of two and a half pounds of salt to each gallon of water gives the water its incredible buoyancy, unique in all Europe.

THE BRITISH SPAS FEDERATION
Westfield Hallow Worcester WR2 6LB
Telephone and Fax 0905 640202

The Federation was originally formed in 1921, as a consortium of British towns and cities with spa interests, but became more of a tourism and promotional body over the years as the therapeutic British spa declined. Today, the Federation represents 12 spa towns with natural springs in Britain, and has two associate members, one in Wales and the other in Ireland.

BSF's main objective is to develop wider public understanding and interest in the many genuine benefits of spa-related health and relaxation. It organises medical seminars to interest doctors and other practitioners in the concept of spas and the value of restorative treatments.

In the early 1990s, *Spa 2000* was launched to heighten interest in British spas and get the waters back on for tasting and bathing. Unfortunately the initiative co-incided with a severe recession when investment was at an all time low. More recently, there has been considerable interest in spas as centres for health and relaxation and several spa towns are now co-operating with private developers to recreate their spa facilities.

In 1993, the BSF published *The Spa Heritage Town Trail*, a free colour brochure sponsored by Schweppes and promoting a 'trail' around the twelve spas of Great Britain, highlighting their unique heritage and culture. Information on individual towns, annual events and copies of the brochure are available from all tourist information centres in the spa towns.

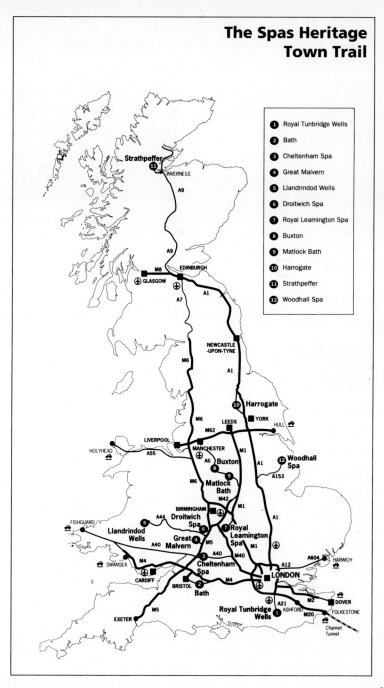

The Spas Heritage Town Trail

1. Royal Tunbridge Wells
2. Bath
3. Cheltenham Spa
4. Great Malvern
5. Llandrindod Wells
6. Droitwich Spa
7. Royal Leamington Spa
8. Buxton
9. Matlock Bath
10. Harrogate
11. Strathpeffer
12. Woodhall Spa

MEMBERS OF
THE BRITISH SPAS FEDERATION

BATH

Tourist Information Centre
The Colonnades 11-13 Bath Street
Avon BA1 1SW
Tel 0225 462831

Bath's hot spa waters have bubbled out of the limestone at 46.5°C for centuries and produce a million litres of water daily. A bacterial organism closed down the last of the treatment facilities in 1978, and although this has now been eliminated, the spa bathing facilities remain closed. Visitors can sip the spa mineral water sold in the famous Pump Room for the modest sum of 35 pence per glass.

Although at present visitors cannot bathe in the spa waters, it is hoped that in the not too distant future, modern spa facilities will once again be available to the public in the uniqe setting of this World Heritage site.

The healing properties of the warm spa water have been appreciated down the centuries and have been beneficial in the treatment of rheumatism, arthritis, high blood pressure and metabolic diseases.

Bath is noted for its elegant, honey-coloured 18th century architecture, Roman remains, magnificent Civic Rooms, museums, galleries, shops and beautiful parks. Thereare also many interesting and varied walks within the city boundaries and in the countryside beyond.

BUXTON

Tourist Information Centre
The Crescent Derbyshire SK17 6B
Tel 0298 25106
(mini-com available)

The market town of Buxton nestles in the Derbyshire hills and is famed for its warm pale blue waters which lie underground for 20 years before coming up to the surface at a temperature of 28°C. Water can be sampled at the drinking fountain by the Crescent in the town centre.

Thermal water is used for orthopaedic treatments at the Devonshire Royal Hospital, and in the spa swimming pool. The water is excellent for bottling and bathing, and benefits rheumatic and arthritic disorders.

Buxton is a friendly town with beautiful buildings and a wide variety of interesting places to visit and things to do as well as an entertainment programme to suit everyone.

234

CHELTENHAM SPA

Tourist Information Centre
77 Promenade   Gloucestershire
GL50 1PP Tel 0242 522878

This attractive town is noted for its lovely gardens, fashionable shops and Regency buildings. No spa bathing facilities here, but Britain's only alkaline spring water is available for drinking in the Pump Room. The spa water is reputed to benefit circulation and digestive disorders.

DROITWICH

Tourist Information Centre
St Richard's House   Victoria Square
Hereford & Worcester WR9 8DS
Tel 0905 774312

Droitwich is the only fully operational health spa in Britain. Bathing in the brine baths is a unique experience, matched only by the Dead Sea.

The new complex, designed on modern lines opened in 1985 and is operated by Compass Healthcare, who run the adjoining private hospital and specialist knee clinic. Over 150,000 visitors use the baths each year. Facilities and treatment areas are being refurbished.

The brine baths are kept free in the mornings for hydrotherapy treatments for patients recovering from such diverse health problems as strokes, arthritis and major orthopaedic surgery. After midday, the spa is open to the public (no more than 20 people at any one time). Other reasonably priced facilities are available in the complex including sauna, massage, beauty treatments and fitness assessments.

The salty water is marvellous for bathing and hydrotherapy because of its buoyancy. Even non-swimmers can relax floating in these unique waters, kept at a constant temperature of 33°C. A spa session costs a very reasonable £5.50 per person or £10 per couple, and includes sauna, brine bath and use of a towel. All sessions should be booked in advance.

The water is not suitable for drinking, of course, but because of its buoyancy is an ideal medium for hydrotherapy and relaxation.

HARROGATE

Tourist Information Centre
Royal Baths Assembly Rooms
Crescent Road   North Yorkshire
HG1 2RR   Tel 0423 525666

Harrogate still retains the elegance of its rich spa heritage. Although bathing facilities closed in 1969, the magnificent Turkish baths in the Royal Baths Assembly Rooms have been fully restored and are now open seven days a week, with separate sessions for men and women. A session lasting two hours costs £6.50. Body and beauty treatments including massage, facials and manicures are now available to visitors to the Turkish baths.

The Royal Pump Room Museum houses the original Sulphur Well, where the health giving but foul tasting water can be sampled. Harrogate's spa water is used to treat rheumatic, digestive and skin troubles.

This elegant North Yorkshire town offers the visitor good hotels, quality shops, beautiful gardens and open spaces, and is surrounded by some of Britain's most beautiful scenery and interesting places to visit.

LEAMINGTON SPA

Tourist Information Centre
South Lodge   Jephson Gardens
The Parade Warwickshire CV32 4AB
Tel 0926 311470
This favourite town of Queen Victoria provides blazing floral displays and quality shopping in the most stylish of settings, and is only minutes away from historic Warwick Castle, Europe's finest mediaeval fortress.

The mildly laxative spa water can be sampled in the fountain of the Pump Room cafe, and tastes salty, but is excellent for hydrotherapy.

Treatment facilities at the Spa Pump Rooms finished at the end of 1990 - until then 60,000 patients a year, mainly NHS referrals, were treated by an outstanding hydro/physiotherapy department.

LLANDRINDOD WELLS

Tourist Information Centre
Town Hall Powys LD1 6AA
Tel 0597 822600
This beautiful little town is set in the rural beauty of Mid Wales, and was a leading Victorian Spa in the days when 'taking the waters' was the fashionable and healthy thing to do. Many people flocked to enjoy the medicinal waters, fresh air and breathtaking scenery of Wales's premier inland holiday resort.

Today, Llandrindod Wells is a thriving holiday town offering many diverse attractions including a Victorian theatre, modern sporting facilities and an annual 9-day Victorian Festival. Spa water cannot be tasted at present, but hopefully will be available for sampling in the Pump Room in the near future.

MALVERN

Tourist Information Centre
Winter Gardens Complex Grange Road
Hereford & Worcester WR14 3HB
Tel 0684 892289

Malvern's spa water flows from springs in the Malvern Hills and is exceptionally pure and ideal for drinking. Malvern water is successfully bottled by Schweppes and exported all over the world. Visitors can sample the water from St Anne's Well and the Holy Well situated outside the town.

Malvern is a charming Victorian town with a picturesque setting and delightful features like original gas lamps. No treatment or bathing facilities are currently available.

MATLOCK BATH

Tourist Information Centre
The Pavilion Derbyshire   DE4 3NR
Tel 0629 55082

Known as "Little Switzerland" because of its rugged scenery and spectacular cable car ride, Matlock Bath is a charming town and the spa water can be sampled at the Victorian pump in the tourist information centre.

No hydrotherapy or spa treatment facilities are available, but the thermal water which emerges from the spring at a constant 20°C can be enjoyed in the swimming pools of the New Bath Hotel and in the children's paddling pool in the park.

In 1990, Albert Rockach's Deepwood Mining company was drilling for minerals in the hills outside the town and struck a major new source of pure mineral water. A bottling plant was set up at the new source. A major new thermal spring was also discovered within the underground caves, but a planned £100 million scheme to build a health and leisure facility around the spring, with hotels, restaurants and car parks has now been abandoned.

ROYAL TUNBRIDGE WELLS

Tourist Information Centre
The Old Fish Market The Pantiles
Kent   TN2 5TN Tel 0892 515675

Royal Tunbridge Wells is Britain's most southerly spa town and is set in an area of outstanding natural beauty. It developed into a fashionable spa resort in 1606 following the discovery of a mineral spring. The striking architecture, fashionable shops and the town's colourful gardens are still enjoyed by today's visitors.

The chalybeate (iron rich) waters can be sampled via 'the dipper' on summer afternoons from the spring inside the entrance to the Pantiles (the colonnaded tree-lined shopping area). The iron water is taken medicinally for blood disorders.

No spa bathing facilities are planned at the moment.

STRATHPEFFER

Tourist Information Centre
The Square   Ross-shire   IV14 9DW
Tel 0997 21415
Nestling in a picturesque valley in the heart of the Scottish Highlands, this Victorian spa's invigorating waters can be sampled in a new pavilion. The Victorian station has also been tastefully restored.

No spa bathing facilities at present, but lots of other attractions including stunning scenery to delight visitors to this charming and historic town.

WOODHALL SPA

Tourist Information Centre
The Cottage Museum   Iddlesleigh
Road   Lincolnshire   LN10 6SH
Tel 0526 53775
A spa in name only! Although a member of the British Spas Federation, the source of the iodine and bromide rich waters became contaminated some years ago, and a new pure source has yet to be laid on.

Woodhall Spa played a great part in both World Wars and Petwood House became the Officers' Mess for the famous 617 'Dam Busters' Squadron. Petwood House is now a luxury hotel, and Woodhall Spa a peaceful and attractive Lincolnshire town set amid pine and birch woods 20 miles from Lincoln.

BSF ASSOCIATE MEMBERS

LISDOONVARNA SPA WELLS
Lisdoonvarna Co Clare Ireland   Tel 065-74023

Lisdoonvarna is a small friendly spa town and a mecca for traditional Irish music and its culture.

The Spa Wells and Health Centre house the principal sulphur springs of Gowlaun, where a range of spa treatments including sulphur baths are available in the Bath House.

The iron and magnesia springs are housed in their own grounds in a pump room adjacent to the park. The Twin Wells comprise iron and sulphur springs and are situated on the edge of the park.

An exciting proposed development of an international quality health spa complete with accommodation is currently under consideration.

TREFRIW WELLS SPA
Trefriw Gwynedd Wales LL27 OJS   Tel 0492 640057

Trefriw Wells Spa is a mineral rich spring bubbling from a Welsh mountainside cleft. Originally discovered by the Romans, the magnificent Cyclopean Bath House built in 1743 is still intact and contains a huge Welsh slate bath and artefacts of times gone by. The Victorian Pump Room and Bath House now houses the tea room, gift shop and museum - open seven days a week all year round.

The iron-rich water is the only fully licensed spa water medicine in the world, and is sold as an easily absorbed iron supplement in sachet form. Spatone Plus™ is particularly valuable to those with iron deficiencies who cannot tolerate manufactured iron preparations. Further clinical trials to extend use of this 'natural' cure are currently being carried out in Cardiff University Hospital.

A GLOSSARY OF

TREATMENTS & THERAPIES

ACUPRESSURE

A gentle finger pressure applied to the meridian points of the body - these are the channels of magnetic energy connecting the organs of the body. A long treatment taking at least 90 minutes.

ACUPUNCTURE

An ancient form of Chinese medicine, again using the meridians of the body to regulate the life energy (Chi). Very fine needles are painlessly inserted to restore function and relieve pain, imparting a relaxed and invigorating effect.

Other types of acupuncture are sometimes offered without use of needles. Instead these use electro and laser treatments.

AROMATHERAPY

A pressure point massage using essential oils with various therapeutic properties specifically chosen for each individual after an initial consultation.

BIO-PEEL

Special facial devised by René Guinot which removes the dead skin cells and leaves the face smoother with a clearer complexion. Gives a real boost to the skin's appearance.

BLITZ JET DOUCHE

A treatment used in continental spas and now popular in the UK. The recipient stands in a tiled area and is massaged from a distance of about 12 feet by a powerful jet of warmed water from a hose. The therapist massages the entire body from feet upwards using this hose - finishing with an optional cold water spray. Quite breathtaking!

BODY SCRUB/ EXFOLIATION

A treatment recommended on its own or as a preparation for other body treatments or tanning. Dead skin cells are removed and the exfoliation cleanses and invigorates the body.

BODY WRAP / HERBAL WRAP / SEAWEED WRAP

Wonderfully relaxing treatment in which the body is covered in various oils and gels and then wrapped in a sheet steamed in aromatic herbs. As the recipient lies gently perspiring, toxins and excess fluid are eliminated from the body.

BUST TREATMENT

An exfoliation treatment is followed by the application of specialised products and massage, designed to tone, firm and strengthen the skin, helping improve bust shape.

CELLU M6

A new electrical driven massage treatment which folds and sucks the skin between two motorised rollers, aiding lymph flow and circulation. It has interchangeable heads and can be used on many parts of the body including the head. Cellu M6 is usually offered as either a stress relief or detoxification treatment.

CATHIODERMIE

Another treatment from René Guinot, which uses a mild electrical current to effect a deep cleanse of the skin. This oxygenates the outer skin layer, improving its texture and encouraging regeneration. The treatment, which can be used on other parts of the body as well as the face, includes a mask and lasts about 90 minutes.

As this is such a thorough cleanse, the skin must be allowed time to recover. Sun-bathing and make-up should be avoided on the same day.

COLONIC IRRIGATION

Washing out of the bowel by means of a gentle enema. An alternative detoxification treatment that is not as bad as it sounds! Available at *Shrubland Hall Health Clinic*.

ELECTROLYSIS

A method of removing unwanted hair permanently, using an electrically charged needle to the hair root. Can be expensive as each hair has to be removed separately. Especially good for removal of facial hair.

FACIAL

The most popular treatment in the beauty salon. The face and neck is thoroughly cleansed, toned and moisturised using products suited to individual skin conditions. There are many types of different facials, some with strangely undescriptive names like Paris and Hollywood. Beauty therapists can explain the differences and advise.

FANGO THERAPY

Application of mineralised mud, mixed with spa water to the consistency of plasticine, heated and used as a poultice to cover joints or areas of the body affected with arthritis or related conditions. The pack retains the heat for at least 30 minutes.

FARADIC EXERCISE

Passive electrically controlled exercise to tone and firm the body, through pads strapped to the muscles causing a tickling or tingling sensation depending on the faradic current used. Slendertone is the most well known type of faradic treatment and several sessions are necessary to effect an improvement.

FLOATARIUM / FLOAT ROOM / FLOATATION TANK

A covered bath or shallow pool containing a saturated solution of Epsom salts in water allowing the body to float effortlessly. After immersion, the lights are turned down until total darkness results. Stress and fatigue are relieved by the profound level of relaxation possible, with no awareness of gravity, temperature, light or sound. An amazing experience.

Springs Hydro now offers a range of 'dry floatation' treatments with the water covered, so the client floats but is not immersed in the saline solution.

G5 MASSAGE

A deep gyratory massage using various electrically driven applicator heads (five originally, hence the name G5) on different parts of the body. The treatment relieves tiredness and tension and helps tone the body. Gives a much stronger massage than is possible using the hands alone.

GALVANIC TREATMENTS

Often used in conjuction with faradic treatments. Galvanic current encourages the absorption of liquids into the skin, by using current-conducting clay and electrodes on parts of the body needing firming, as in Ionithermie treatments.

HELLERWORK

A therapy designed to restore the body's balance, returning it to a relaxed and more youthful state by releasing built-up tensions and stress. Combines manipulation of connective body tissue with discussion on affects of mental attitudes on the body, teaching the client to become aware of movements that keep the body supple and tension-free.

Now offered at *Champneys* and some progressive health clubs.

HOMŒOPATHY

A form of alternative medicine which boosts the body's healing ability by using highly diluted and specially prepared forms of plant, mineral and animal substances. The remedies are prepared taking into account the personality as well as the symptoms of the individual.

HYDROTHERAPY

Therapeutic treatment involving the use of water in its application.

Many different forms of treatment - bathing or exercising muscles and joints in a warm therapeutic pool, hot and cold compresses to improve blood flow to diseased areas or reduce inflammation and swelling, cold water wraps for various disorders, hot and cold baths (see Sitz baths), jet sprays and inhalation therapy to aid respiratory problems.

Heated thermal baths are used extensively in spas along with modified exercise to aid arthritis and mobility. Bathing in warm spa water cleanses the pores, improves circulation and exercises the muscles. Bathers should always lie down for about 30 minutes afterwards and take care getting out of the pool, as hot/warm water lowers blood pressure and can cause dizziness.

IONITHERMIE

A range of facial and slimming treatments for correction of cellulite and improvement of skin and muscle tone. The treatment uses gentle galvanic stimuli with thermal clay and biologically active natural ingredients. The strength of the stimuli can be varied according to need and tolerance! Can result in immediate inch loss.

INFRA-RED

Treatment uses healing infra-red light to treat painful muscles and other parts of the body. The lamps are placed over the affected area helping muscles relax and increasing the circulation of the blood.

IRIDOLOGY

A form of complementary medicine which uses the study of the iris as a form of diagnosis. Iridology claims to reveal genetic weaknesses and tendencies in the body which may be causing health problems. Lifestyle and diet changes can then be made to help overcome these.

KARWENDEL

A continental treatment using fossil oils to relax and refresh the body. The thick tarry substance is rich in nutrients and added to a warm, therapeutic bath, stimulating the circulation and helping to clear up problem skin. Beneficial to sufferers of psoriasis and other skin conditions.

KINESIOLOGY

A therapy used to diagnose food allergies and other conditions using acupressure massage, testing muscle strength to check energy flow. Pressure would be applied to patient's raised arm while different foods are held in the mouth. Weakness of arm muscle indicates sensitivity to a food.

KNEIPP THERAPY

A cold water treatment used extensively in Europe but less frequently in the UK. It works through the reaction of the body to being stimulated by the cold, and improves blood supply, metabolism and helps strengthen the nervous system. Treatment consists of herbal baths or body packs (see *Signal Box Health Farm* entry for full description). Not as barbaric as it sounds as all procedures are carefully monitored at every stage, and the treatment is only given to a warm body in a well heated room.

MASSAGE

The most popular and available treatment in all health farms and beauty salons. Swedish body massage is the type most generally given, and uses long sweeping movements interspersed with kneading and pummelling. Fatigue and tension, but NOT, unfortunately fat, are rubbed away with the help of scented oils to reduce friction.

Very relaxing and especially beneficial to the neck and shoulder areas.

NEEDLE SHOWERS

An overhead shower with additional water outlets placed at different body levels to give a horizontal spray massage. Pleasantly invigorating.

MOOR PEAT BATH

A hot or warm bath lasting about 20 minutes, to which a mixture of liquid peat has been added. The treatment finishes with a lie down in a warm room. Good for rheumatism sufferers.

OSTEOPATHY

The manipulation of the spine to relieve back pain, sciatica, neck and shoulder pains and various other conditions of the body.

PARAFFIN WAX BATHS

Not a bath for immersion! A thick layer of warm wax is brushed over the body which is then wrapped up to keep warm. As the body perspires, the heat draws out toxins, cleansing the pores and softening the skin.

PARAFFIN WAX FOR HANDS AND FEET

A treatment to help relieve the discomforts of arthritis, rheumatism and circulatory problems. The warmth and cleansing effects combine to leave the skin feeling soft.

PHYSIOTHERAPY

The application of various techniques including electrical muscle stimulation, remedial exercise in water and with apparatus to restore or improve the health and mobility of the body.

Especially useful in treating sports injuries.

REFLEXOLOGY

A foot massage in which pressure points in the toes and feet which correspond with other parts of the body are massaged and stimulated. Hitherto unknown health problems can sometimes be detected in this relaxing treatment.

ROLFING

A structural bodywork technique, formulated by American biochemist Ida Rolf, aimed at improving posture and health by realigning physical body structures. Involves massage and manipulation of body's connective tissue. Not widely known or available in the UK.

SALT RUB

A brisk body rub given after showering. Salt is massaged all over the body by hand or with a loofah. A salt rub is often given prior to a hydrotherapy massage bath.

Very invigorating, leaves the skin soft and glowing.

SAUNA

A wooden-lined room complete with wooden benches for sitting or reclining. The room is heated with dry heat to around 40°C or more, making the body sweat profusely - a cold plunge or shower afterwards closes the pores and leaves the body glowing.

This popular heat treatment originated in Finland, and is found in virtually all health farms and health clubs.

SCOTTISH DOUCHE

A shower of alternating hot and cold water jets to stimulate the spinal column and tone up the circulation and nervous systems of the body.

SCLEROTHERAPY

The treatment of broken capillaries (thread veins) using a fine gauge needle to inject a solution of glycerine chromate into each blood vessel. This blanches the skin and causes the blood vessel to go into spasm and its walls to collapse. As no more blood flows through the vessel, it loses its red colour. Treatment description sounds worse than it is! Relatively painless procedure that feels like tiny pin-pricks. Each vessel is treated two or three times and repeat sessions may be necessary to achieve a good result.

SHIATSU

An oriental body therapy similar to acupressure.

The practitioner uses his/her elbows, knees, feet, palms and fingers to press along the meridian lines of the body. Shiatsu restores balance or 'oneness' by summoning energy to and from parts of the body that need it. Very therapeutic and effective in the relief of insomnia, pain and tension.

SITZ BATHS

A hip bath composed of two parts, one filled with hot water the other cold. The patient sits in the hot water with feet in the cold for a few minutes and then alternates. An effective natural treatment to improve circulation and as an aid in prostate and some gynaecological conditions.

STEAM BATH

A popular heat treatment given in its own enclosure, using steam to promote perspiration and help remove body toxins.

Like the sauna, the steam room has shelving to sit or recline on - menthol vapours can be added to the steam to aid inhalation.

STEAM CABINET

A relaxing treatment lasting about 30 minutes - unlike the steam room, the head remains outside the cabinet and is not exposed to the steam as the rest of the body gently perspires inside. Hotter than a steam room and available at many health farms - should be followed by 30 minutes relaxation.

THALASSOTHERAPY

The therapeutic use of sea-water, seaweeds and other marine components. Most popular in French spas, it is now becoming a favourite treatment in the UK too. Thalassotherapy programmes include algae baths, wraps and masks.

TURKISH BATHS

Real Turkish baths are a series of increasingly hot and humid steam rooms complete with marble slabs for reclining as the body perspires. The procedure is reversed to cool down before finishing with a tepid or cold shower and a rest. Steam rooms are sometimes incorrectly called Turkish baths.

The spa town of *Harrogate* has a splendid example of a Turkish bath in all its glory.

UNDERWATER MASSAGE

Massage given in a warm bath by high pressure jets of water within the bath and sometimes combined with peat or seaweed. The process is helpful in breaking down cellulite and improving the circulation, but is not suitable for those with a raised blood pressure or who bruise easily.

Underwater massage can also be given by a therapist with a hand held, high pressure hose.

WAXING

Removal of unwanted hair from the body and face using a warm wax thinly applied. Muslin strips are pressed onto the hairs which should be at least 1/4" long, and then removed.

Can be uncomfortable, but regrowth will be softer and take longer to show.

VITAL HARMONY

A Decleor treatment involving body exfoliation combined with aromatherapy oils to improve the elasticity of the skin. Slimming and relaxing, it leaves the body feeling smoother and firmer.

YOGA

A system of training mind and body which originated in India and is particularly helpful in the management of stress-related problems.

There are several forms of yoga, the best known one in Western countries is Hatha yoga, which uses postures and exercises emphasising the importance of breathing and relaxation.

HEALTHY BREAKS
in Britain and Ireland

Alphabetical listing of establishments featured

Dedicated Health Farms and Resorts

Self-catering villages with spa and treatment facilities

Name	Section	Page No.
Castle Oaks Holiday Village	Ireland	211
Dalfaber Resort	Scotland	192
Elveden Forest - Center Parcs	Central	120
Lakeland Village	Northern	167
Langdale Village	Northern	151
Longleat Forest - Center Parcs	South-west	104
Plas Talgarth	Wales	176
Sherwood Forest - Center Parcs	Central	136

Hotels and establishments with spa and treatment facilities

Name	Section	Page No.
Aghadoe Heights Hotel	Ireland	210
Armathwaite Hall	Northern	144
Auchrannie Hotel	Scotland	184
Barnham Broom	Central	116
Bath Spa Hotel	South-west	92
Beadlow Manor	Southern	40
Bedruthen Steps	South-west	93
Belfry	Central	117
Belton Woods	Central	118
Berkeley Hotel	London	20
Blunsdon House	South-west	94
Botley Park	Southern	41
Bowfield Hotel	Scotland	185
Brandshatch Place	Southern	42
Breadsall Priory	Central	119
Bridgewood Manor	Southern	43
Burrendale Hotel	Ireland	211
Buxted Park	Southern	45
Cairndale Hotel	Scotland	186
Cameron House	Scotland	187
Careys Manor	Southern	46
Carlton Hotel	Southern	47
Chewton Glen	Southern	50
Cliveden	Southern	51

LATE ENTRY

Details of Ireland's first residential thalassotherapy centre reached us after we went to press, but such an interesting development deserves a special late mention.

Rochestown Park Hotel
Cork Ireland
Tel 021 892233 Fax 021 892178
Thalassotherapy Centre   Tel 021 894949   Fax 021 8955050

Ireland's first thalassotherapy centre opened in April 1994 and is based at the Rochestown Park Hotel in Cork, a comfortable modern hotel with 63 en suite bedrooms and a fully equipped leisure centre with indoor swimming pool.

The Centre is under the medical direction of Dr Christian Jost . Consultation and medical advice is included in all thalassotherapy programmes with the number of sessions decided according to need. Thalassotherapy programmes include two treatments per 75 minute session and cost IR£25 each.

Four special programmes are currently available: *Toning, Post-natal, Slimming* and *Heavy legs.*

The Centre is equipped with a thalassotherapy pool filled with warmed sea water, with counter currents, neck showers, wall water jets and a gymnastic area. Other facilities incorporating use of sea water include a multijets shower bed, hydrojet and a computerised massage bath.

Treatments

A wide range of therapeutic treatments are available including sea water wraps, brumisation (inhalation of micronized sea water), muscle toning, pressotherapy (lympathic drainage and fluid retention treatment), electrolipolysis (reduction of local fatty deposits by insertion of probe) and dermabrasion for post acne scars, stretch marks and burns.

Body and beauty treatments are also available and include full body massage IR£35; thalassotherapy treatments from IR£25; facials from IR£30; eyelash tint IR6; red thread vein and blood spot treatment IR£20; milia removal IR£10; skin tag removal from IR£10; waxing from IR£3; advanced electrolysis treatment from IR£13.

Tariff

Special rates are available for users of the Thalassotherapy Centre and include accommodation in the Rochestown Park Hotel and use of the leisure facilities.

One Day Treatment with overnight accommodation, breakfast and thalassotherapy (five treatments) IR£100 single, IR£90 per person sharing double room .

Weekend Treatment (two days) with overnight accommodation, breakfast and thalassotherapy (14 treatments) IR£212 single, IR£192 per person sharing double room.

Lunch from IR£5.25 to IR£12, dinner from IR£9 to approximately IR£23.

Further information and travel directions from the hotel or through our new booking service (see page 253).

LATE ENTRY 2

Stop The World
Hornblotton House Hornblotton Shepton Mallet
Somerset BA4 6SB

Tel 0963 824100 Fax 0963 824643

Programmes designed to cleanse and rejuvenate body and spirit are offered at this peaceful country house, surrounded by 50 acres of beautiful Somerset countryside. Courses lasting four, five or six days are offered on various dates throughout the year and incorporate good food, gentle exercise, meditation and a caring atmosphere. Relaxation weekends are also available.

No more than ten guests stay at any one time, and the delicious vegetarian meals are relaxed and informal. Fresh flowers, essential oils and candles decorate and perfume the rooms, creating a feeling of peace and relaxation. Bedrooms are homely and comfortable with single, double and shared accommodation available.

Treatments
Various treatments (body massage, pedicures, facials) are incorporated in all programmes - extra ones available subject to availability.

Tariff
£785 per person for six night *Cleansing and Detoxification Programme* ; *Basic Programme* £450 for five nights; £435 for four nights; *Relaxation Weekend* £295 per person.

Travel Directions
Hornblotton is 7 miles south of Shepton Mallet on A37.
Nearest railway station Castle Cary approximately 3 miles.

NEW READER SERVICE

Discovery Books
and leading spa consultants **Erna Low**
are pleased to offer *Healthy Breaks* readers a free
advisory and booking service.

If, after reading this book, you require further help or
information about any of the establishments featured,
just call one of our telephone numbers
and we will do our best to help.

0932 346201
(Discovery Books)

071-584 2841
(Erna Low Consultants Ltd)

We will be pleased to reserve your healthy break for
you at the best rates currently available.

Special Offer!

If you use our service to book your healthy break,
when we publish the *Healthy Breaks Cook Book*
you will be sent a free copy.
On receipt of your booking we will send you a
Spas Worldwide Brochure.

Telephone for further details and a reservation form.

*Erna Low Travel Consultants Limited are established travel
agents specialising in spa vacations at home and overseas.*

PHOTO CREDITS

All photographs and illustrations in this book appear courtesy of the entries and Spa towns except for the following which are gratefully acknowledged. Page 6 Chewton Glen, Hampshire; Page 9 Royal Club Evian, France; Page 12 Hyatt Carlton Tower, London; Page 14 Center Parcs, Nottinghamshire; Page 37 Champneys, Hertfordshire; Pages 230/231 Droitwich Brine Baths.